IT'S PAR FOR THE COURSE, CHARLIE BROWN

CHARLES M. SCHULZ

Ballantine Books New York

Copyright © 2005 United Feature Syndicate
Foreword copyright © 2005 Johnny Miller

Published in the United States by Ballantine Books,
an imprint of The Random House Publishing Group,
a division of Random House, Inc., New York.

Ballantine and colophon are registered trademarks
of Random House, Inc.

The comic strips in this book were originally published
in newspapers worldwide.

Cataloging-in-Publication Data can be obtained from
the publisher upon request.

ISBN 0-345-46415-X

Printed in the United States of America

Ballantine Books website address: www.ballantinebooks.com

2 4 6 8 9 7 5 3 1

First Edition

Design by Diane Hobbing of Snap-Haus Graphics

IT'S PAR FOR THE COURSE, CHARLIE BROWN

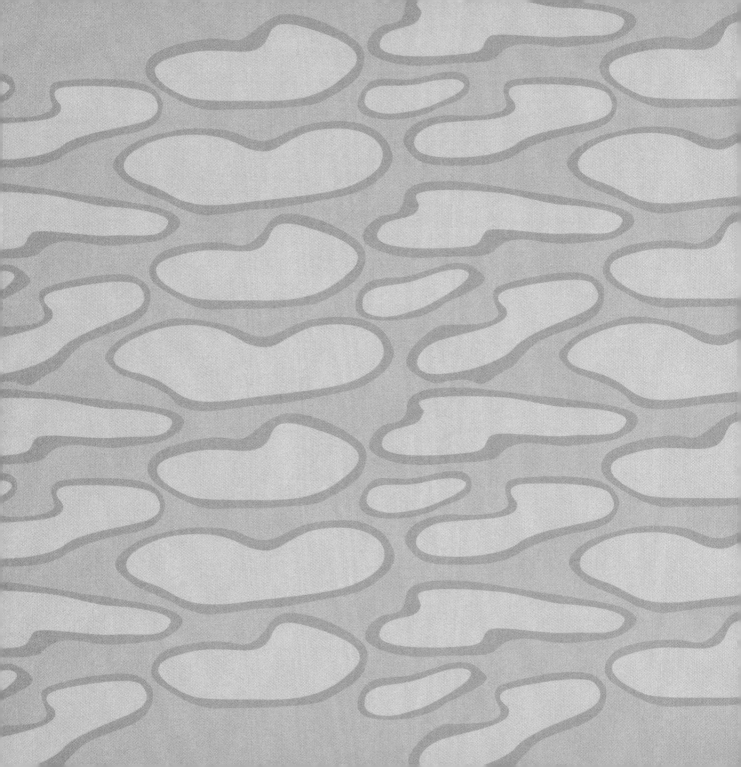

FOREWORD BY JOHNNY MILLER

I first met Charles Schulz in the early '70s through some friends from the Napa Valley who arranged for us to play together in the Bing Crosby Pro-Am tournament. By then I had met a lot of celebrities, but meeting the creator of *Peanuts* was a real treat. I grew up with that comic strip; it was my favorite, along with *Beetle Bailey.* And no matter how old or successful you are, when you meet a hero from your childhood for the first time, it's like you're a kid all over again.

My friends had known Charles for years, and they called him by his nickname, Sparky. He invited me to do the same, but I couldn't make myself do it. It didn't feel right. So at first I called him Mr. Schulz, then Charles, just like Peppermint Patty calls Charlie Brown. But that was as informal as I ever got. I guess I just respected him too much.

We really hit it off for some reason. I felt he was a genius at what he did, and he called me a genius at what I did, so maybe we had a bit of a mutual admiration going. We played together quite a bit after that first Bing Crosby; we played in charity events and privately, just for the fun of it.

He would ask for lessons sometimes, and I enjoyed helping him with his swing. He had a really nice swing, a grooved swing. It was sort of like a Sam Snead come-over: just a little over the top, which produced a bit of a fade. It was a good shot, a reliable shot. Charles had a good short game and he was a good putter. He was a pretty darn good golfer, actually. Which isn't to say that he was happy with his game. What golfer ever is?

I still remember the first hole I played with Charles. He missed an easy putt, a three-footer, and a single word came out of his mouth: "Rats!" I fell on the green laughing. But he didn't say it as a joke. A person's real, true self always comes out on the golf course, and deep down inside, Charles Schulz *was* Charlie Brown. He really was.

People think of Charlie Brown as a failure. But you know what? He was a competitor. And so was Charles. He wanted to excel on the golf course as much as he did when he sat down at the drawing board. Not in the sense of wanting to show off or anything. Just in doing his best in a quiet way.

But he definitely carried Charlie Brown around with him inside. He asked me once about a time I made three birdies in a row. He just couldn't understand it. For him, if he made a good putt on one hole, by the time he got to the next hole, the cup would have somehow shrunken down to the size of a thimble. For me, it was the opposite: With every good putt I made, the cup just kept getting bigger.

He was a man of few words, but they were always the right words. Just like with that missed putt. It wasn't twelve sentences with the word *rats* at the end; it was just *rats,* you know? He didn't need to say more. And that's something I've tried to apply in my career as a commentator. I don't go for long analysis; my style is more short little blurbs. And of course you have to know when to shut up and let the action speak for itself.

What makes these golf cartoons so great is that they capture the central fact of the game, which is that golf is the ultimate game of frustration. It brings out all our self-doubts and insecurities like no other game I know. Every golfer has been there. I sure have—in the late '70s, when I was in a pretty big slump, my whole life felt like one long *Peanuts* cartoon. You have to keep it in perspective, keep your sense of humor. That's why these cartoons are so great. I mean, they're tragic, but they're funny, too. And even if you don't play golf, it's impossible not to read them and see some part of your own life in there and laugh at yourself just a bit. It's really amazing to me how much meaning and feeling Charles could put into four or five little boxes, with just a few words. But I guess that's what made him the best.

I miss him. I think of him often, especially when that MetLife blimp goes cruising by. He was a great supporter of the game and a great friend.

I believe that after his family and *Peanuts,* golf was his biggest love. He loved all sports, really. Hockey, tennis, baseball, football: They're all in his cartoons. But I think Charles had a special feeling for golf, because it was a sport that he could still play late in his life and get a lot of enjoyment from. He needed the release, the competitiveness.

Man, he was nuts about the game of golf.

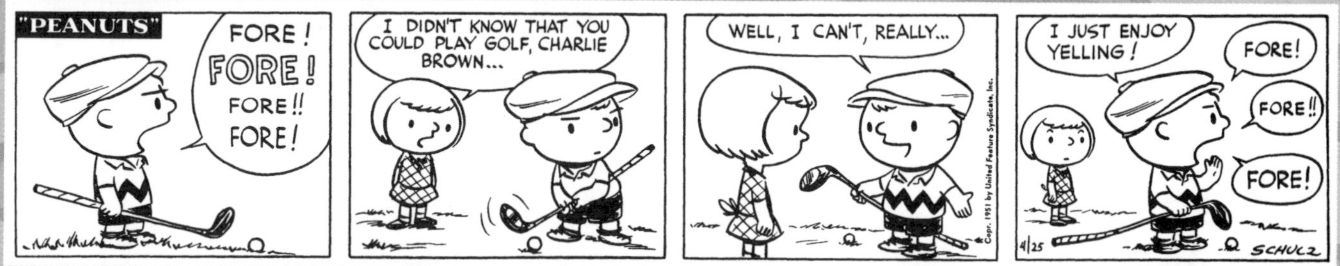
"PEANUTS"
FORE! FORE! FORE!! FORE!
I DIDN'T KNOW THAT YOU COULD PLAY GOLF, CHARLIE BROWN...
WELL, I CAN'T, REALLY...
Copr. 1951 by United Feature Syndicate, Inc.
I JUST ENJOY YELLING!
FORE!
FORE!!
FORE!
4/25
SCHULZ

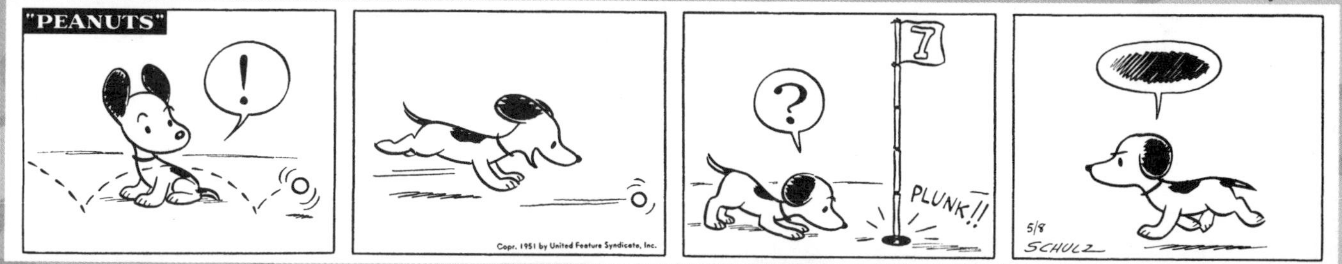
"PEANUTS"
!
Copr. 1951 by United Feature Syndicate, Inc.
7
?
PLUNK!!
5/8
SCHULZ

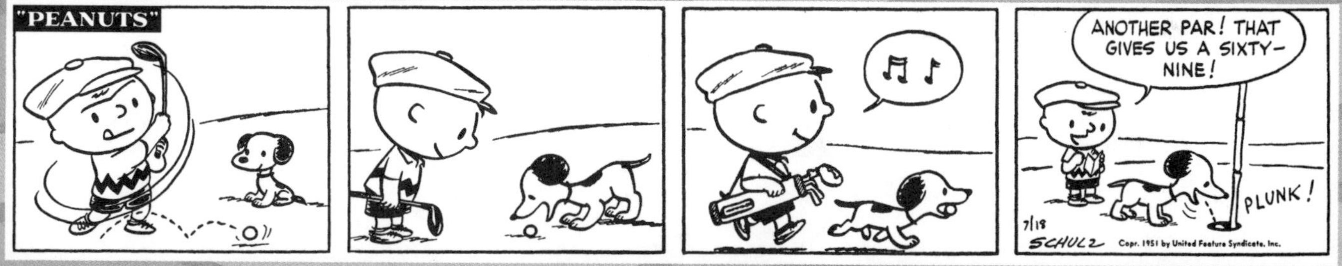
"PEANUTS"
ANOTHER PAR! THAT GIVES US A SIXTY-NINE!
PLUNK!
7/18
SCHULZ
Copr. 1951 by United Feature Syndicate, Inc.

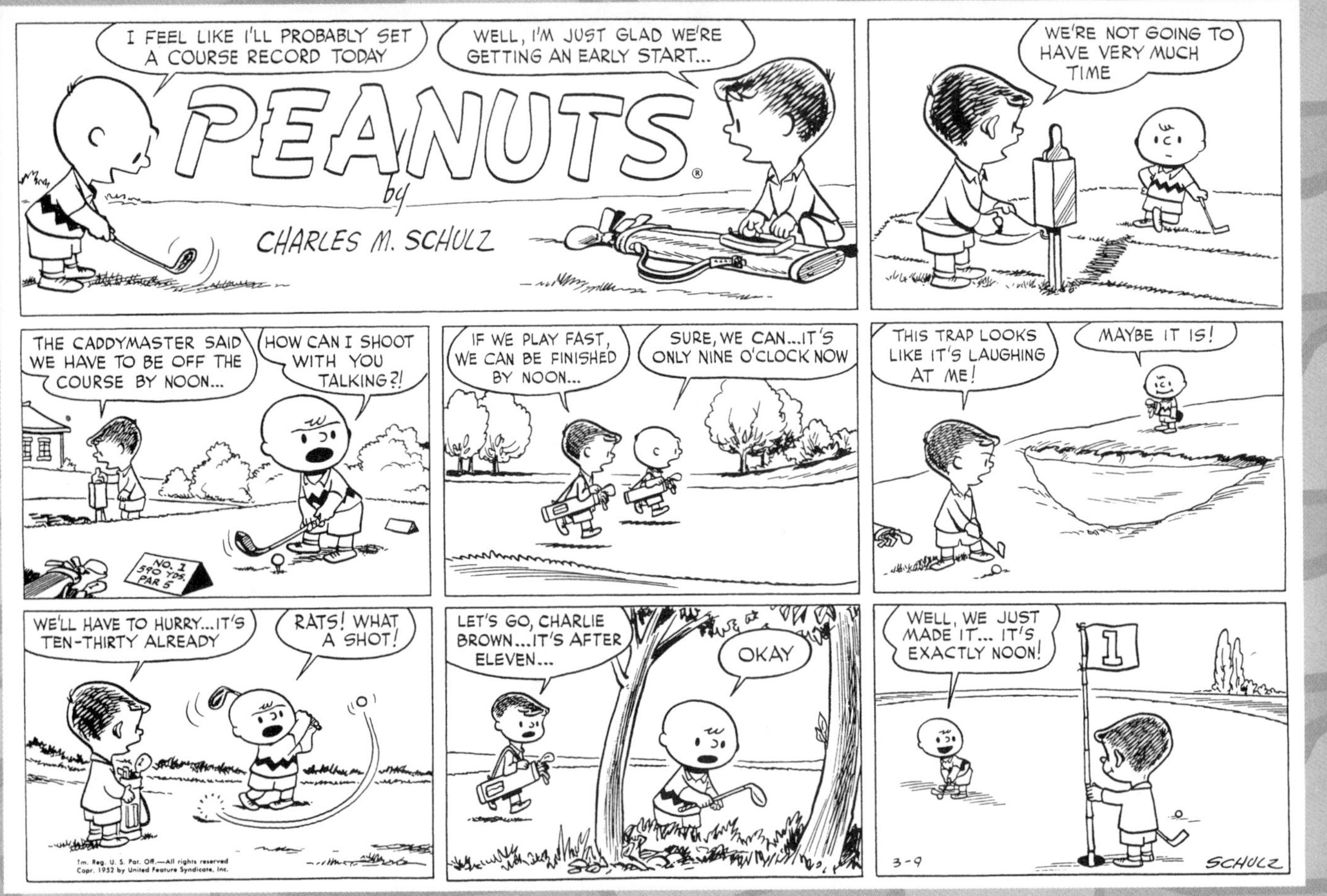
I FEEL LIKE I'LL PROBABLY SET A COURSE RECORD TODAY
WELL, I'M JUST GLAD WE'RE GETTING AN EARLY START...
PEANUTS
by
CHARLES M. SCHULZ
WE'RE NOT GOING TO HAVE VERY MUCH TIME
THE CADDYMASTER SAID WE HAVE TO BE OFF THE COURSE BY NOON...
HOW CAN I SHOOT WITH YOU TALKING?!
NO. 1 590 YDS. PAR 5
IF WE PLAY FAST, WE CAN BE FINISHED BY NOON...
SURE, WE CAN...IT'S ONLY NINE O'CLOCK NOW
THIS TRAP LOOKS LIKE IT'S LAUGHING AT ME!
MAYBE IT IS!
WE'LL HAVE TO HURRY...IT'S TEN-THIRTY ALREADY
RATS! WHAT A SHOT!
Tm. Reg. U. S. Pat. Off.—All rights reserved
Copr. 1952 by United Feature Syndicate, Inc.
LET'S GO, CHARLIE BROWN...IT'S AFTER ELEVEN...
OKAY
WELL, WE JUST MADE IT... IT'S EXACTLY NOON!
1
3-9
SCHULZ

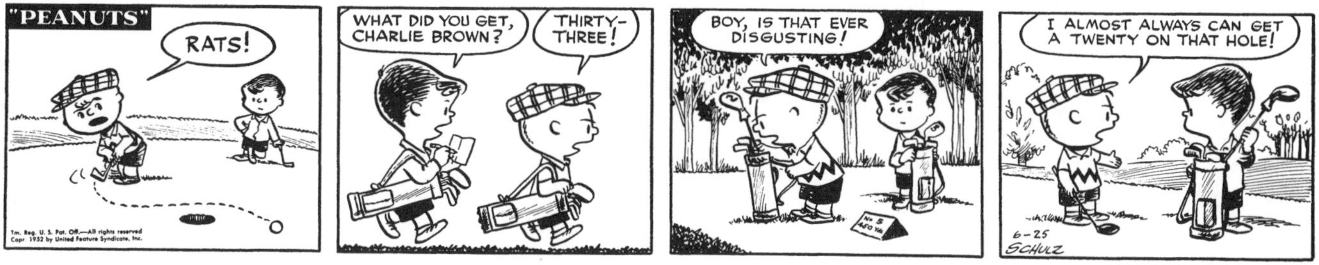
"PEANUTS"
RATS!
Tm. Reg. U. S. Pat. Off.—All rights reserved
Copr 1952 by United Feature Syndicate, Inc.
WHAT DID YOU GET, CHARLIE BROWN?
THIRTY-THREE!
BOY, IS THAT EVER DISGUSTING!
I ALMOST ALWAYS CAN GET A TWENTY ON THAT HOLE!
6-25
SCHULZ

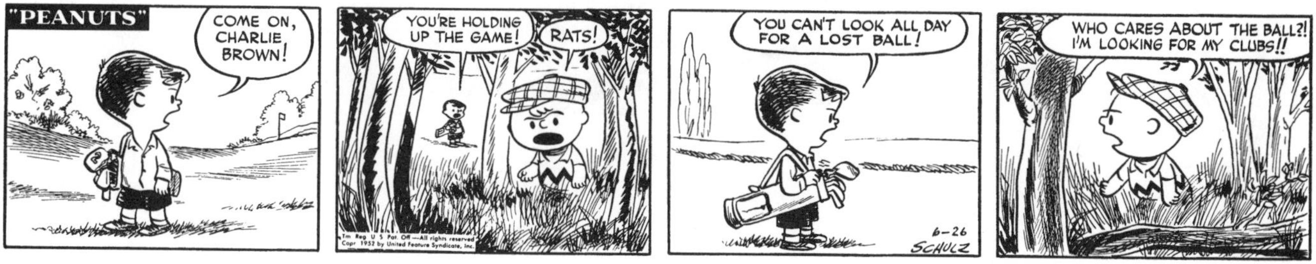
"PEANUTS"
COME ON, CHARLIE BROWN!
YOU'RE HOLDING UP THE GAME!
RATS!
Tm. Reg. U. S. Pat. Off.—All rights reserved
Copr 1952 by United Feature Syndicate, Inc.
YOU CAN'T LOOK ALL DAY FOR A LOST BALL!
6-26
SCHULZ
WHO CARES ABOUT THE BALL?! I'M LOOKING FOR MY CLUBS!!

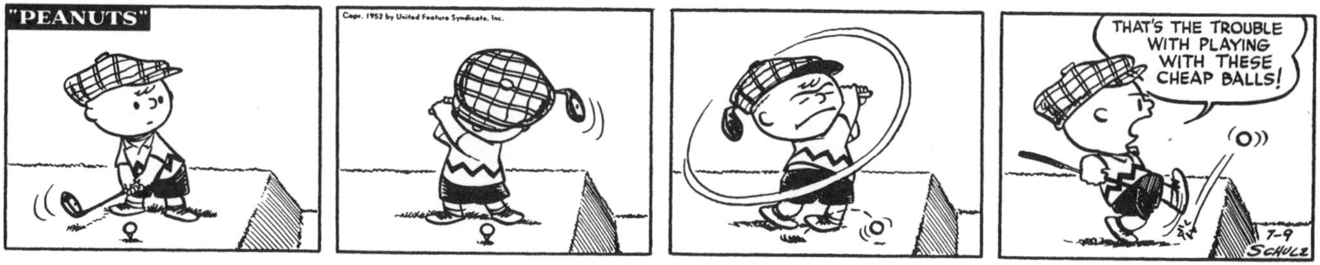
"PEANUTS"
Copr. 1952 by United Feature Syndicate, Inc.
THAT'S THE TROUBLE WITH PLAYING WITH THESE CHEAP BALLS!
7-9
SCHULZ

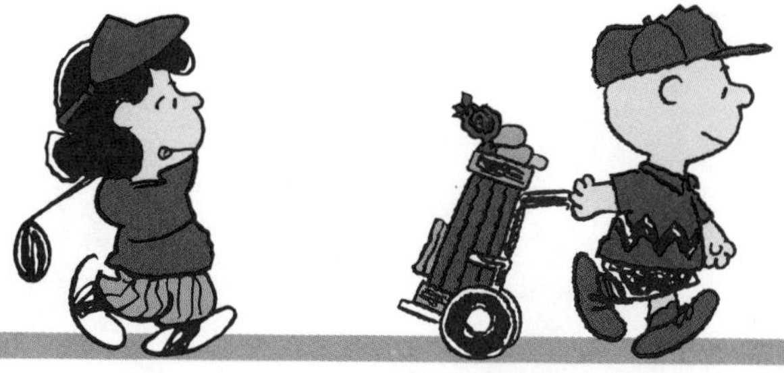

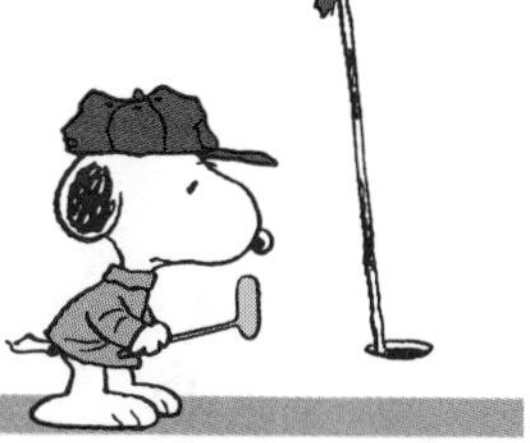

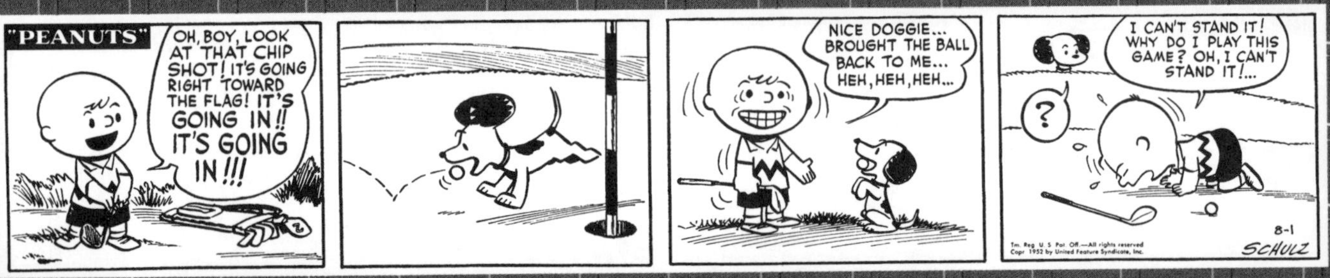
"PEANUTS"
OH, BOY, LOOK AT THAT CHIP SHOT! IT'S GOING RIGHT TOWARD THE FLAG! IT'S GOING IN!! IT'S GOING IN!!!
NICE DOGGIE... BROUGHT THE BALL BACK TO ME... HEH, HEH, HEH...
?
I CAN'T STAND IT! WHY DO I PLAY THIS GAME? OH, I CAN'T STAND IT!...
Tm. Reg. U. S. Pat. Off.—All rights reserved Copr. 1952 by United Feature Syndicate, Inc.
8-1
SCHULZ

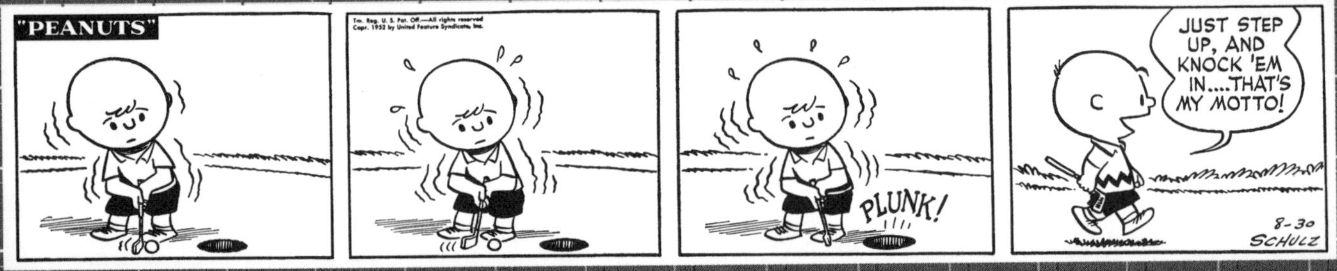
"PEANUTS"
Tm. Reg. U. S. Pat. Off.—All rights reserved Copr. 1952 by United Feature Syndicate, Inc.
PLUNK!
JUST STEP UP, AND KNOCK 'EM IN....THAT'S MY MOTTO!
8-30
SCHULZ

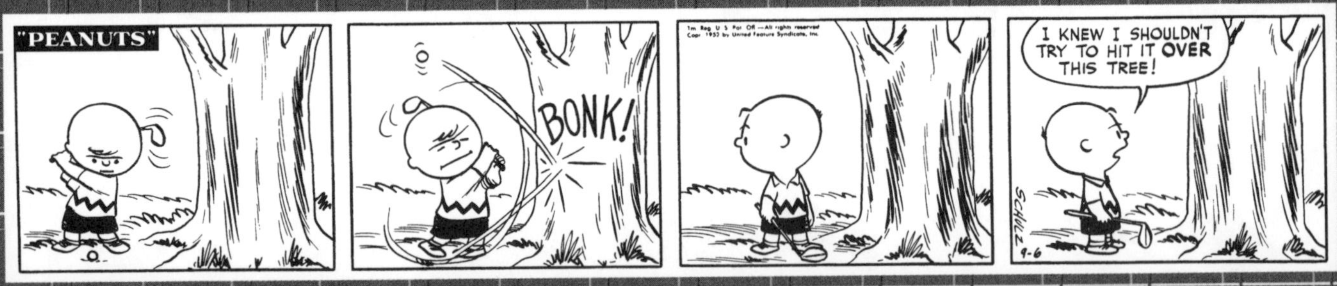
"PEANUTS"
BONK!
Tm. Reg. U. S. Pat. Off.—All rights reserved Copr. 1952 by United Feature Syndicate, Inc.
SCHULZ
9-6
I KNEW I SHOULDN'T TRY TO HIT IT **OVER** THIS TREE!

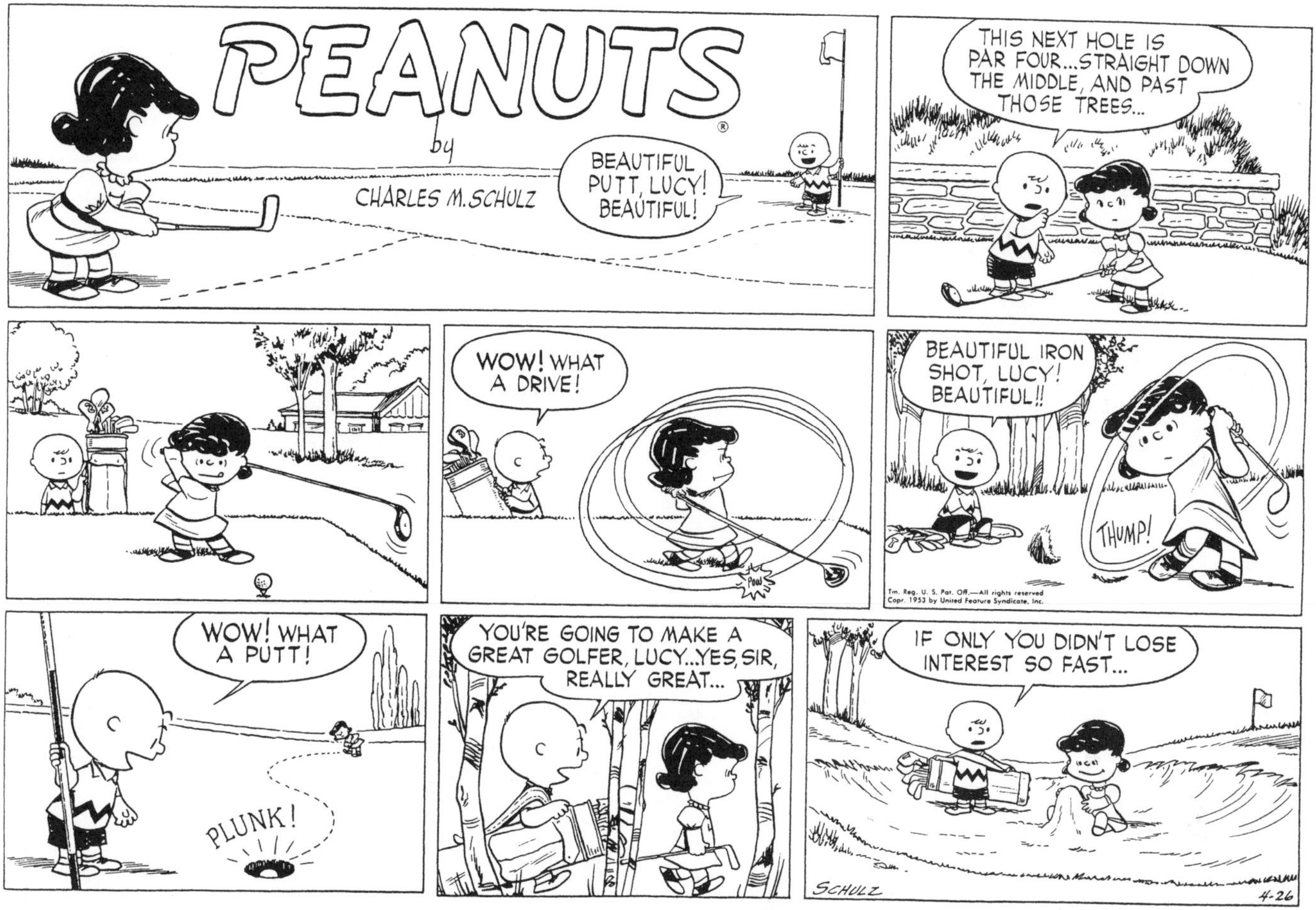
PEANUTS
by
CHARLES M. SCHULZ
BEAUTIFUL PUTT, LUCY! BEAUTIFUL!
THIS NEXT HOLE IS PAR FOUR...STRAIGHT DOWN THE MIDDLE, AND PAST THOSE TREES...
WOW! WHAT A DRIVE!
POW
BEAUTIFUL IRON SHOT, LUCY! BEAUTIFUL!!
THUMP!
Tm. Reg. U. S. Pat. Off.—All rights reserved
Copr. 1953 by United Feature Syndicate, Inc.
WOW! WHAT A PUTT!
PLUNK!
YOU'RE GOING TO MAKE A GREAT GOLFER, LUCY...YES, SIR, REALLY GREAT...
IF ONLY YOU DIDN'T LOSE INTEREST SO FAST...
SCHULZ
4-26

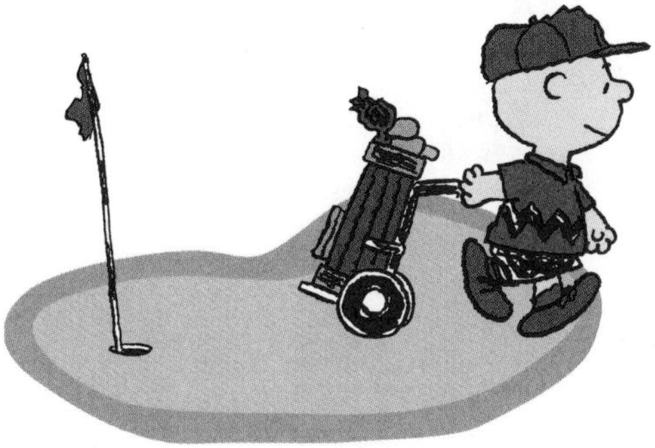

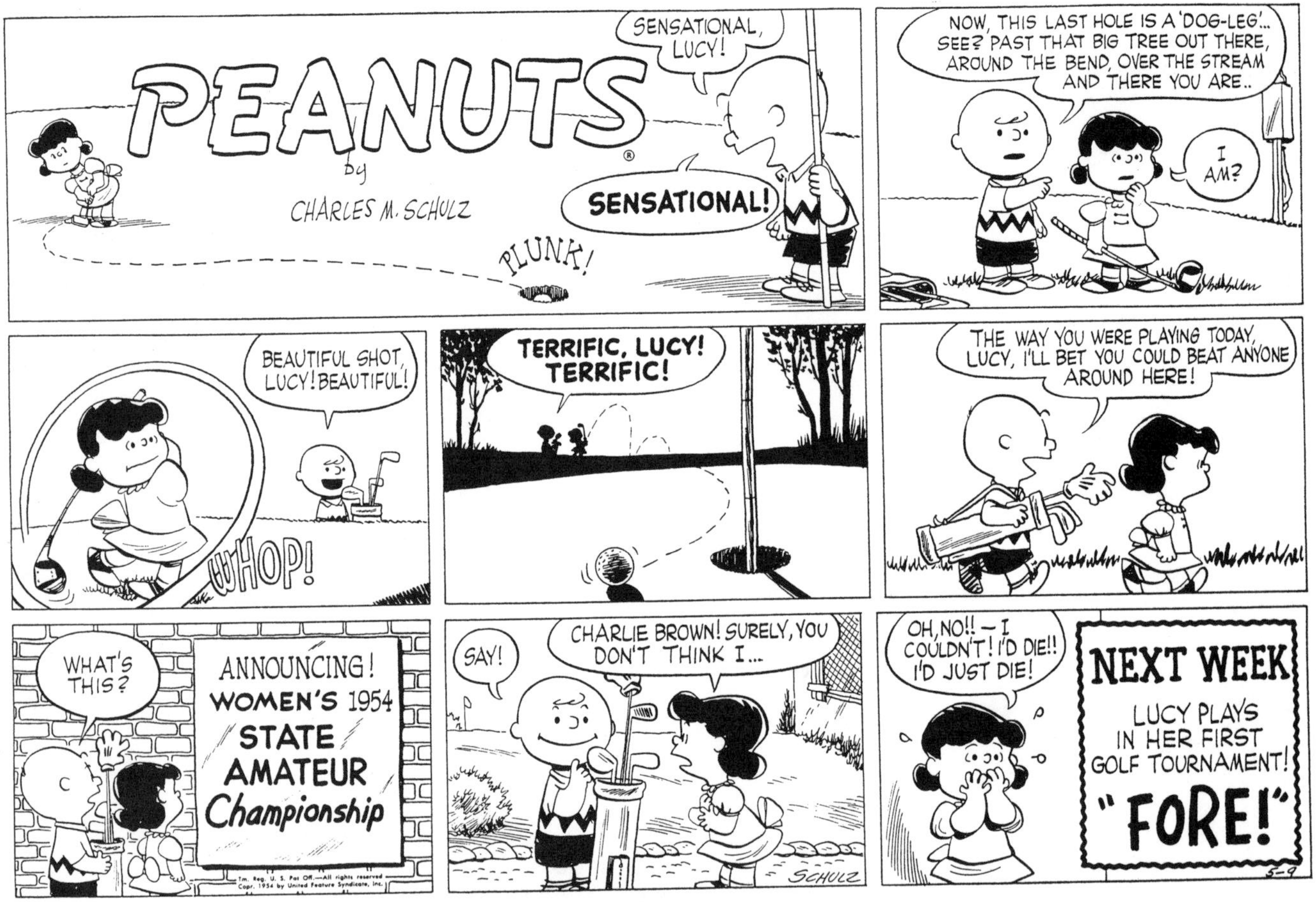

PEANUTS
by
CHARLES M. SCHULZ
SENSATIONAL, LUCY!
SENSATIONAL!
PLUNK!
NOW, THIS LAST HOLE IS A 'DOG-LEG'.. SEE? PAST THAT BIG TREE OUT THERE, AROUND THE BEND, OVER THE STREAM AND THERE YOU ARE..
I AM?
BEAUTIFUL SHOT, LUCY! BEAUTIFUL!
WHOP!
TERRIFIC, LUCY! TERRIFIC!
THE WAY YOU WERE PLAYING TODAY, LUCY, I'LL BET YOU COULD BEAT ANYONE AROUND HERE!
WHAT'S THIS?
ANNOUNCING! WOMEN'S 1954 STATE AMATEUR Championship
Tm. Reg. U. S. Pat Off.—All rights reserved
Copr. 1954 by United Feature Syndicate, Inc.
SAY!
CHARLIE BROWN! SURELY, YOU DON'T THINK I...
SCHULZ
OH, NO!! — I COULDN'T! I'D DIE!! I'D JUST DIE!
NEXT WEEK
LUCY PLAYS IN HER FIRST GOLF TOURNAMENT!
"FORE!"
5-9

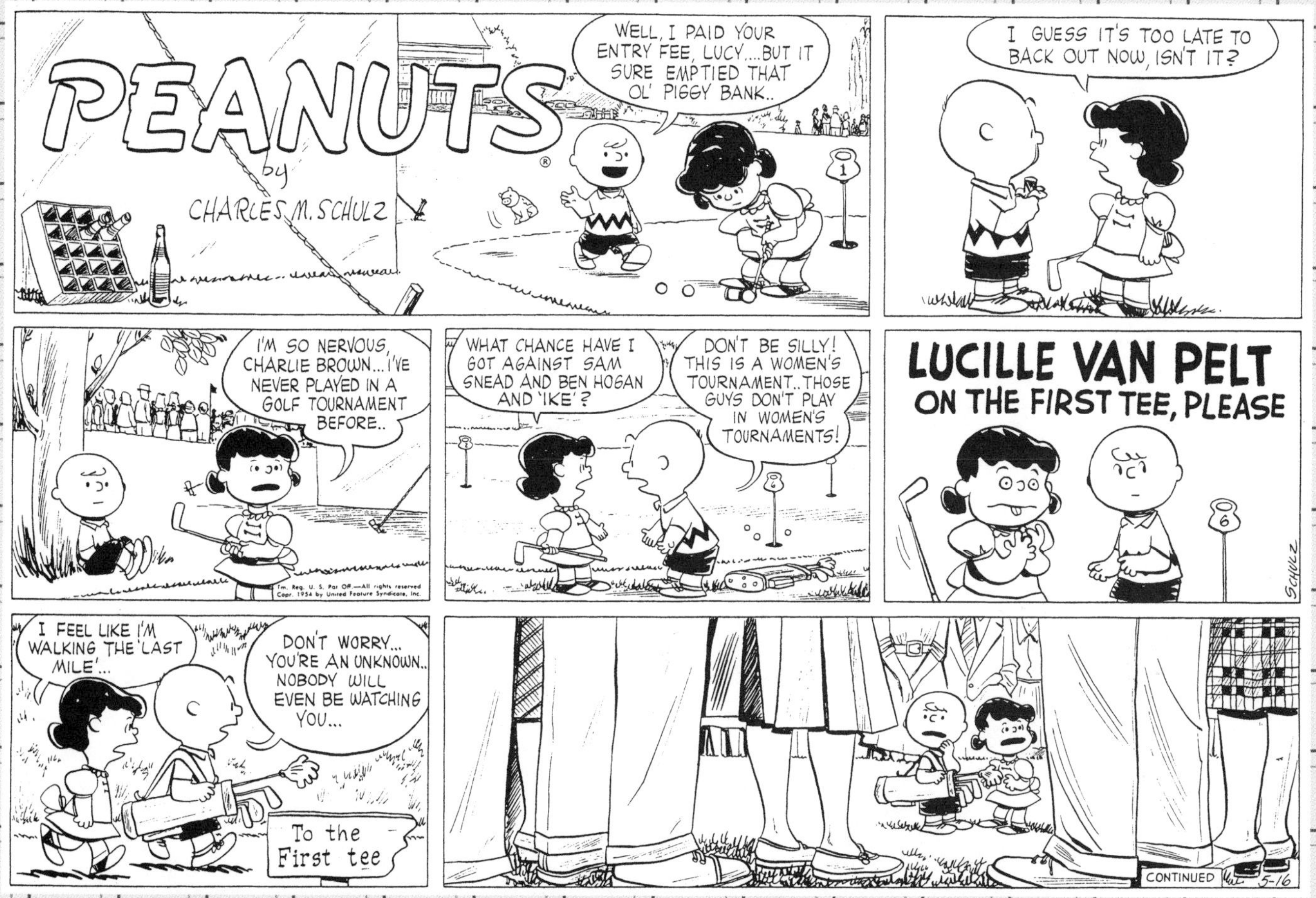
PEANUTS
by
CHARLES M. SCHULZ
WELL, I PAID YOUR ENTRY FEE, LUCY....BUT IT SURE EMPTIED THAT OL' PIGGY BANK..
I GUESS IT'S TOO LATE TO BACK OUT NOW, ISN'T IT?
I'M SO NERVOUS, CHARLIE BROWN...I'VE NEVER PLAYED IN A GOLF TOURNAMENT BEFORE..
Tm. Reg. U. S. Pat Off.—All rights reserved Copr. 1954 by United Feature Syndicate, Inc.
WHAT CHANCE HAVE I GOT AGAINST SAM SNEAD AND BEN HOGAN AND 'IKE'?
DON'T BE SILLY! THIS IS A WOMEN'S TOURNAMENT..THOSE GUYS DON'T PLAY IN WOMEN'S TOURNAMENTS!
LUCILLE VAN PELT ON THE FIRST TEE, PLEASE
SCHULZ
I FEEL LIKE I'M WALKING THE 'LAST MILE'...
DON'T WORRY... YOU'RE AN UNKNOWN.. NOBODY WILL EVEN BE WATCHING YOU...
To the First tee
CONTINUED
5-16

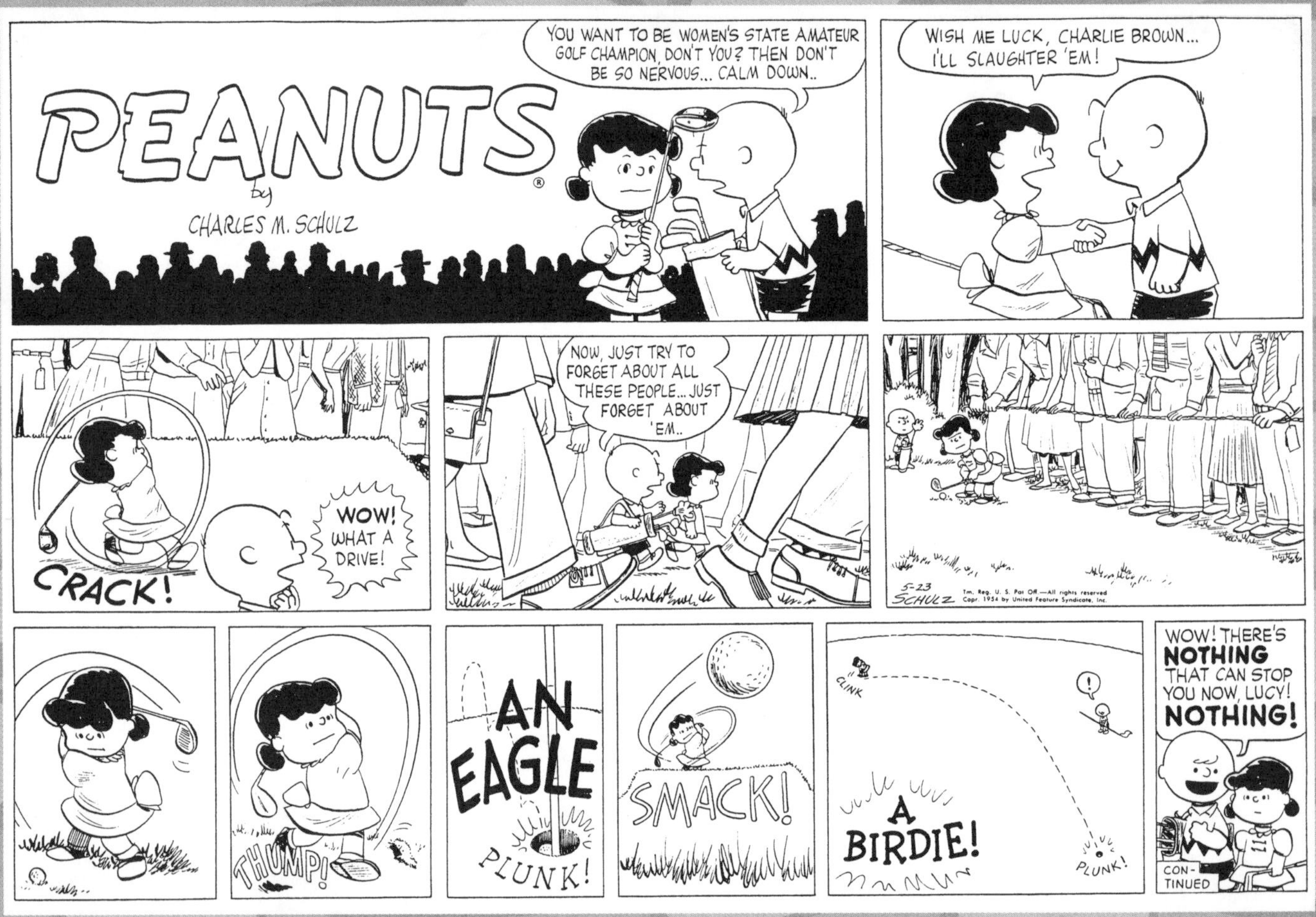
PEANUTS
by
CHARLES M. SCHULZ
YOU WANT TO BE WOMEN'S STATE AMATEUR GOLF CHAMPION, DON'T YOU? THEN DON'T BE SO NERVOUS... CALM DOWN..
WISH ME LUCK, CHARLIE BROWN... I'LL SLAUGHTER 'EM!
CRACK!
WOW! WHAT A DRIVE!
NOW, JUST TRY TO FORGET ABOUT ALL THESE PEOPLE... JUST FORGET ABOUT 'EM..
5-23
SCHULZ
Tm. Reg. U. S. Pat. Off.—All rights reserved
Copr. 1954 by United Feature Syndicate, Inc.
THUMP!
AN EAGLE
PLUNK!
SMACK!
CLINK
!
A BIRDIE!
PLUNK!
WOW! THERE'S NOTHING THAT CAN STOP YOU NOW, LUCY! NOTHING!
CON-TINUED

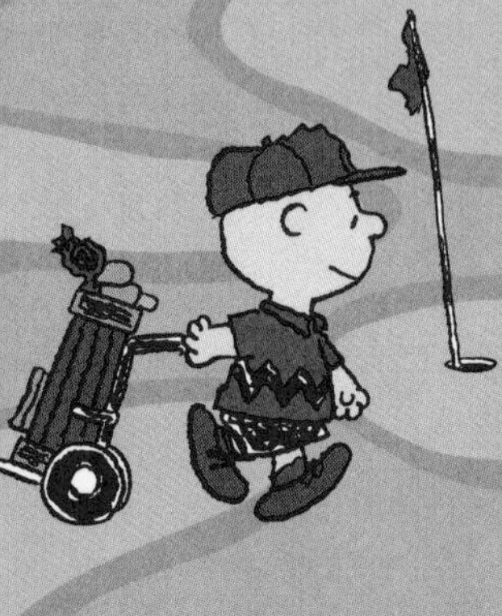

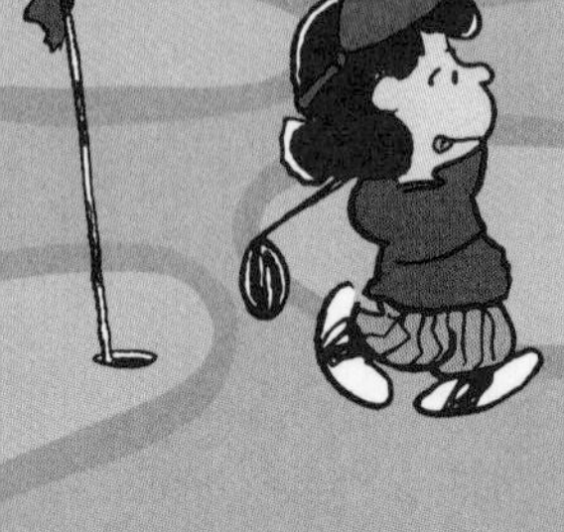

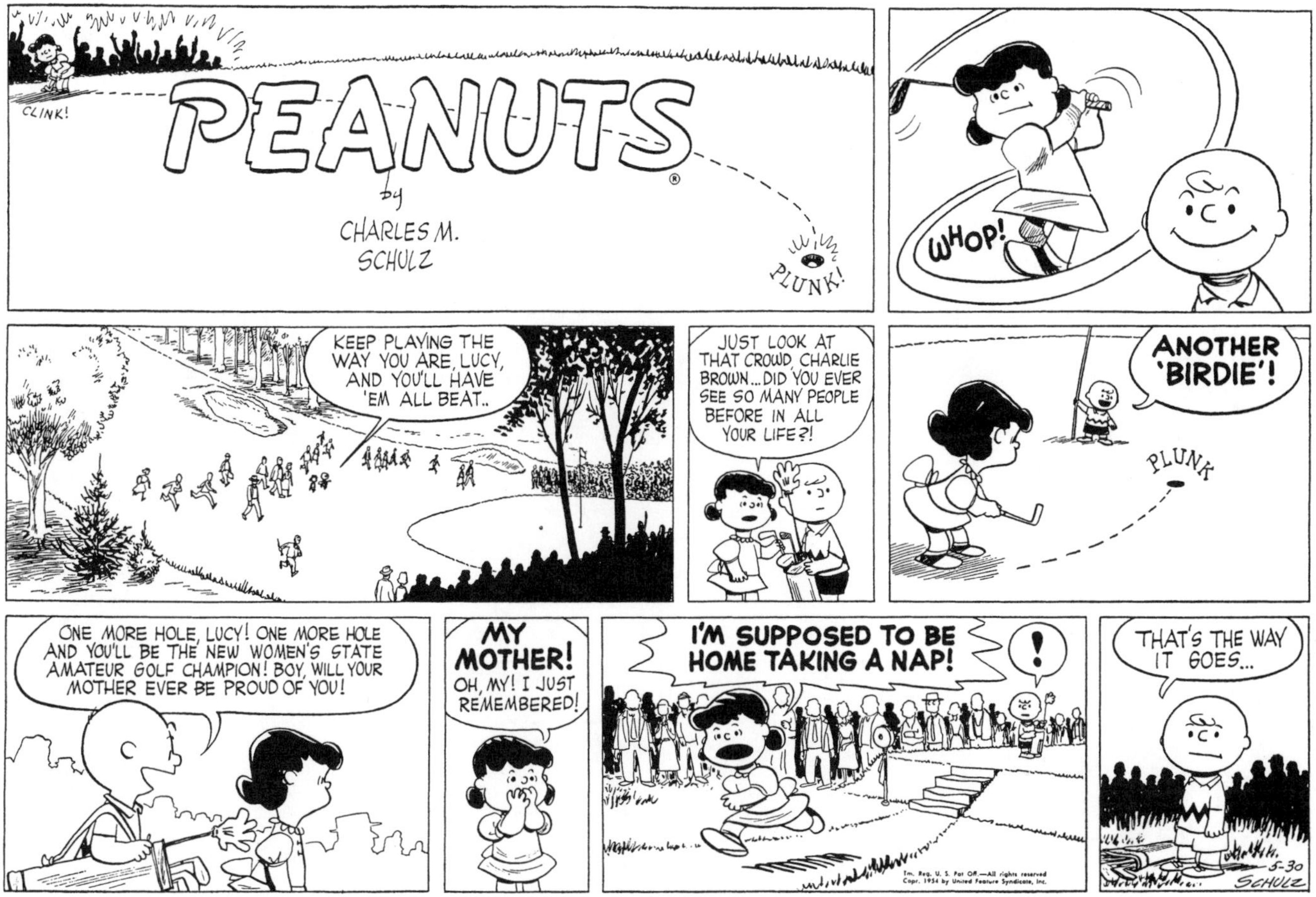
CLINK!
PEANUTS
by
CHARLES M.
SCHULZ
PLUNK!
WHOP!
KEEP PLAYING THE WAY YOU ARE, LUCY, AND YOU'LL HAVE 'EM ALL BEAT..
JUST LOOK AT THAT CROWD, CHARLIE BROWN...DID YOU EVER SEE SO MANY PEOPLE BEFORE IN ALL YOUR LIFE?!
ANOTHER 'BIRDIE'!
PLUNK
ONE MORE HOLE, LUCY! ONE MORE HOLE AND YOU'LL BE THE NEW WOMEN'S STATE AMATEUR GOLF CHAMPION! BOY, WILL YOUR MOTHER EVER BE PROUD OF YOU!
MY MOTHER! OH, MY! I JUST REMEMBERED!
I'M SUPPOSED TO BE HOME TAKING A NAP!
!
Tm. Reg. U. S. Pat. Off.—All rights reserved
Copr. 1954 by United Feature Syndicate, Inc.
THAT'S THE WAY IT GOES...
5-30
SCHULZ

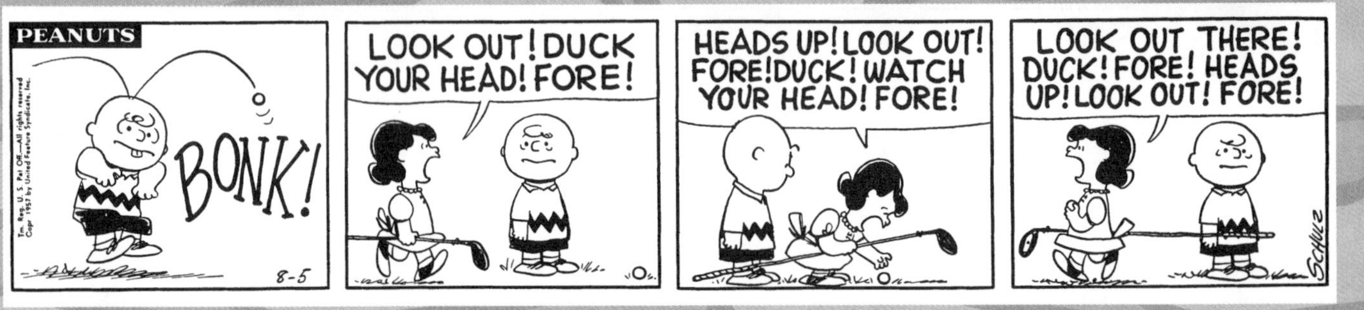
PEANUTS
BONK!
8-5
LOOK OUT! DUCK YOUR HEAD! FORE!
HEADS UP! LOOK OUT! FORE! DUCK! WATCH YOUR HEAD! FORE!
LOOK OUT, THERE! DUCK! FORE! HEADS UP! LOOK OUT! FORE!
SCHULZ

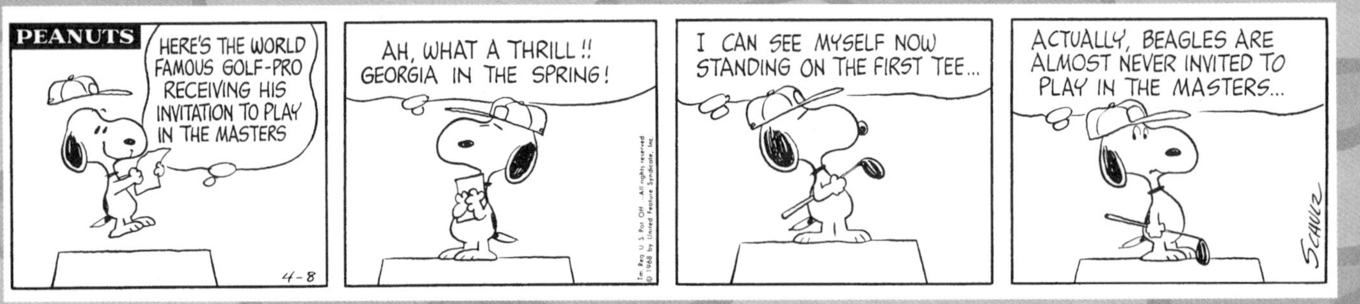
PEANUTS
HERE'S THE WORLD FAMOUS GOLF-PRO RECEIVING HIS INVITATION TO PLAY IN THE MASTERS
4-8
AH, WHAT A THRILL!! GEORGIA IN THE SPRING!
I CAN SEE MYSELF NOW STANDING ON THE FIRST TEE...
ACTUALLY, BEAGLES ARE ALMOST NEVER INVITED TO PLAY IN THE MASTERS...
SCHULZ

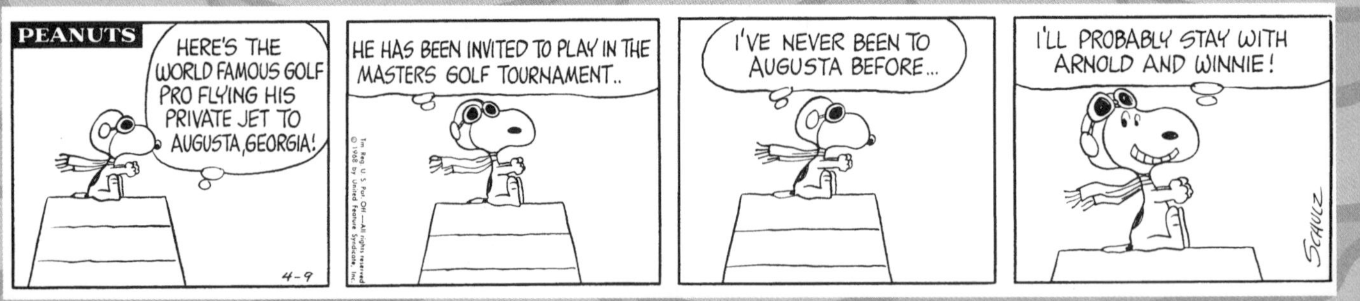
PEANUTS
HERE'S THE WORLD FAMOUS GOLF PRO FLYING HIS PRIVATE JET TO AUGUSTA, GEORGIA!
4-9
HE HAS BEEN INVITED TO PLAY IN THE MASTERS GOLF TOURNAMENT..
I'VE NEVER BEEN TO AUGUSTA BEFORE...
I'LL PROBABLY STAY WITH ARNOLD AND WINNIE!
SCHULZ

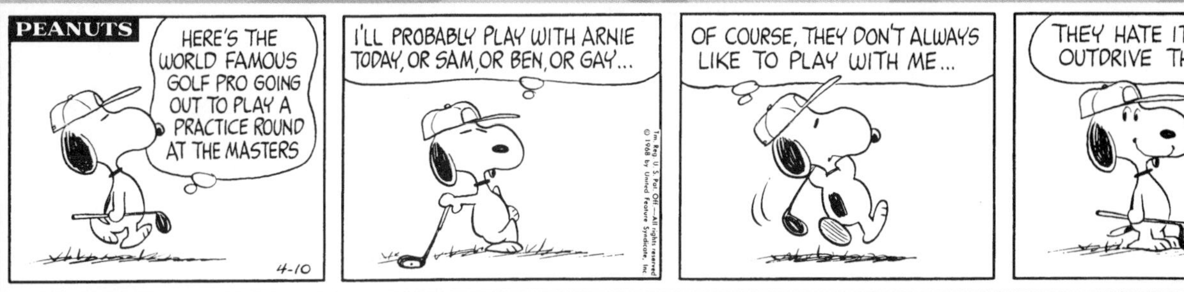
PEANUTS
HERE'S THE WORLD FAMOUS GOLF PRO GOING OUT TO PLAY A PRACTICE ROUND AT THE MASTERS
4-10
I'LL PROBABLY PLAY WITH ARNIE TODAY, OR SAM, OR BEN, OR GAY...
Tm. Reg. U.S. Pat. Off.—All rights reserved © 1968 by United Feature Syndicate, Inc.
OF COURSE, THEY DON'T ALWAYS LIKE TO PLAY WITH ME...
THEY HATE IT WHEN I OUTDRIVE THEM!
SCHULZ

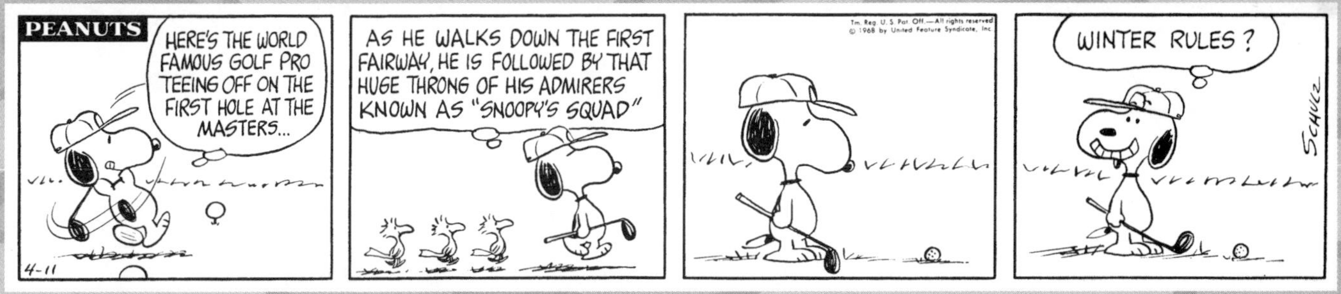
PEANUTS
HERE'S THE WORLD FAMOUS GOLF PRO TEEING OFF ON THE FIRST HOLE AT THE MASTERS...
4-11
AS HE WALKS DOWN THE FIRST FAIRWAY, HE IS FOLLOWED BY THAT HUGE THRONG OF HIS ADMIRERS KNOWN AS "SNOOPY'S SQUAD"
Tm. Reg. U.S. Pat. Off.—All rights reserved © 1968 by United Feature Syndicate, Inc.
WINTER RULES?
SCHULZ

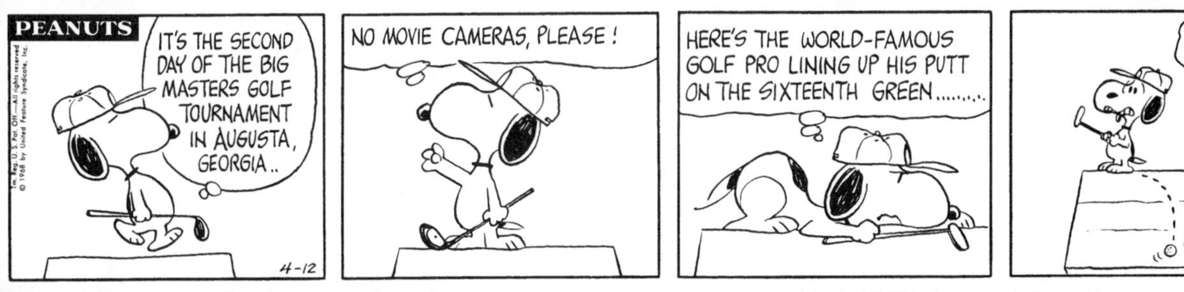
PEANUTS
IT'S THE SECOND DAY OF THE BIG MASTERS GOLF TOURNAMENT IN AUGUSTA, GEORGIA..
Tm. Reg. U.S. Pat. Off.—All rights reserved © 1968 by United Feature Syndicate, Inc.
4-12
NO MOVIE CAMERAS, PLEASE!
HERE'S THE WORLD-FAMOUS GOLF PRO LINING UP HIS PUTT ON THE SIXTEENTH GREEN........
SCHULZ

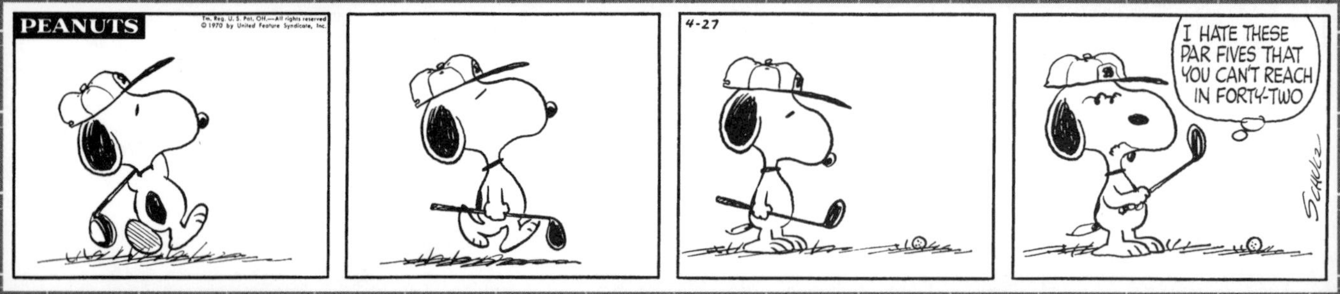
PEANUTS
Tm. Reg. U. S. Pat. Off.—All rights reserved © 1970 by United Feature Syndicate, Inc.
4-27
I HATE THESE PAR FIVES THAT YOU CAN'T REACH IN FORTY-TWO
SCHULZ

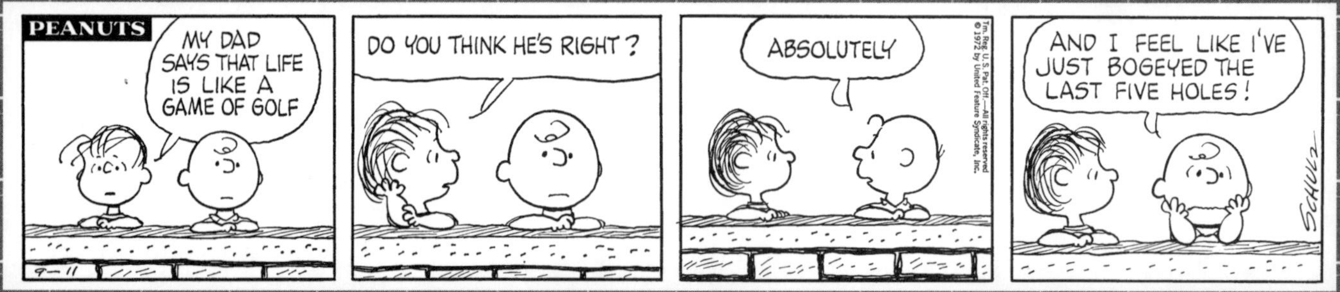
PEANUTS
MY DAD SAYS THAT LIFE IS LIKE A GAME OF GOLF
9-11
DO YOU THINK HE'S RIGHT ?
ABSOLUTELY
Tm. Reg. U. S. Pat. Off.—All rights reserved © 1972 by United Feature Syndicate, Inc.
AND I FEEL LIKE I'VE JUST BOGEYED THE LAST FIVE HOLES !
SCHULZ

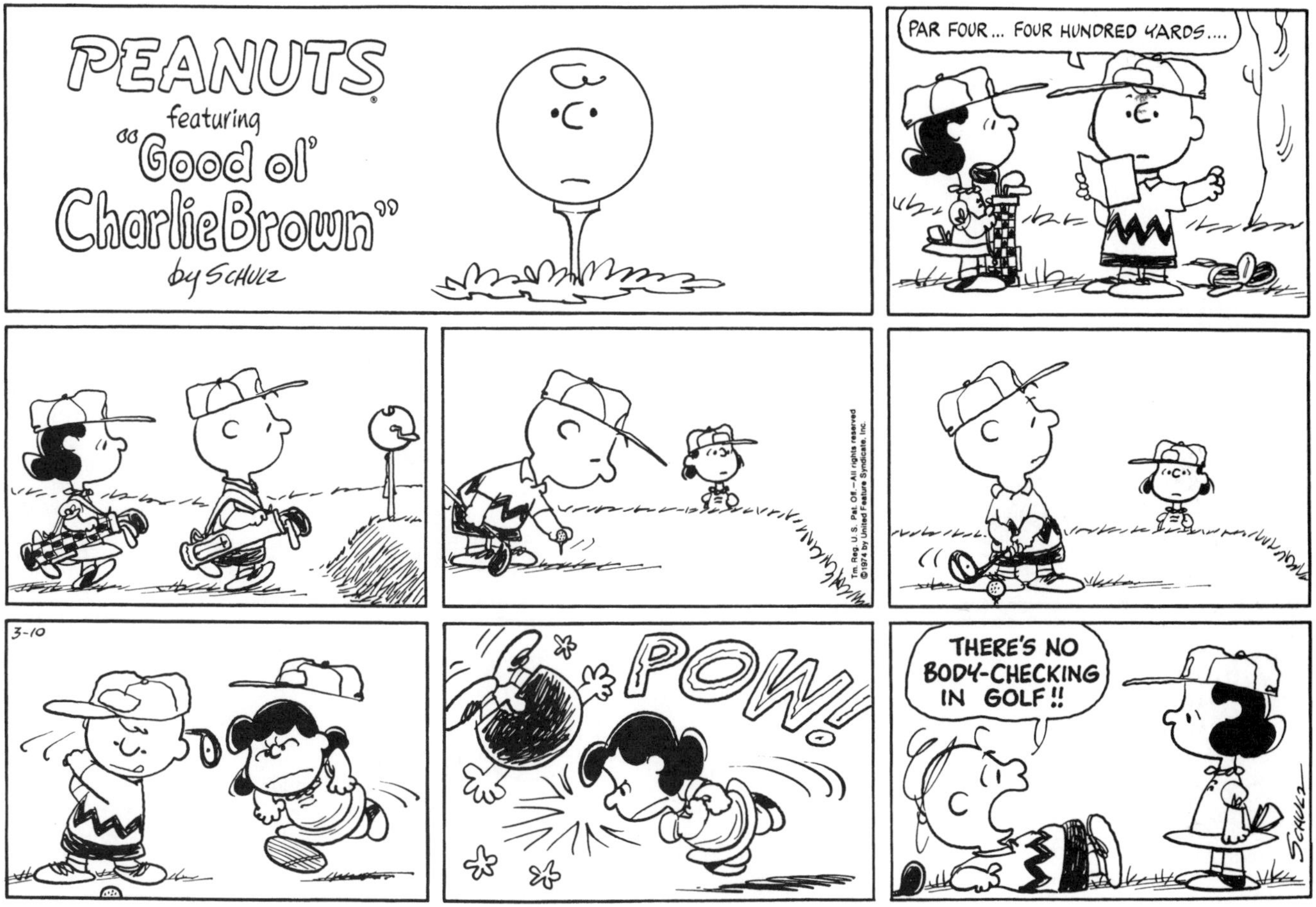
PEANUTS
featuring
"Good ol' Charlie Brown"
by SCHULZ
PAR FOUR... FOUR HUNDRED YARDS....
Tm. Reg. U.S. Pat. Off.—All rights reserved
©1974 by United Feature Syndicate, Inc.
3-10
POW!
THERE'S NO BODY-CHECKING IN GOLF!!
SCHULZ

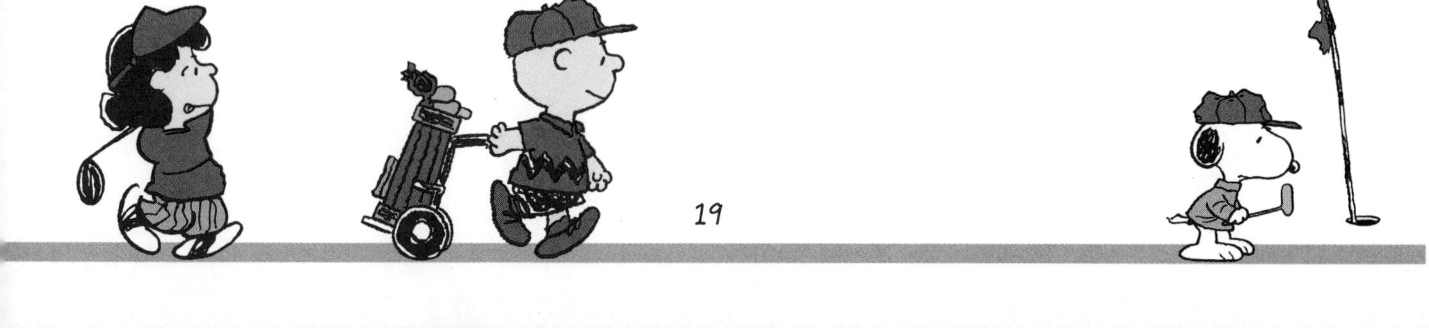

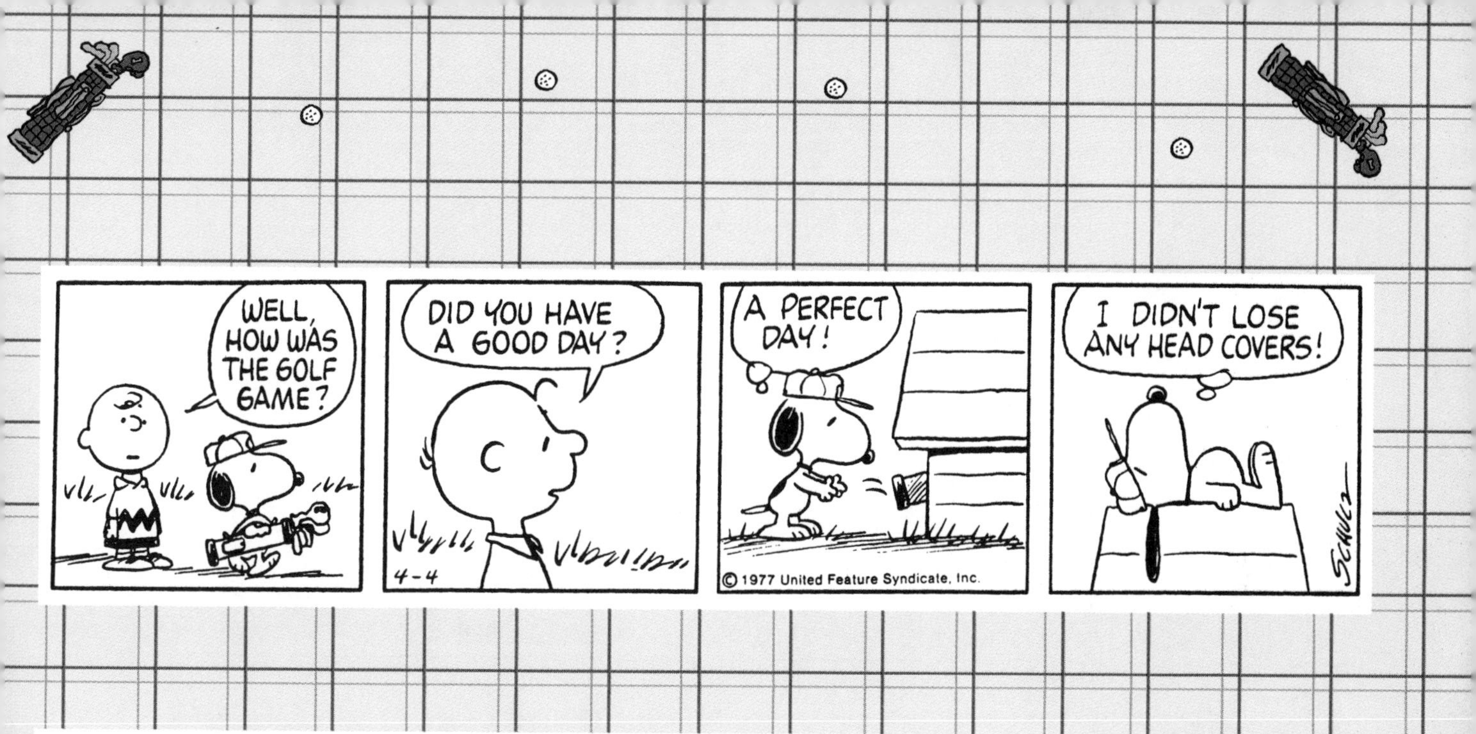
WELL, HOW WAS THE GOLF GAME?
DID YOU HAVE A GOOD DAY?
4-4
A PERFECT DAY!
© 1977 United Feature Syndicate, Inc.
I DIDN'T LOSE ANY HEAD COVERS!
SCHULZ

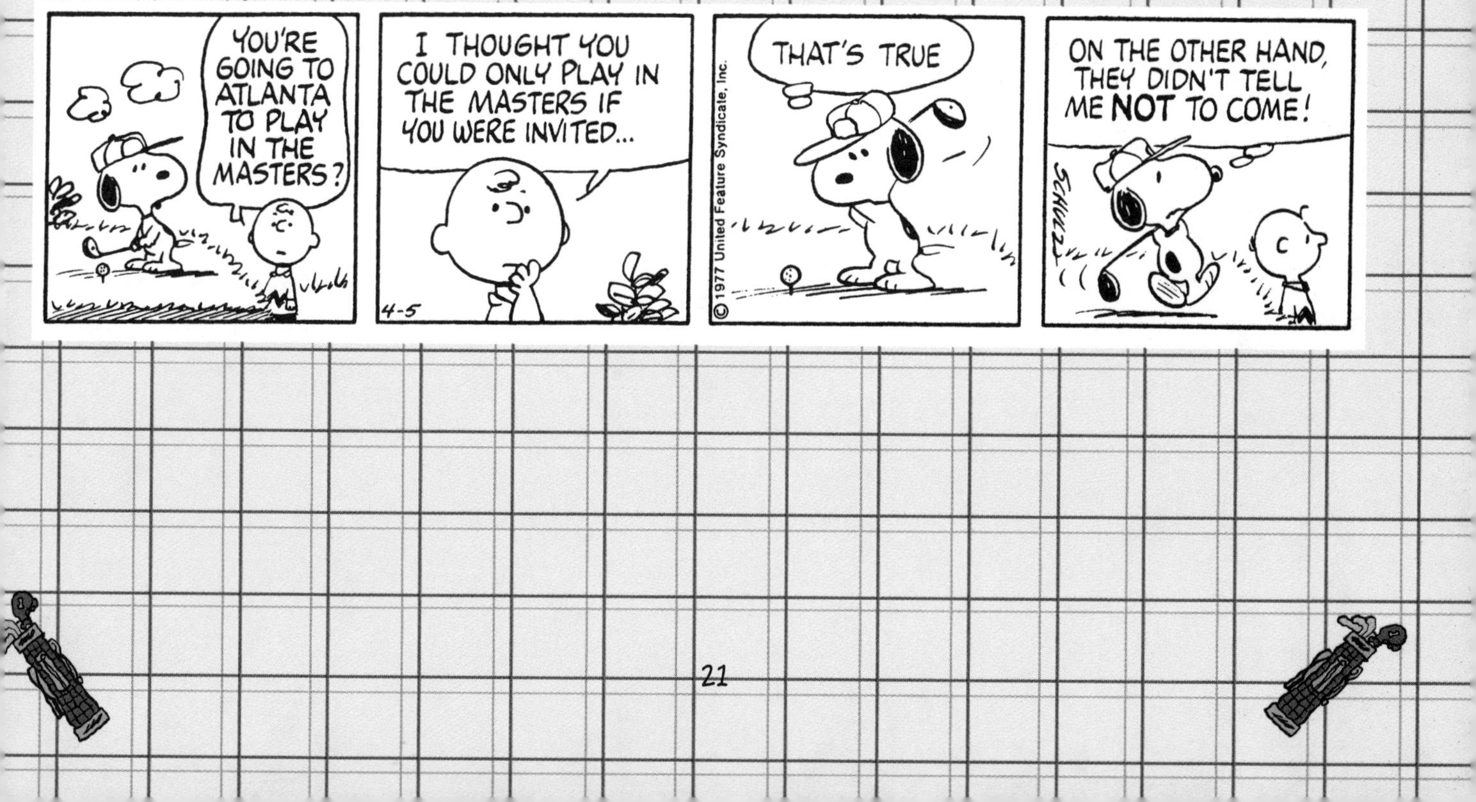
YOU'RE GOING TO ATLANTA TO PLAY IN THE MASTERS?
I THOUGHT YOU COULD ONLY PLAY IN THE MASTERS IF YOU WERE INVITED...
4-5
© 1977 United Feature Syndicate, Inc.
THAT'S TRUE
ON THE OTHER HAND, THEY DIDN'T TELL ME **NOT** TO COME!
SCHULZ

© 1977 United Feature Syndicate, Inc.
GOOD GRIEF, DON'T GO OUT OF BOUNDS!
HIT A TREE! HIT A BUILDING!
HIT A HOUSEWIFE!
4-6
SCHULZ

OTHER GOLFERS ARE LUCKY...
© 1977 United Feature Syndicate, Inc.
THEY HAVE CADDIES WHO TAKE THE FLAG OUT OF THE HOLE...
MY CADDY FALLS IN THE HOLE!
4-7
SCHULZ

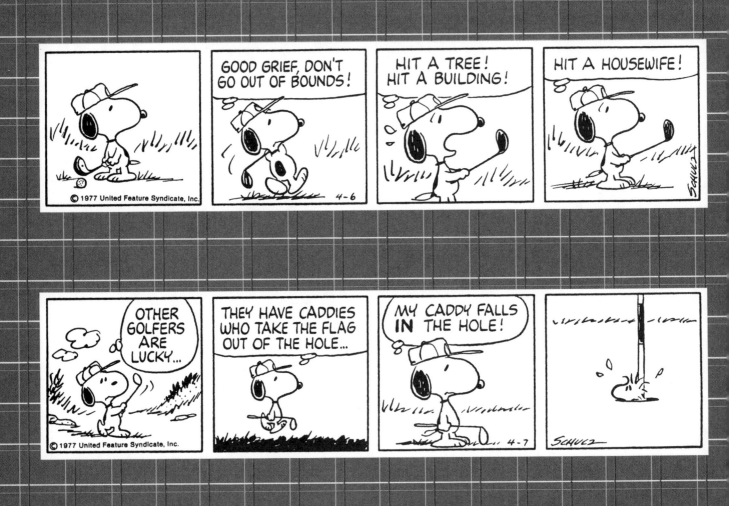

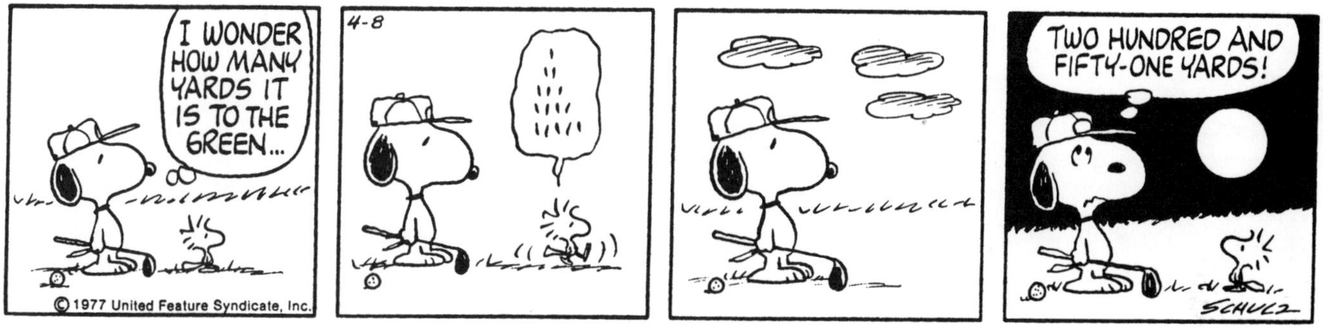
I WONDER HOW MANY YARDS IT IS TO THE GREEN...
© 1977 United Feature Syndicate, Inc.
4-8
TWO HUNDRED AND FIFTY-ONE YARDS!
SCHULZ

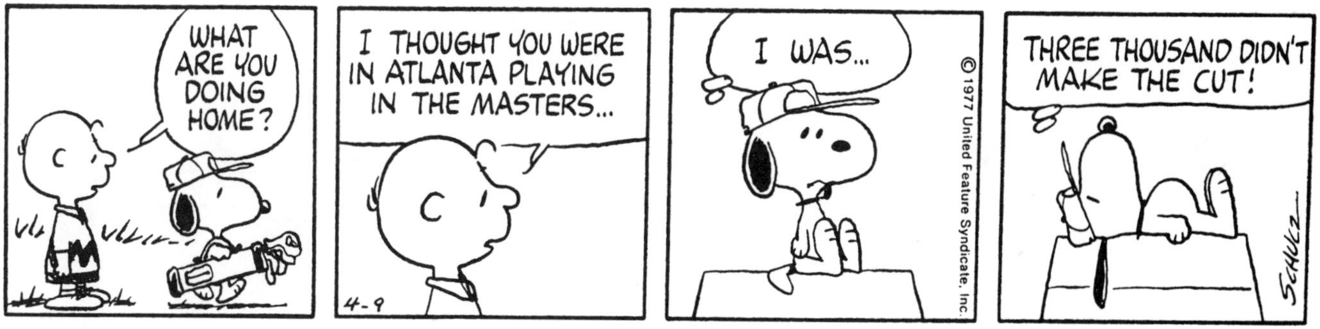
WHAT ARE YOU DOING HOME?
I THOUGHT YOU WERE IN ATLANTA PLAYING IN THE MASTERS...
4-9
I WAS...
© 1977 United Feature Syndicate, Inc.
THREE THOUSAND DIDN'T MAKE THE CUT!
SCHULZ

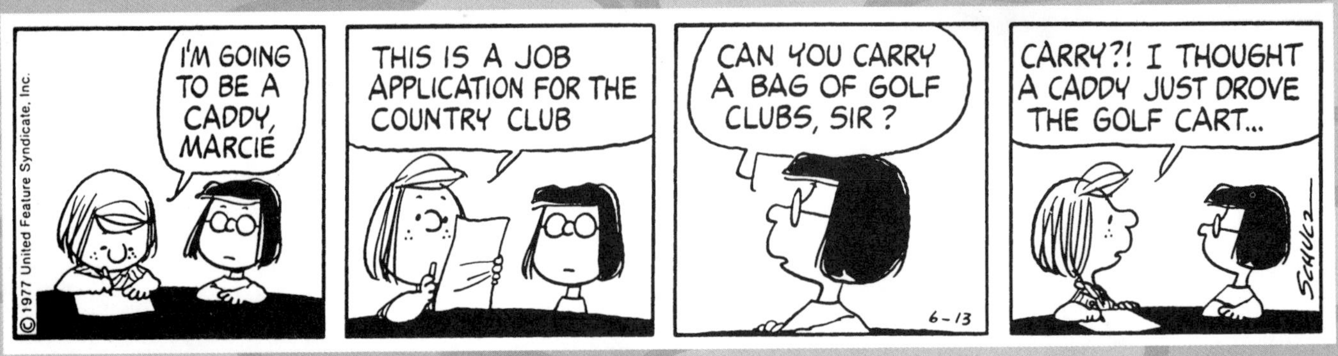
© 1977 United Feature Syndicate, Inc.
I'M GOING TO BE A CADDY, MARCIE
THIS IS A JOB APPLICATION FOR THE COUNTRY CLUB
CAN YOU CARRY A BAG OF GOLF CLUBS, SIR?
6-13
CARRY?! I THOUGHT A CADDY JUST DROVE THE GOLF CART...
SCHULZ

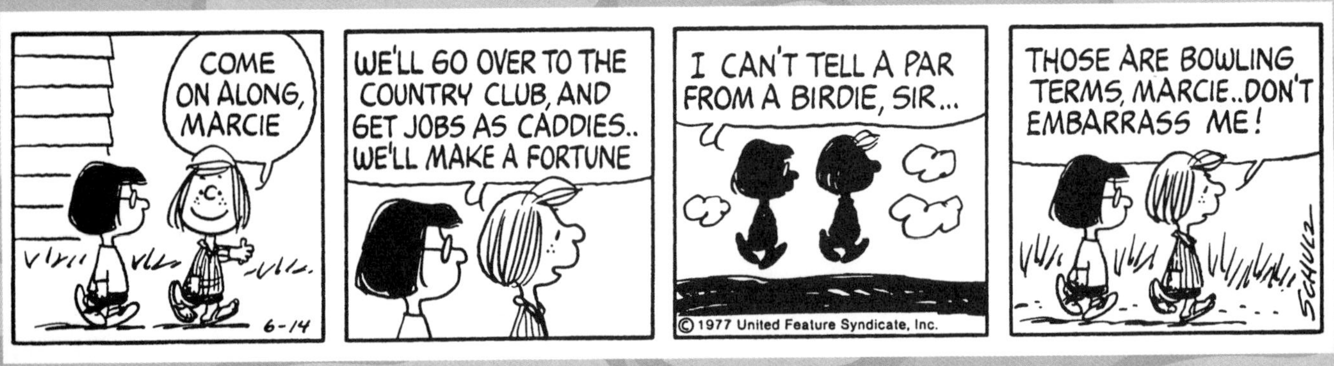
COME ON ALONG, MARCIE
6-14
WE'LL GO OVER TO THE COUNTRY CLUB, AND GET JOBS AS CADDIES.. WE'LL MAKE A FORTUNE
I CAN'T TELL A PAR FROM A BIRDIE, SIR...
© 1977 United Feature Syndicate, Inc.
THOSE ARE BOWLING TERMS, MARCIE..DON'T EMBARRASS ME!
SCHULZ

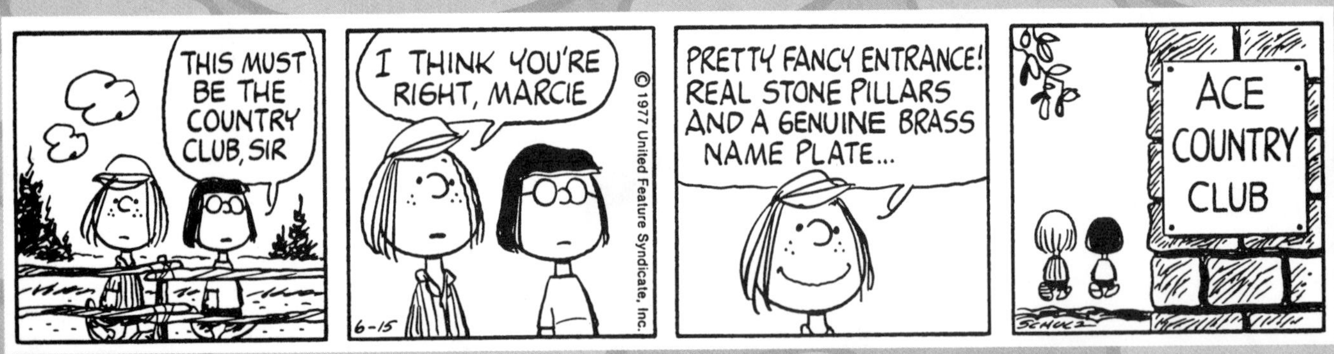
THIS MUST BE THE COUNTRY CLUB, SIR
I THINK YOU'RE RIGHT, MARCIE
6-15
© 1977 United Feature Syndicate, Inc.
PRETTY FANCY ENTRANCE! REAL STONE PILLARS AND A GENUINE BRASS NAME PLATE...
ACE COUNTRY CLUB
SCHULZ

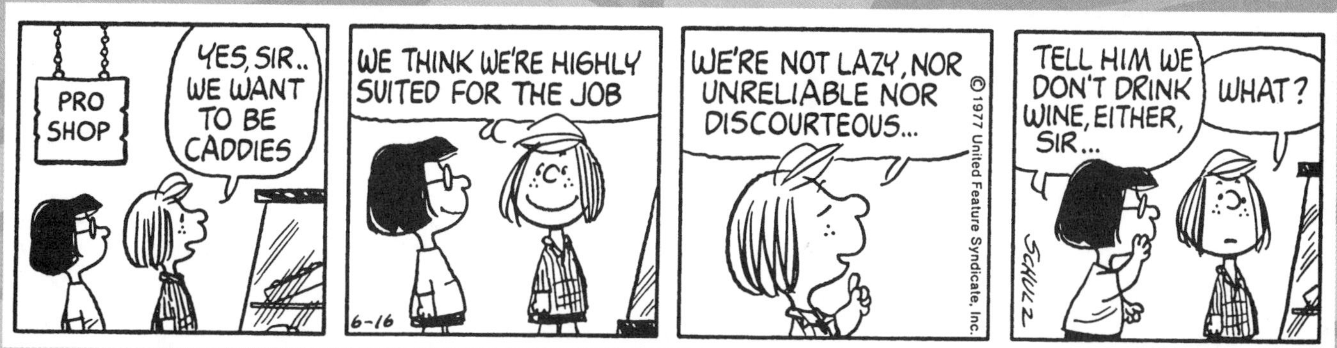
PRO SHOP
YES, SIR.. WE WANT TO BE CADDIES
WE THINK WE'RE HIGHLY SUITED FOR THE JOB
6-16
WE'RE NOT LAZY, NOR UNRELIABLE NOR DISCOURTEOUS...
© 1977 United Feature Syndicate, Inc.
TELL HIM WE DON'T DRINK WINE, EITHER, SIR...
WHAT?
SCHULZ

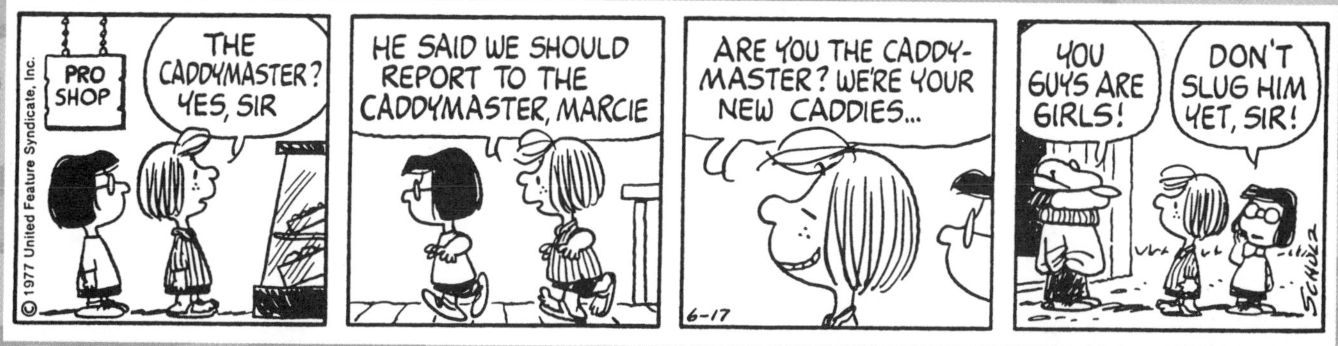
© 1977 United Feature Syndicate, Inc.
PRO SHOP
THE CADDYMASTER? YES, SIR
HE SAID WE SHOULD REPORT TO THE CADDYMASTER, MARCIE
ARE YOU THE CADDY-MASTER? WE'RE YOUR NEW CADDIES...
6-17
YOU GUYS ARE GIRLS!
DON'T SLUG HIM YET, SIR!
SCHULZ

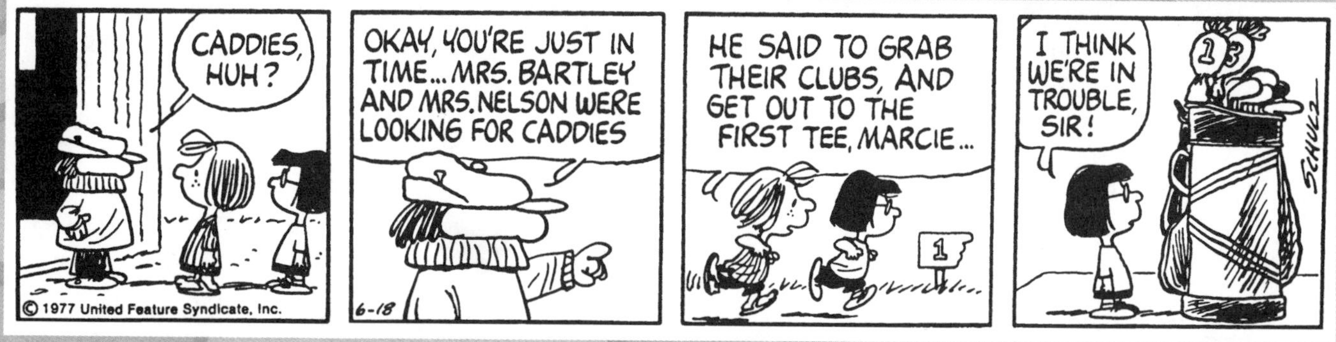
CADDIES, HUH?
© 1977 United Feature Syndicate, Inc.
OKAY, YOU'RE JUST IN TIME... MRS. BARTLEY AND MRS. NELSON WERE LOOKING FOR CADDIES
6-18
HE SAID TO GRAB THEIR CLUBS, AND GET OUT TO THE FIRST TEE, MARCIE...
1
I THINK WE'RE IN TROUBLE, SIR!
SCHULZ

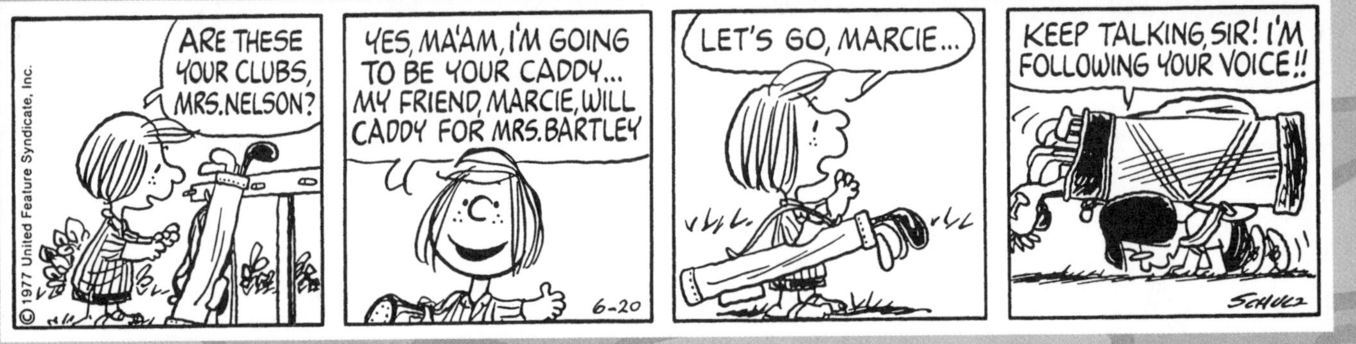
© 1977 United Feature Syndicate, Inc.
ARE THESE YOUR CLUBS, MRS. NELSON?
YES, MA'AM, I'M GOING TO BE YOUR CADDY... MY FRIEND, MARCIE, WILL CADDY FOR MRS. BARTLEY
6-20
LET'S GO, MARCIE...
KEEP TALKING, SIR! I'M FOLLOWING YOUR VOICE!!
SCHULZ

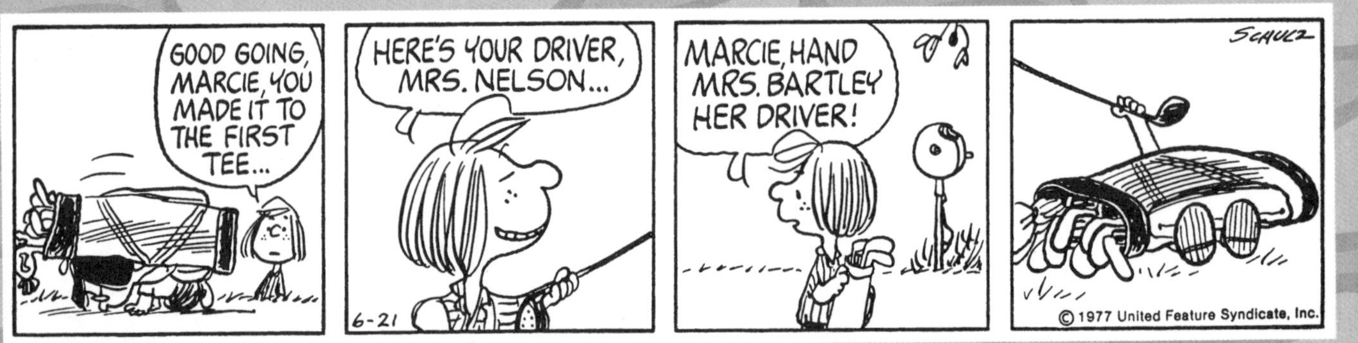
GOOD GOING, MARCIE, YOU MADE IT TO THE FIRST TEE...
HERE'S YOUR DRIVER, MRS. NELSON...
6-21
MARCIE, HAND MRS. BARTLEY HER DRIVER!
SCHULZ
© 1977 United Feature Syndicate, Inc.

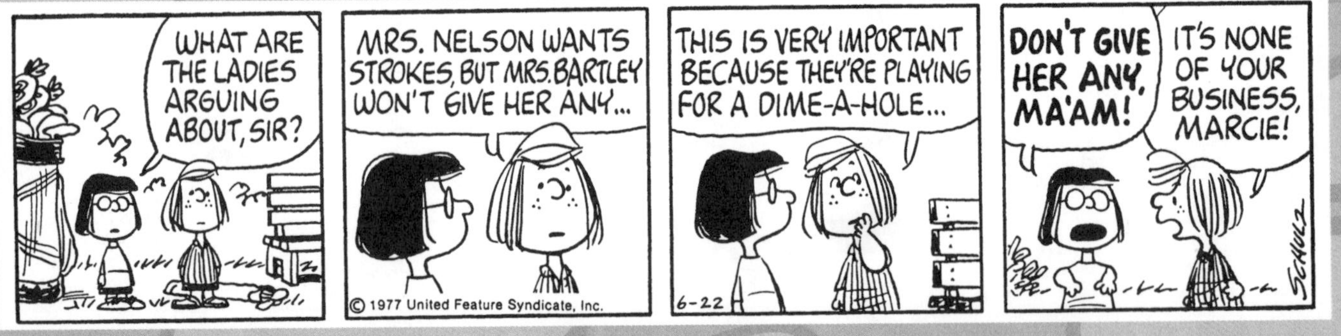
WHAT ARE THE LADIES ARGUING ABOUT, SIR?
MRS. NELSON WANTS STROKES, BUT MRS. BARTLEY WON'T GIVE HER ANY...
© 1977 United Feature Syndicate, Inc.
THIS IS VERY IMPORTANT BECAUSE THEY'RE PLAYING FOR A DIME-A-HOLE...
6-22
DON'T GIVE HER ANY, MA'AM!
IT'S NONE OF YOUR BUSINESS, MARCIE!
SCHULZ

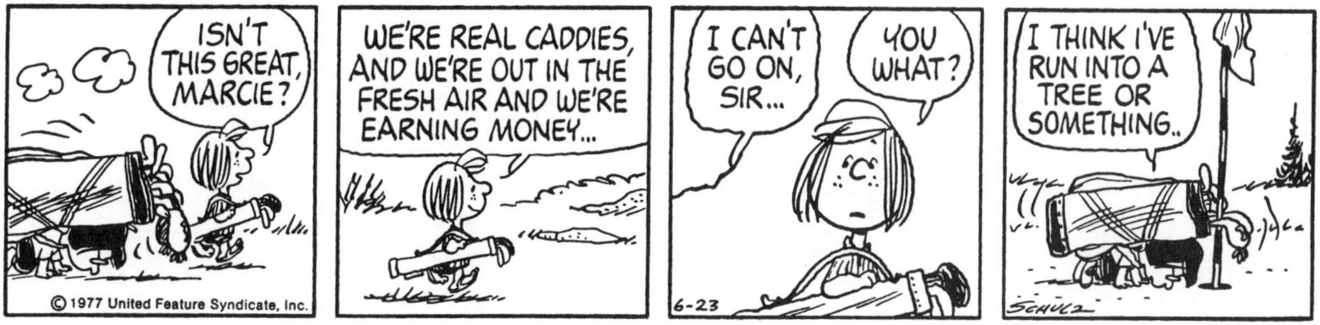
ISN'T THIS GREAT, MARCIE?
© 1977 United Feature Syndicate, Inc.
WE'RE REAL CADDIES, AND WE'RE OUT IN THE FRESH AIR AND WE'RE EARNING MONEY...
I CAN'T GO ON, SIR...
YOU WHAT?
6-23
I THINK I'VE RUN INTO A TREE OR SOMETHING..
SCHULZ

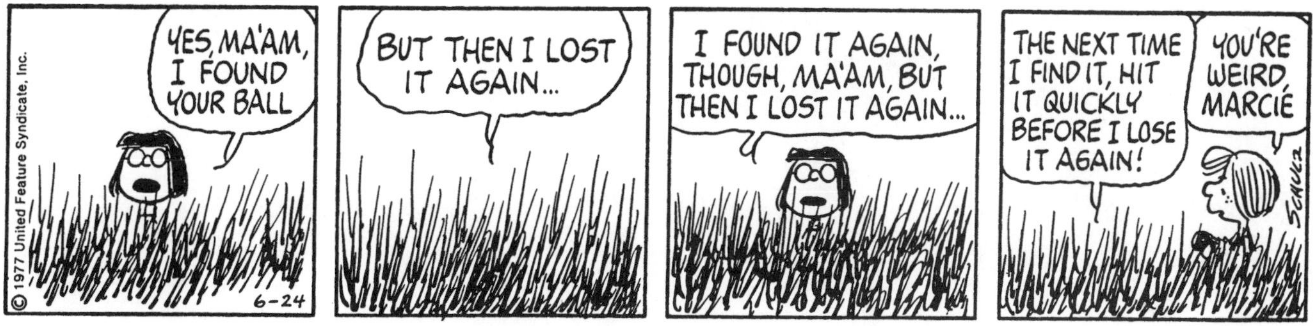
© 1977 United Feature Syndicate, Inc.
YES, MA'AM, I FOUND YOUR BALL
6-24
BUT THEN I LOST IT AGAIN...
I FOUND IT AGAIN, THOUGH, MA'AM, BUT THEN I LOST IT AGAIN...
THE NEXT TIME I FIND IT, HIT IT QUICKLY BEFORE I LOSE IT AGAIN!
YOU'RE WEIRD, MARCIE
SCHULZ

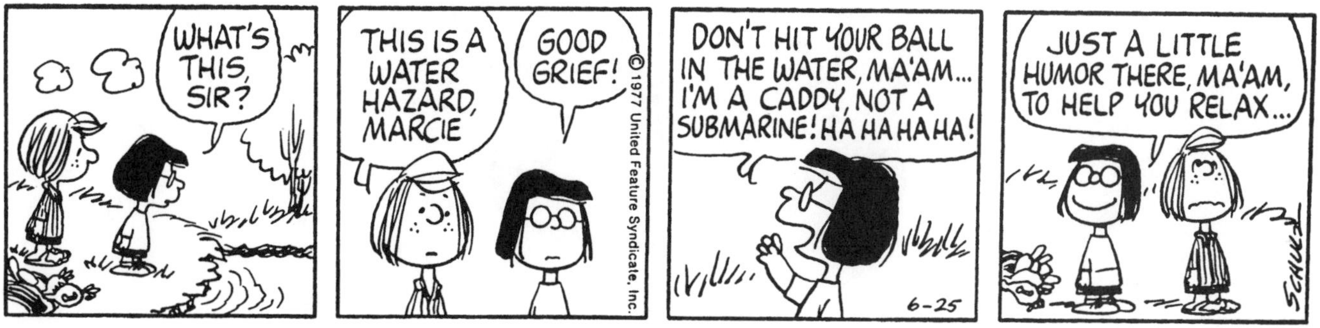
WHAT'S THIS, SIR?
THIS IS A WATER HAZARD, MARCIE
GOOD GRIEF!
© 1977 United Feature Syndicate, Inc.
DON'T HIT YOUR BALL IN THE WATER, MA'AM... I'M A CADDY, NOT A SUBMARINE! HA HA HA HA!
6-25
JUST A LITTLE HUMOR THERE, MA'AM, TO HELP YOU RELAX...
SCHULZ

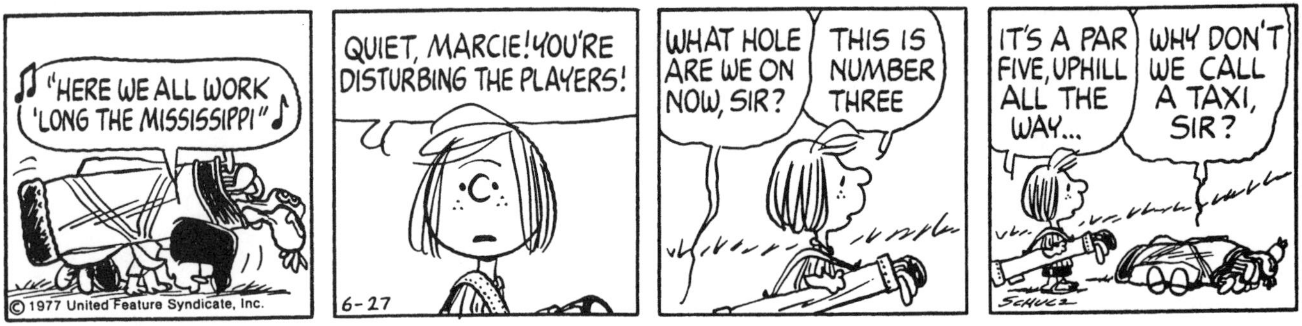
♫ "HERE WE ALL WORK 'LONG THE MISSISSIPPI" ♪
© 1977 United Feature Syndicate, Inc.
QUIET, MARCIE! YOU'RE DISTURBING THE PLAYERS!
6-27
WHAT HOLE ARE WE ON NOW, SIR?
THIS IS NUMBER THREE
IT'S A PAR FIVE, UPHILL ALL THE WAY...
WHY DON'T WE CALL A TAXI, SIR?
SCHULZ

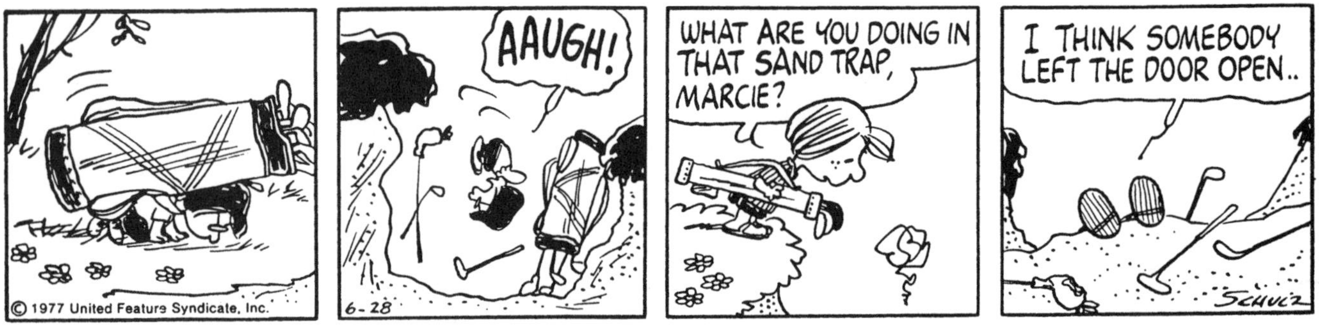
© 1977 United Feature Syndicate, Inc.
AAUGH!
6-28
WHAT ARE YOU DOING IN THAT SAND TRAP, MARCIE?
I THINK SOMEBODY LEFT THE DOOR OPEN..
SCHULZ

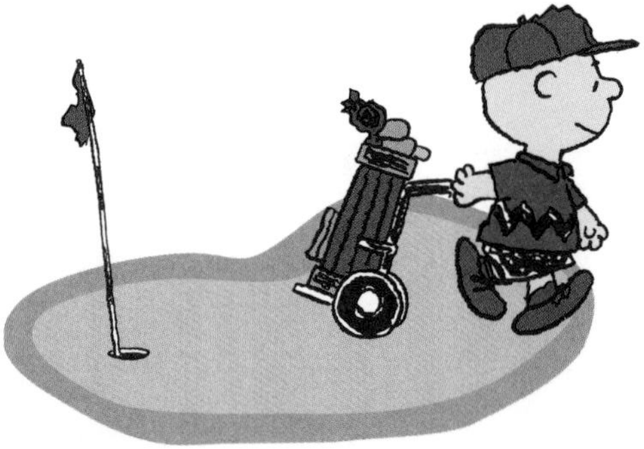

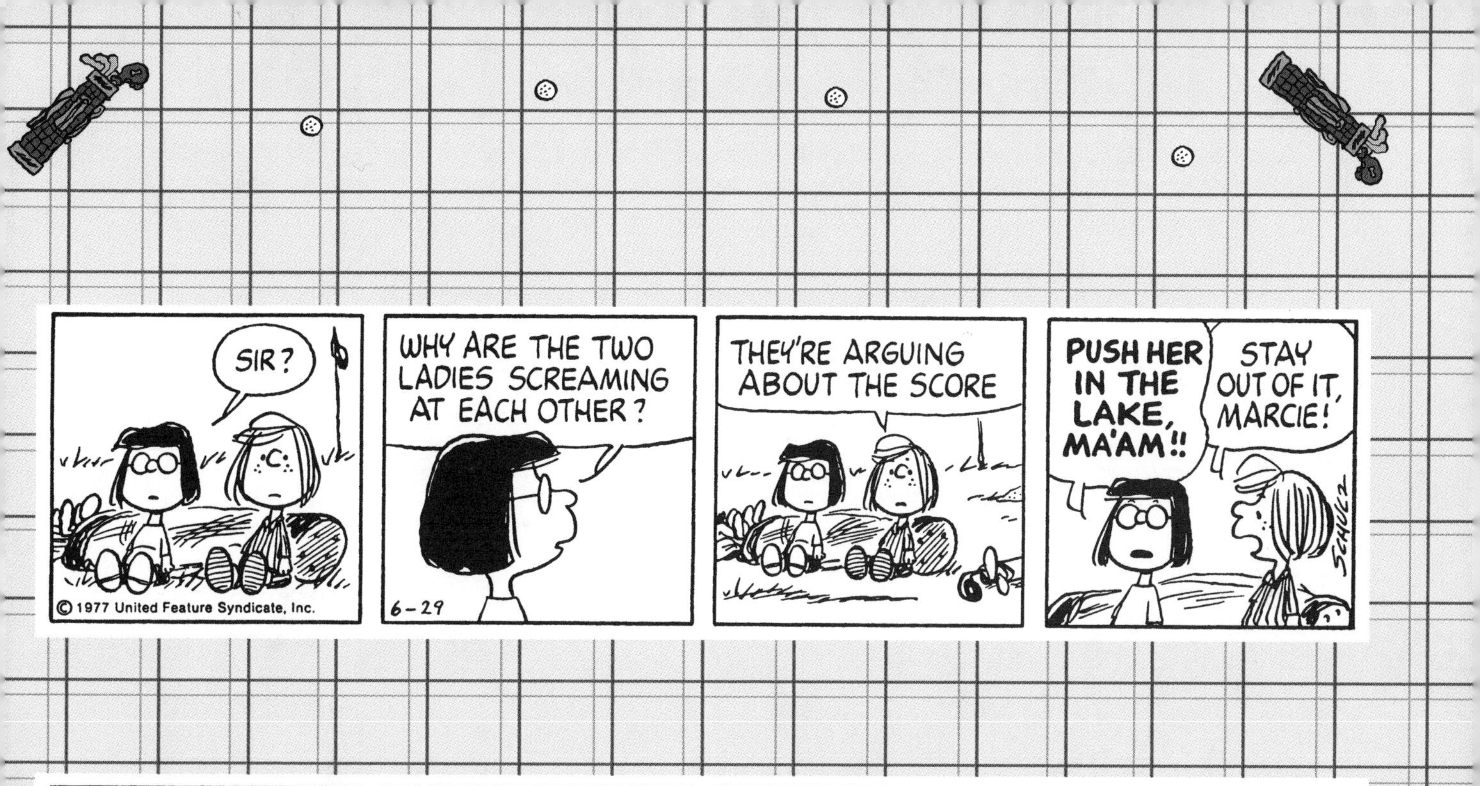
SIR?
© 1977 United Feature Syndicate, Inc.
WHY ARE THE TWO LADIES SCREAMING AT EACH OTHER?
6-29
THEY'RE ARGUING ABOUT THE SCORE
PUSH HER IN THE LAKE, MA'AM!!
STAY OUT OF IT, MARCIE!
SCHULZ

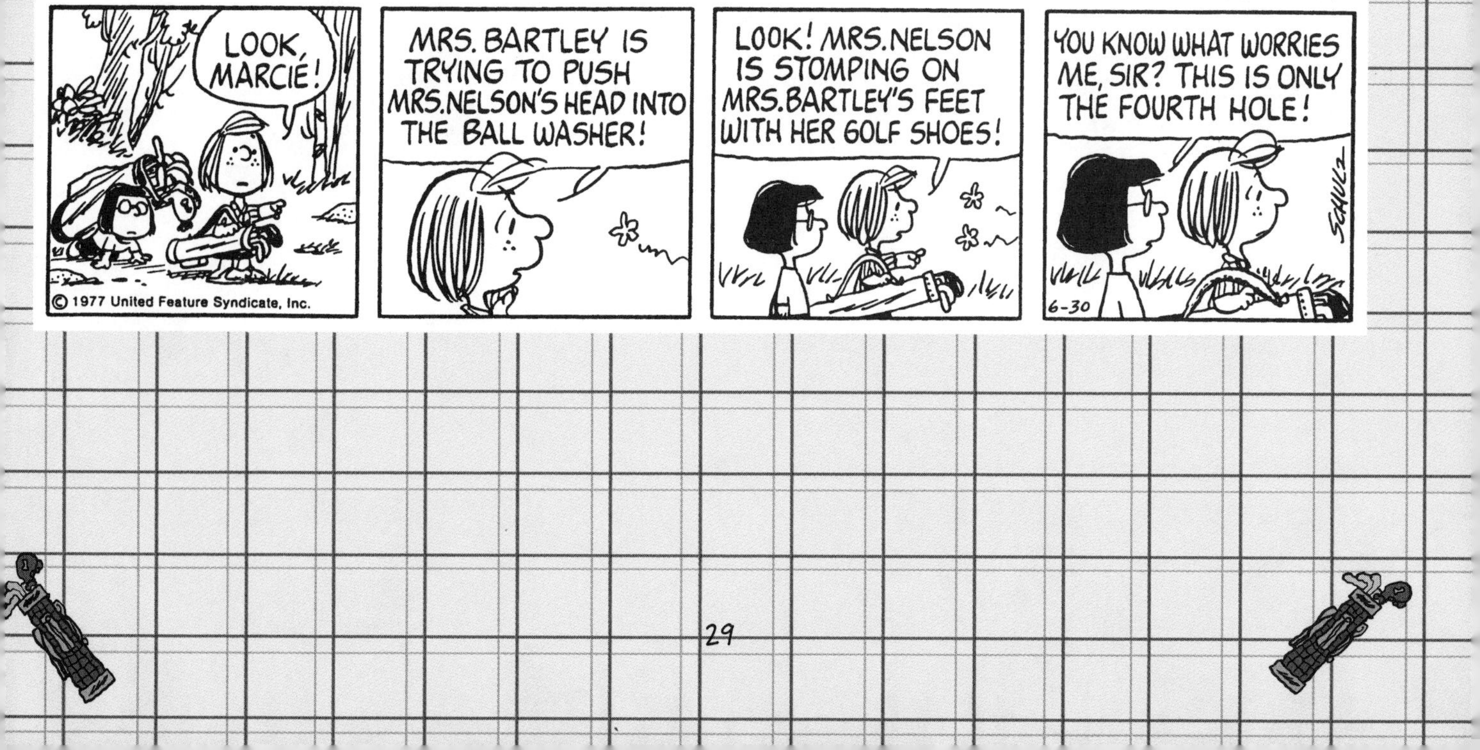
LOOK, MARCIE!
© 1977 United Feature Syndicate, Inc.
MRS. BARTLEY IS TRYING TO PUSH MRS. NELSON'S HEAD INTO THE BALL WASHER!
LOOK! MRS. NELSON IS STOMPING ON MRS. BARTLEY'S FEET WITH HER GOLF SHOES!
YOU KNOW WHAT WORRIES ME, SIR? THIS IS ONLY THE FOURTH HOLE!
SCHULZ
6-30

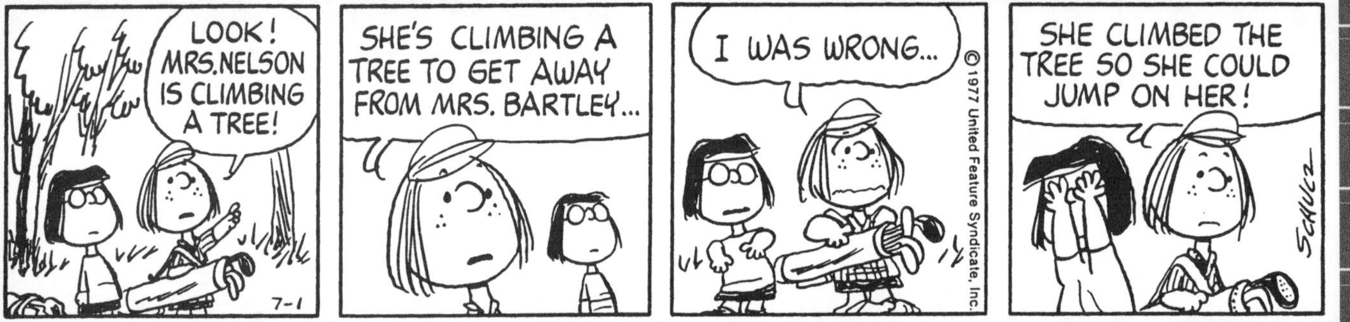
LOOK! MRS.NELSON IS CLIMBING A TREE!
7-1
SHE'S CLIMBING A TREE TO GET AWAY FROM MRS. BARTLEY...
I WAS WRONG...
© 1977 United Feature Syndicate, Inc.
SHE CLIMBED THE TREE SO SHE COULD JUMP ON HER!
SCHULZ

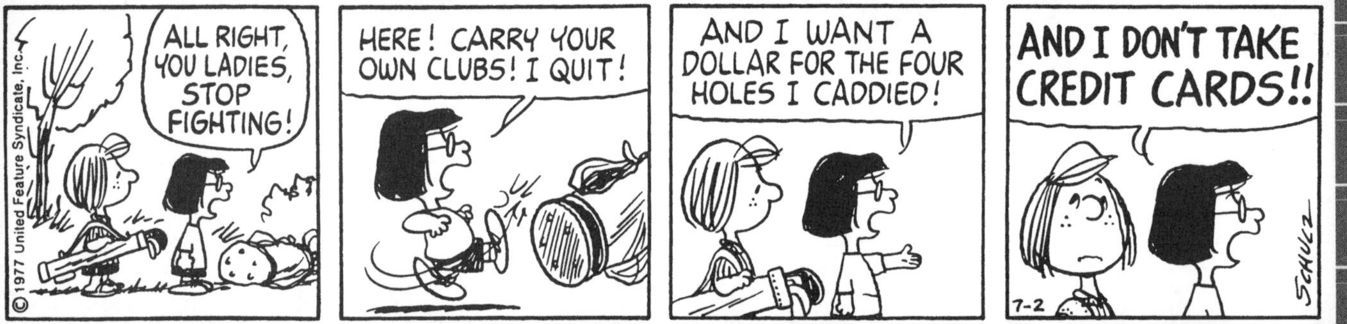
© 1977 United Feature Syndicate, Inc.
ALL RIGHT, YOU LADIES, STOP FIGHTING!
HERE! CARRY YOUR OWN CLUBS! I QUIT!
AND I WANT A DOLLAR FOR THE FOUR HOLES I CADDIED!
AND I DON'T TAKE CREDIT CARDS!!
7-2
SCHULZ

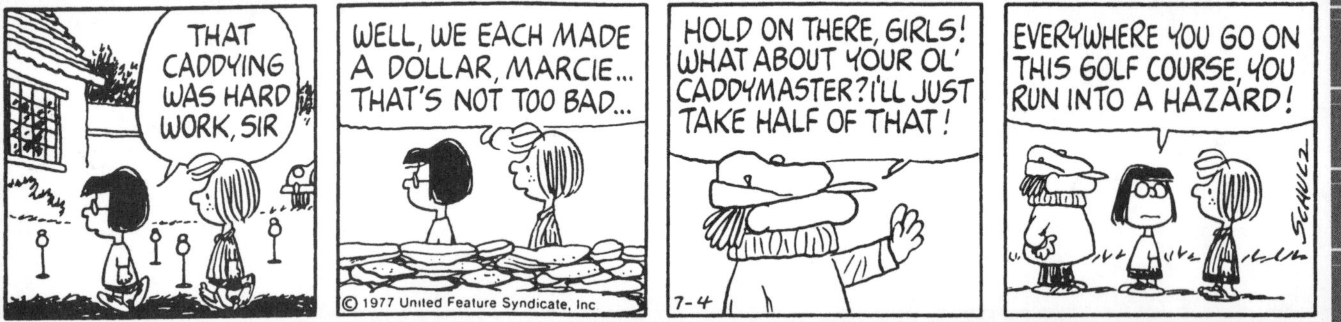
THAT CADDYING WAS HARD WORK, SIR
WELL, WE EACH MADE A DOLLAR, MARCIE... THAT'S NOT TOO BAD...
© 1977 United Feature Syndicate, Inc
HOLD ON THERE, GIRLS! WHAT ABOUT YOUR OL' CADDYMASTER? I'LL JUST TAKE HALF OF THAT!
7-4
EVERYWHERE YOU GO ON THIS GOLF COURSE, YOU RUN INTO A HAZARD!
SCHULZ

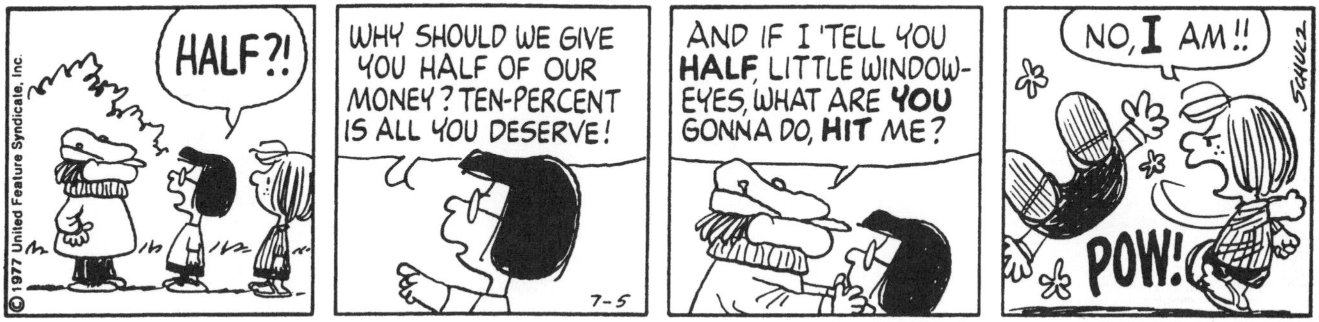
© 1977 United Feature Syndicate, Inc.
HALF?!
WHY SHOULD WE GIVE YOU HALF OF OUR MONEY? TEN-PERCENT IS ALL YOU DESERVE!
7-5
AND IF I TELL YOU **HALF**, LITTLE WINDOW-EYES, WHAT ARE **YOU** GONNA DO, **HIT** ME?
NO, **I** AM!!
POW!
SCHULZ

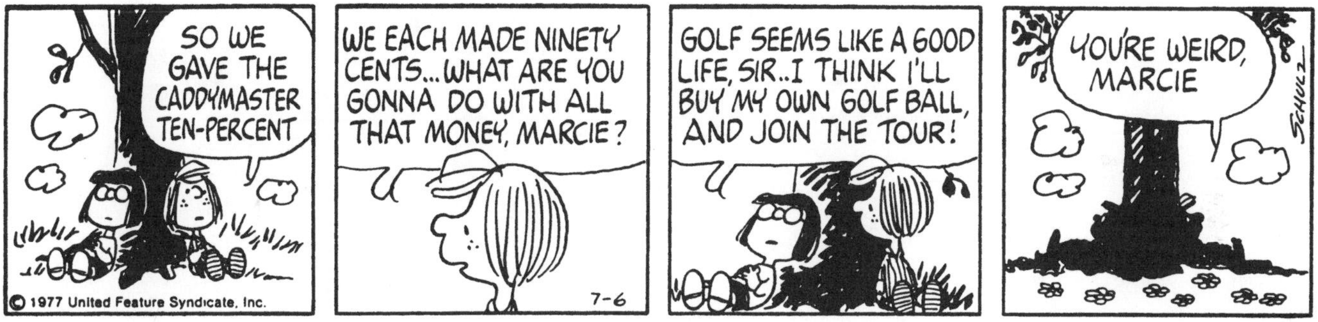
SO WE GAVE THE CADDYMASTER TEN-PERCENT
© 1977 United Feature Syndicate, Inc.
WE EACH MADE NINETY CENTS...WHAT ARE YOU GONNA DO WITH ALL THAT MONEY, MARCIE?
7-6
GOLF SEEMS LIKE A GOOD LIFE, SIR..I THINK I'LL BUY MY OWN GOLF BALL, AND JOIN THE TOUR!
YOU'RE WEIRD, MARCIE
SCHULZ

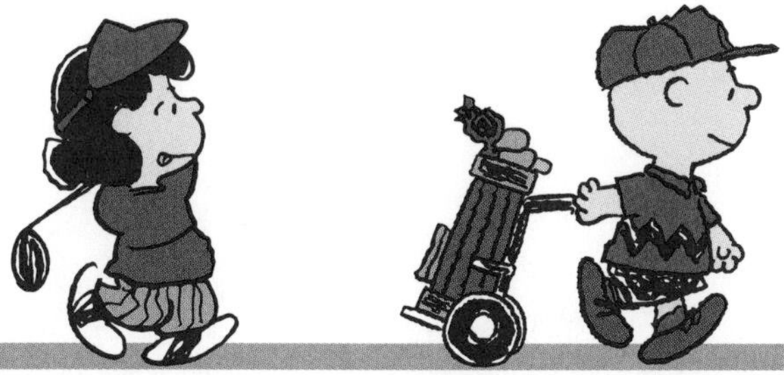

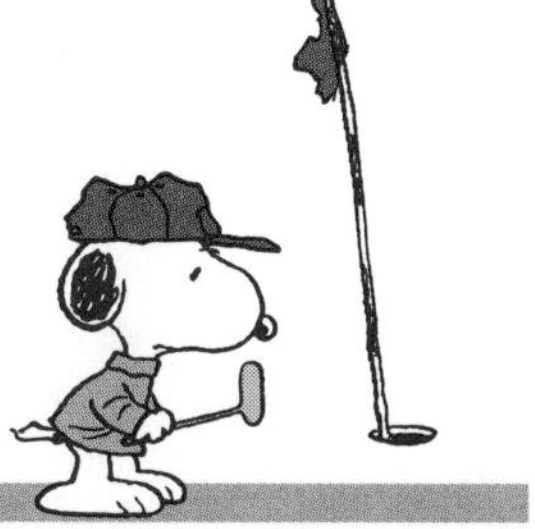

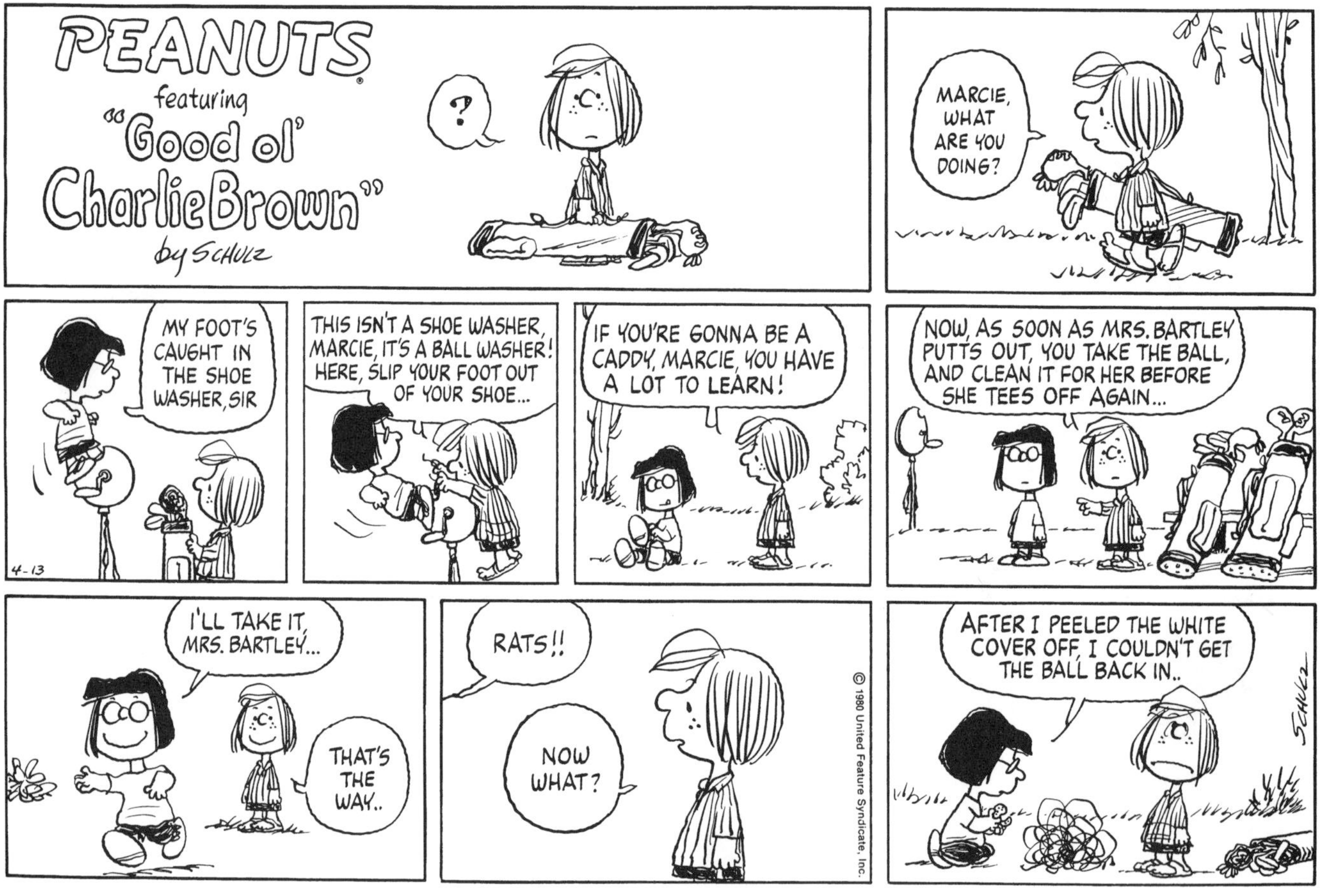
PEANUTS
featuring
"Good ol' Charlie Brown"
by SCHULZ
?
MARCIE, WHAT ARE YOU DOING?
MY FOOT'S CAUGHT IN THE SHOE WASHER, SIR
4-13
THIS ISN'T A SHOE WASHER, MARCIE, IT'S A BALL WASHER! HERE, SLIP YOUR FOOT OUT OF YOUR SHOE...
IF YOU'RE GONNA BE A CADDY, MARCIE, YOU HAVE A LOT TO LEARN!
NOW, AS SOON AS MRS. BARTLEY PUTTS OUT, YOU TAKE THE BALL, AND CLEAN IT FOR HER BEFORE SHE TEES OFF AGAIN...
I'LL TAKE IT, MRS. BARTLEY...
THAT'S THE WAY..
RATS!!
NOW WHAT?
AFTER I PEELED THE WHITE COVER OFF, I COULDN'T GET THE BALL BACK IN..
SCHULZ
© 1980 United Feature Syndicate, Inc.

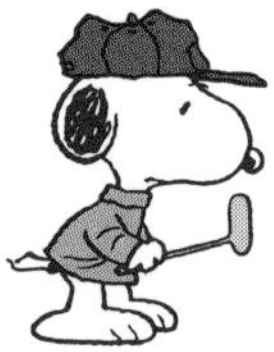

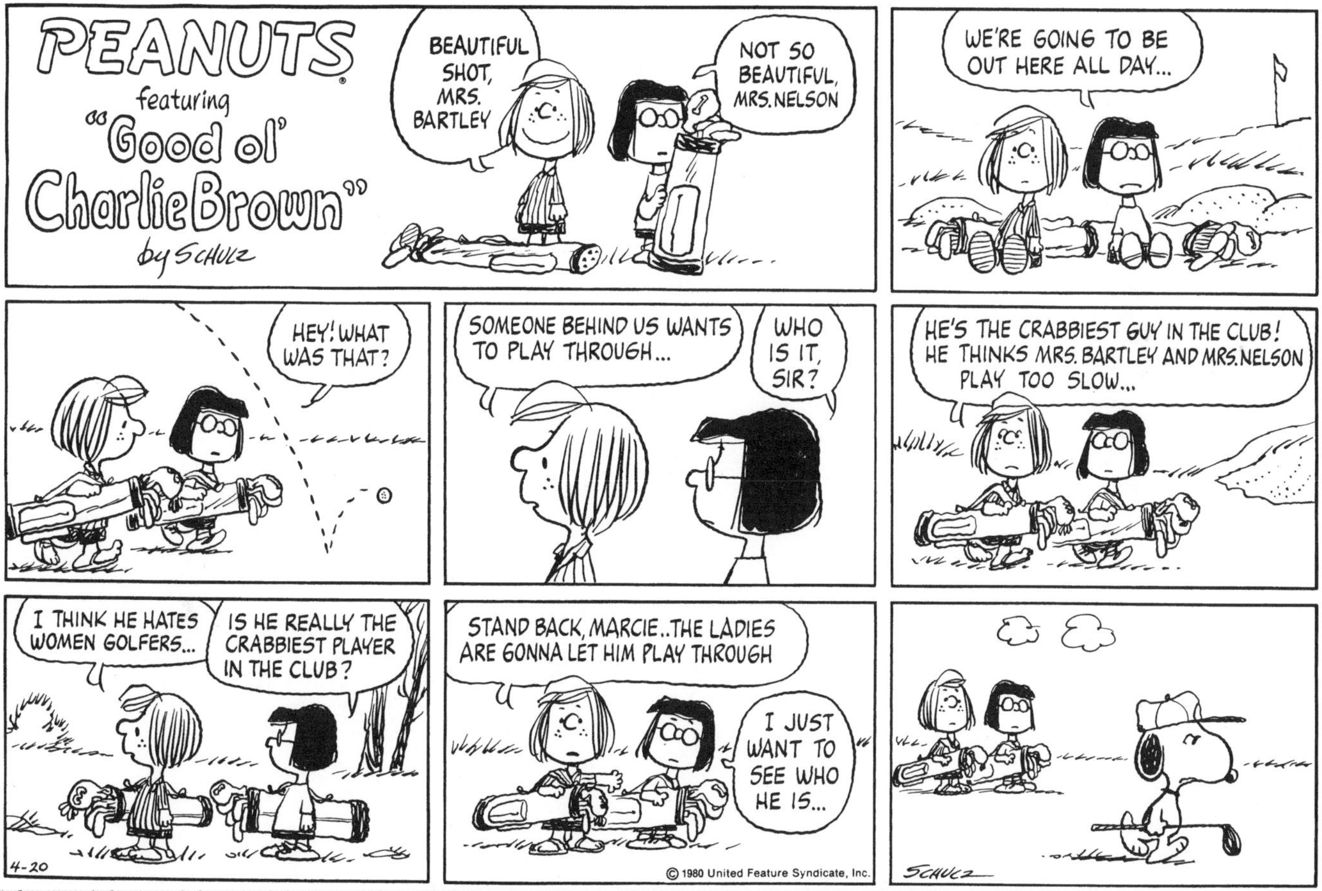
PEANUTS
featuring "Good ol' CharlieBrown"
by SCHULZ
BEAUTIFUL SHOT, MRS. BARTLEY
NOT SO BEAUTIFUL, MRS. NELSON
WE'RE GOING TO BE OUT HERE ALL DAY...
HEY! WHAT WAS THAT?
SOMEONE BEHIND US WANTS TO PLAY THROUGH...
WHO IS IT, SIR?
HE'S THE CRABBIEST GUY IN THE CLUB! HE THINKS MRS. BARTLEY AND MRS. NELSON PLAY TOO SLOW...
I THINK HE HATES WOMEN GOLFERS...
IS HE REALLY THE CRABBIEST PLAYER IN THE CLUB?
4-20
STAND BACK, MARCIE..THE LADIES ARE GONNA LET HIM PLAY THROUGH
I JUST WANT TO SEE WHO HE IS...
© 1980 United Feature Syndicate, Inc.
SCHULZ

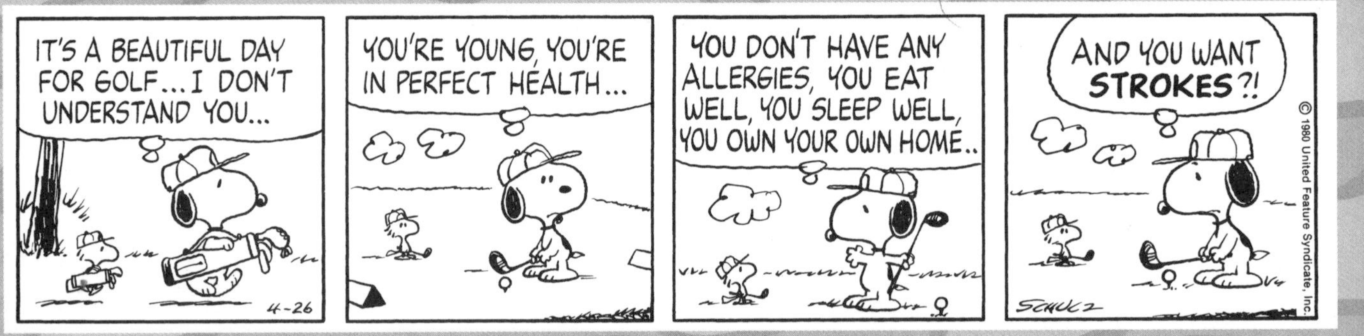
IT'S A BEAUTIFUL DAY FOR GOLF... I DON'T UNDERSTAND YOU...
4-26
YOU'RE YOUNG, YOU'RE IN PERFECT HEALTH...
YOU DON'T HAVE ANY ALLERGIES, YOU EAT WELL, YOU SLEEP WELL, YOU OWN YOUR OWN HOME..
AND YOU WANT **STROKES**?!
SCHULZ
© 1980 United Feature Syndicate, Inc.

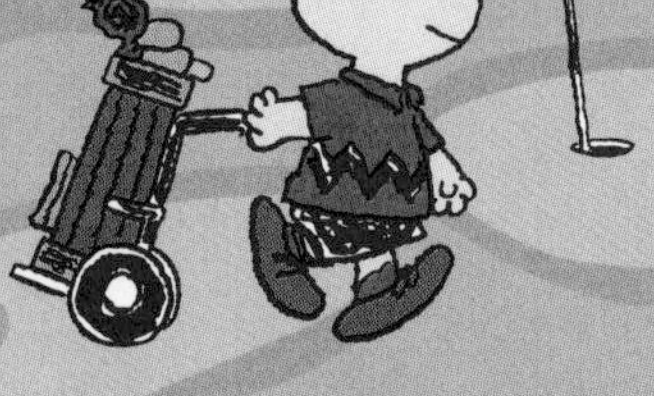

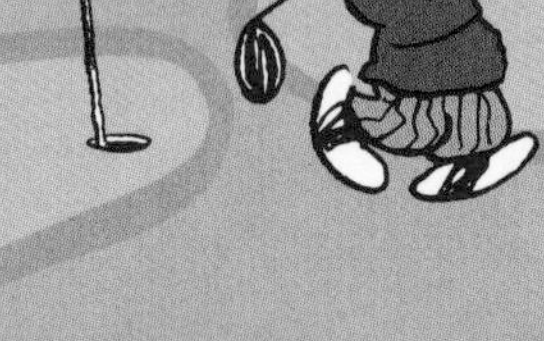

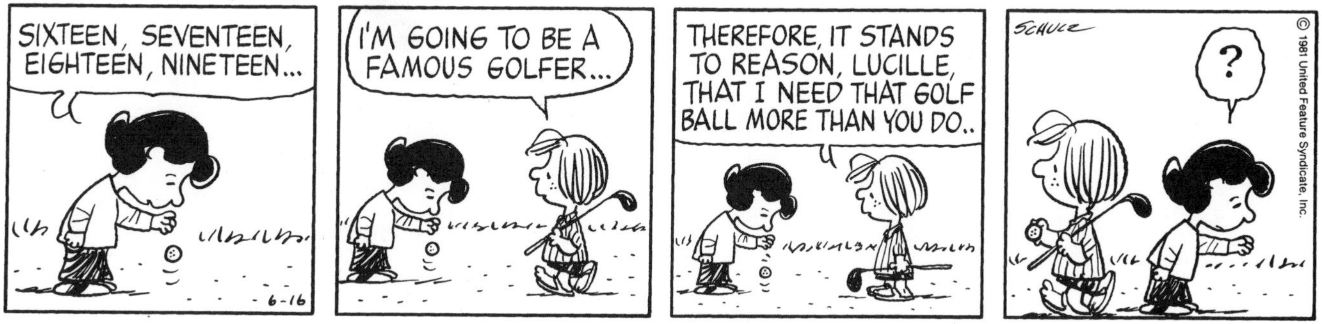
SIXTEEN, SEVENTEEN, EIGHTEEN, NINETEEN...
6-16
I'M GOING TO BE A FAMOUS GOLFER...
THEREFORE, IT STANDS TO REASON, LUCILLE, THAT I NEED THAT GOLF BALL MORE THAN YOU DO..
SCHULZ
?
© 1981 United Feature Syndicate, Inc.

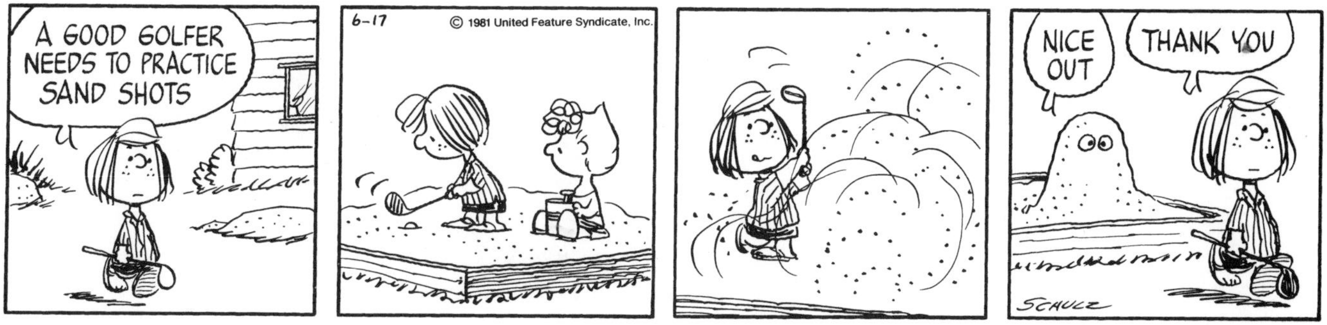
A GOOD GOLFER NEEDS TO PRACTICE SAND SHOTS
6-17
© 1981 United Feature Syndicate, Inc.
NICE OUT
THANK YOU
SCHULZ

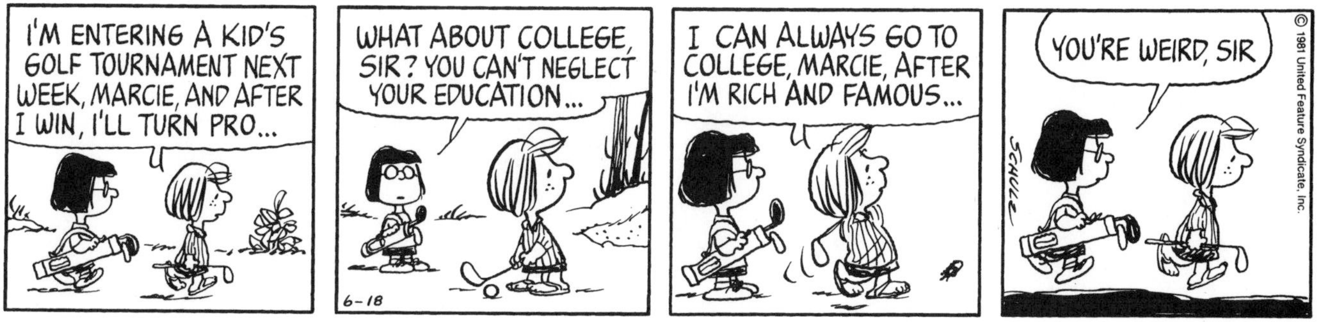
I'M ENTERING A KID'S GOLF TOURNAMENT NEXT WEEK, MARCIE, AND AFTER I WIN, I'LL TURN PRO...
WHAT ABOUT COLLEGE, SIR? YOU CAN'T NEGLECT YOUR EDUCATION...
6-18
I CAN ALWAYS GO TO COLLEGE, MARCIE, AFTER I'M RICH AND FAMOUS...
SCHULZ
YOU'RE WEIRD, SIR
© 1981 United Feature Syndicate, Inc.

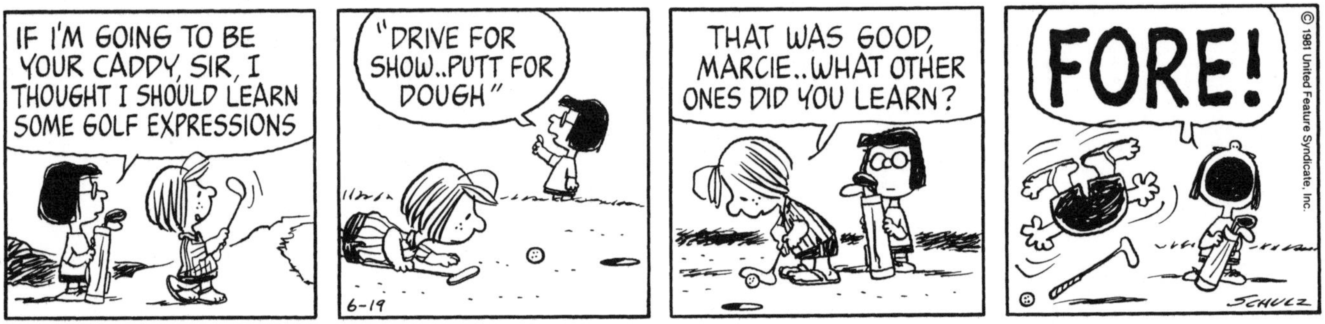
IF I'M GOING TO BE YOUR CADDY, SIR, I THOUGHT I SHOULD LEARN SOME GOLF EXPRESSIONS
"DRIVE FOR SHOW..PUTT FOR DOUGH"
6-19
THAT WAS GOOD, MARCIE..WHAT OTHER ONES DID YOU LEARN?
FORE!
© 1981 United Feature Syndicate, Inc.
SCHULZ

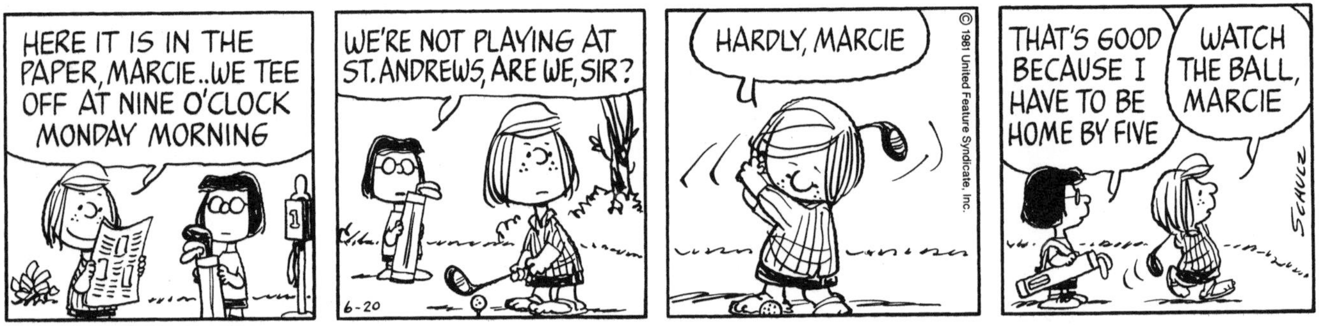
HERE IT IS IN THE PAPER, MARCIE..WE TEE OFF AT NINE O'CLOCK MONDAY MORNING
1
WE'RE NOT PLAYING AT ST. ANDREWS, ARE WE, SIR?
6-20
HARDLY, MARCIE
© 1981 United Feature Syndicate, Inc.
THAT'S GOOD BECAUSE I HAVE TO BE HOME BY FIVE
WATCH THE BALL, MARCIE
SCHULZ

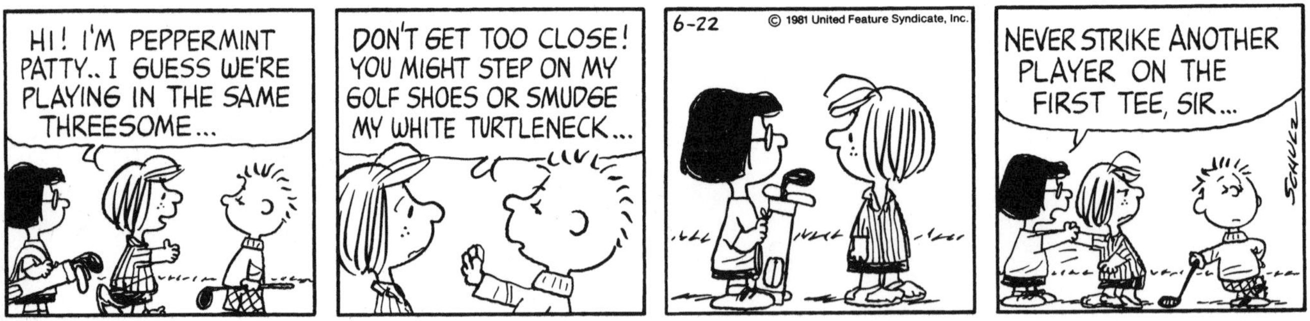
HI! I'M PEPPERMINT PATTY.. I GUESS WE'RE PLAYING IN THE SAME THREESOME...
DON'T GET TOO CLOSE! YOU MIGHT STEP ON MY GOLF SHOES OR SMUDGE MY WHITE TURTLENECK...
6-22
© 1981 United Feature Syndicate, Inc.
NEVER STRIKE ANOTHER PLAYER ON THE FIRST TEE, SIR...
SCHULZ

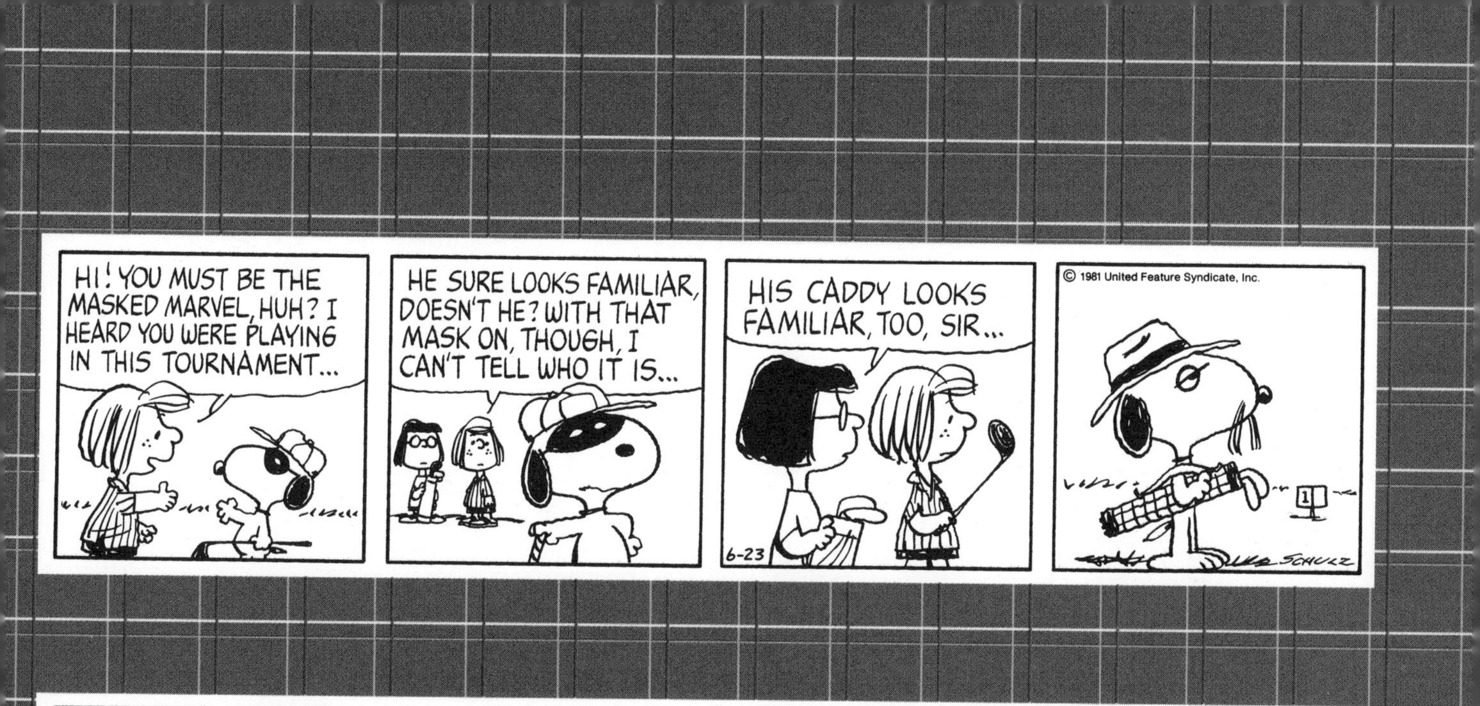
HI! YOU MUST BE THE MASKED MARVEL, HUH? I HEARD YOU WERE PLAYING IN THIS TOURNAMENT...
HE SURE LOOKS FAMILIAR, DOESN'T HE? WITH THAT MASK ON, THOUGH, I CAN'T TELL WHO IT IS...
HIS CADDY LOOKS FAMILIAR, TOO, SIR...
6-23
© 1981 United Feature Syndicate, Inc.
1
SCHULZ

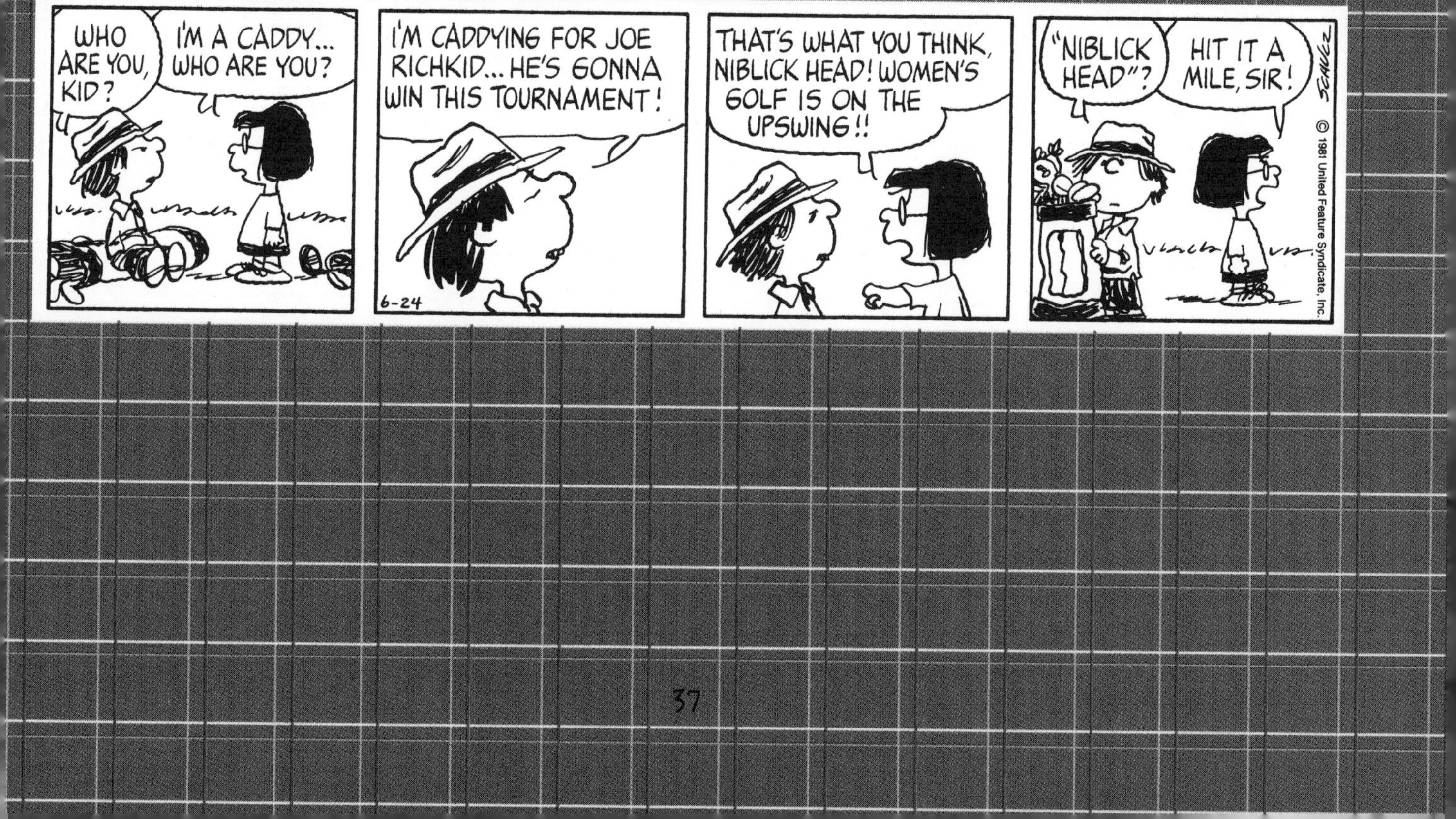
WHO ARE YOU, KID?
I'M A CADDY... WHO ARE YOU?
I'M CADDYING FOR JOE RICHKID... HE'S GONNA WIN THIS TOURNAMENT!
6-24
THAT'S WHAT YOU THINK, NIBLICK HEAD! WOMEN'S GOLF IS ON THE UPSWING!!
"NIBLICK HEAD"?
HIT IT A MILE, SIR!
SCHULZ
© 1981 United Feature Syndicate, Inc.

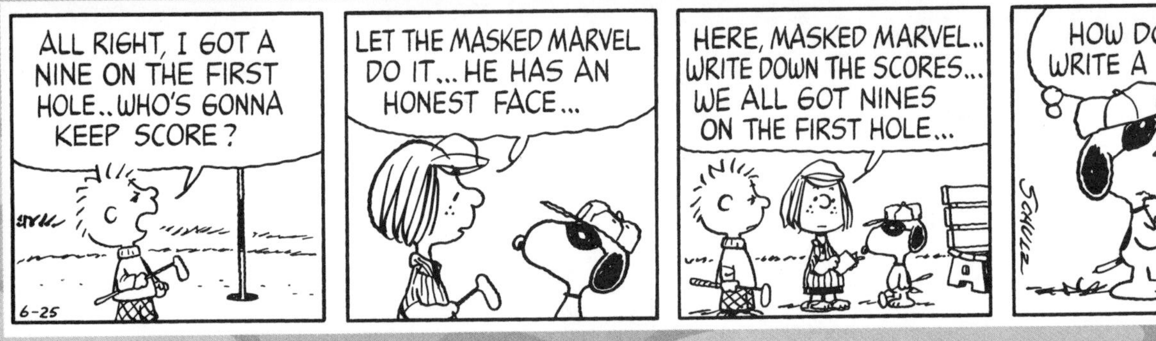
ALL RIGHT, I GOT A NINE ON THE FIRST HOLE..WHO'S GONNA KEEP SCORE?
6-25
LET THE MASKED MARVEL DO IT... HE HAS AN HONEST FACE...
HERE, MASKED MARVEL.. WRITE DOWN THE SCORES... WE ALL GOT NINES ON THE FIRST HOLE...
HOW DO YOU WRITE A NINE?
SCHULZ
© 1981 United Feature Syndicate, Inc.

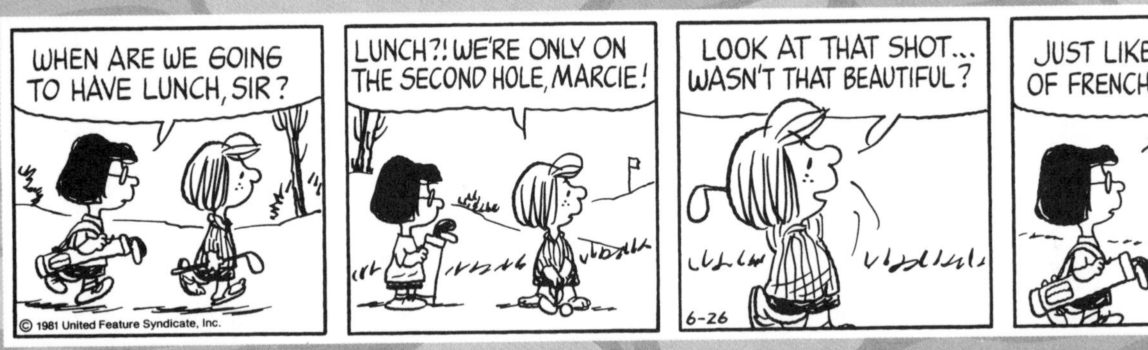
WHEN ARE WE GOING TO HAVE LUNCH, SIR?
© 1981 United Feature Syndicate, Inc.
LUNCH?! WE'RE ONLY ON THE SECOND HOLE, MARCIE!
LOOK AT THAT SHOT... WASN'T THAT BEAUTIFUL?
6-26
JUST LIKE A PLATE OF FRENCH FRIES, SIR..
SCHULZ

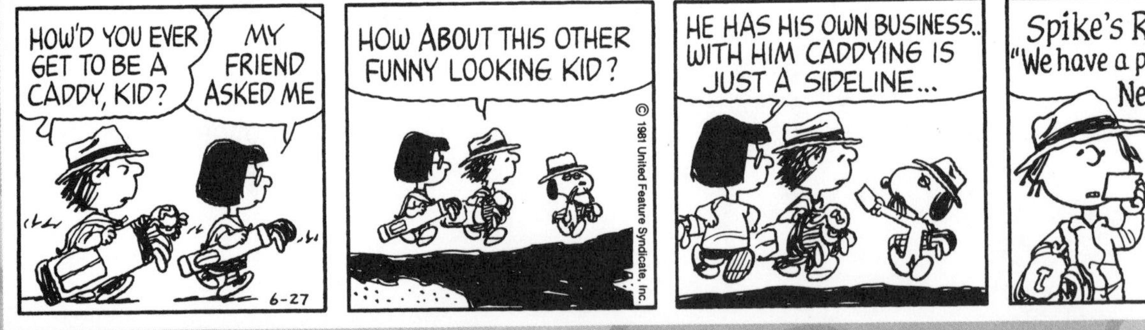
HOW'D YOU EVER GET TO BE A CADDY, KID?
MY FRIEND ASKED ME
6-27
HOW ABOUT THIS OTHER FUNNY LOOKING KID?
© 1981 United Feature Syndicate, Inc.
HE HAS HIS OWN BUSINESS.. WITH HIM CADDYING IS JUST A SIDELINE...
Spike's Real Estate
"We have a place for you."
Needles, Calif.
SCHULZ

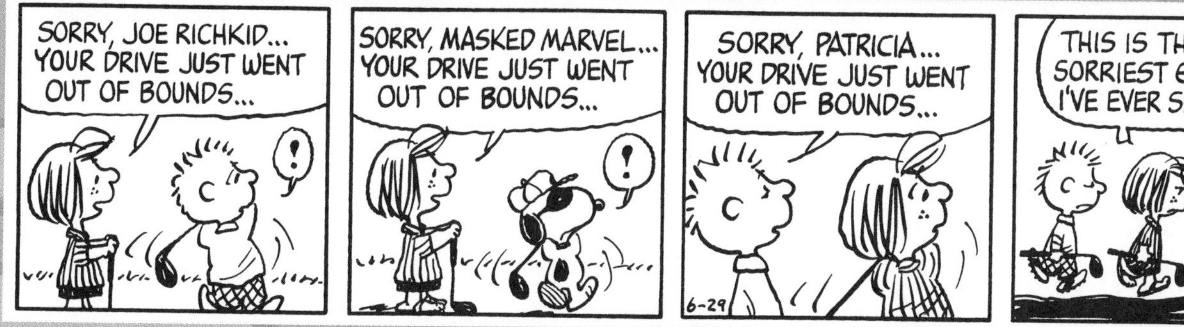
SORRY, JOE RICHKID... YOUR DRIVE JUST WENT OUT OF BOUNDS...
!
SORRY, MASKED MARVEL... YOUR DRIVE JUST WENT OUT OF BOUNDS...
!
SORRY, PATRICIA... YOUR DRIVE JUST WENT OUT OF BOUNDS...
THIS IS THE SORRIEST GROUP I'VE EVER SEEN!
© 1981 United Feature Syndicate, Inc.

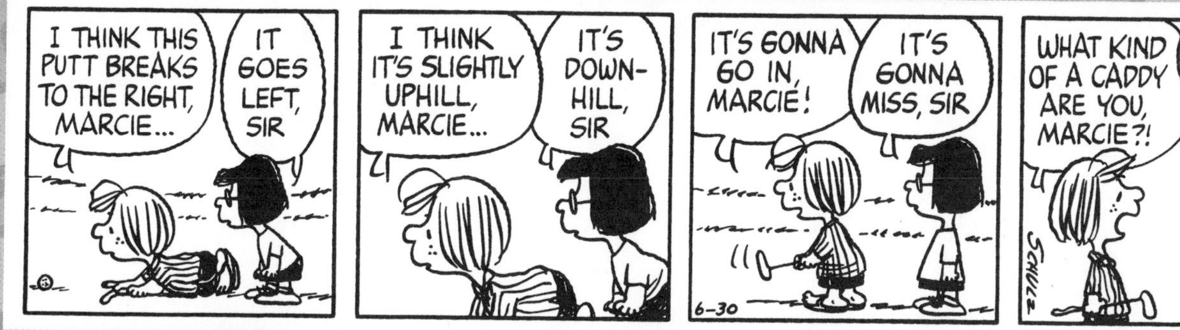
I THINK THIS PUTT BREAKS TO THE RIGHT, MARCIE...
IT GOES LEFT, SIR
I THINK IT'S SLIGHTLY UPHILL, MARCIE...
IT'S DOWN-HILL, SIR
IT'S GONNA GO IN, MARCIE!
IT'S GONNA MISS, SIR
WHAT KIND OF A CADDY ARE YOU, MARCIE?!
TYPICAL, SIR
© 1981 United Feature Syndicate, Inc.

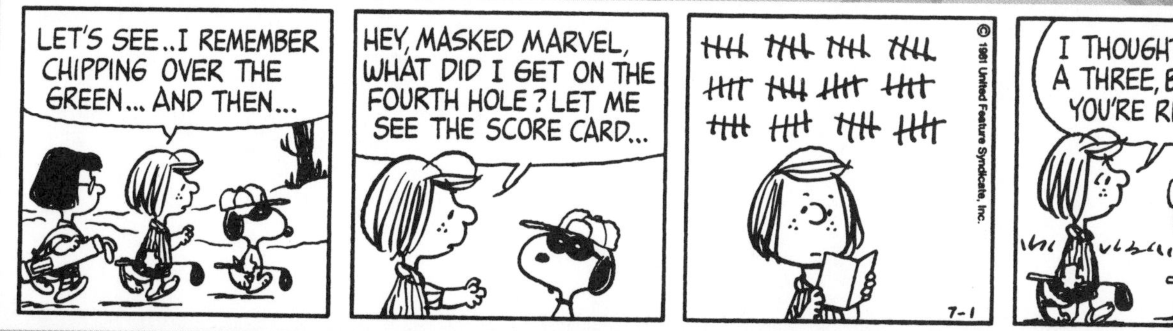
LET'S SEE..I REMEMBER CHIPPING OVER THE GREEN... AND THEN...
HEY, MASKED MARVEL, WHAT DID I GET ON THE FOURTH HOLE? LET ME SEE THE SCORE CARD...
© 1981 United Feature Syndicate, Inc.
I THOUGHT I HAD A THREE, BUT MAYBE YOU'RE RIGHT...

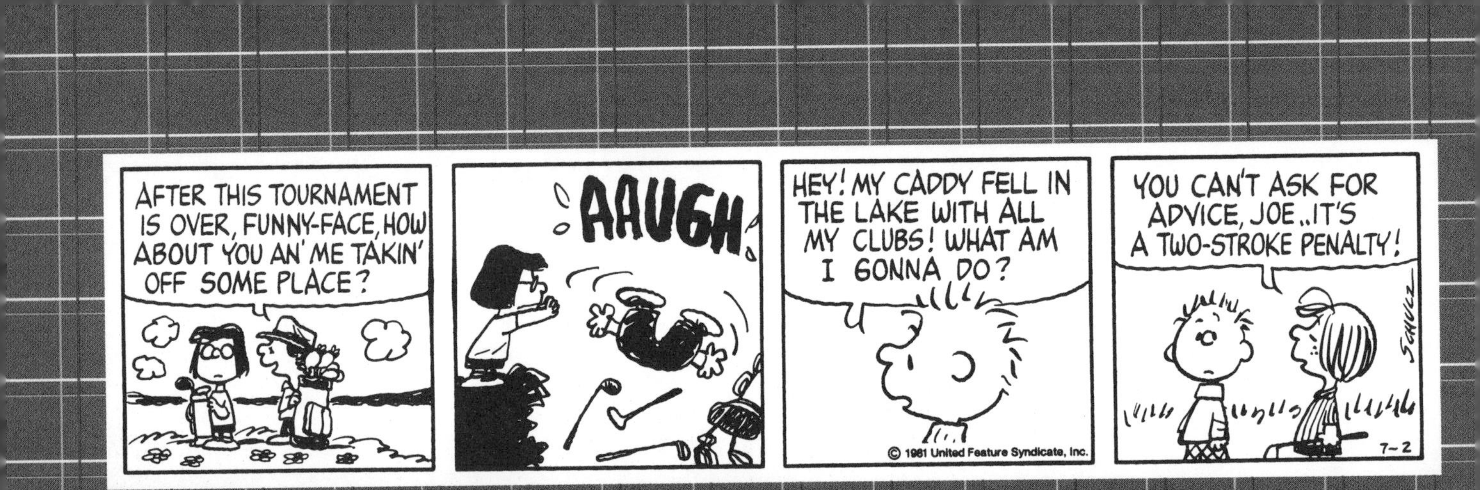
AFTER THIS TOURNAMENT IS OVER, FUNNY-FACE, HOW ABOUT YOU AN' ME TAKIN' OFF SOME PLACE?
AAUGH
HEY! MY CADDY FELL IN THE LAKE WITH ALL MY CLUBS! WHAT AM I GONNA DO?
© 1981 United Feature Syndicate, Inc.
YOU CAN'T ASK FOR ADVICE, JOE..IT'S A TWO-STROKE PENALTY!
SCHULZ
7-2

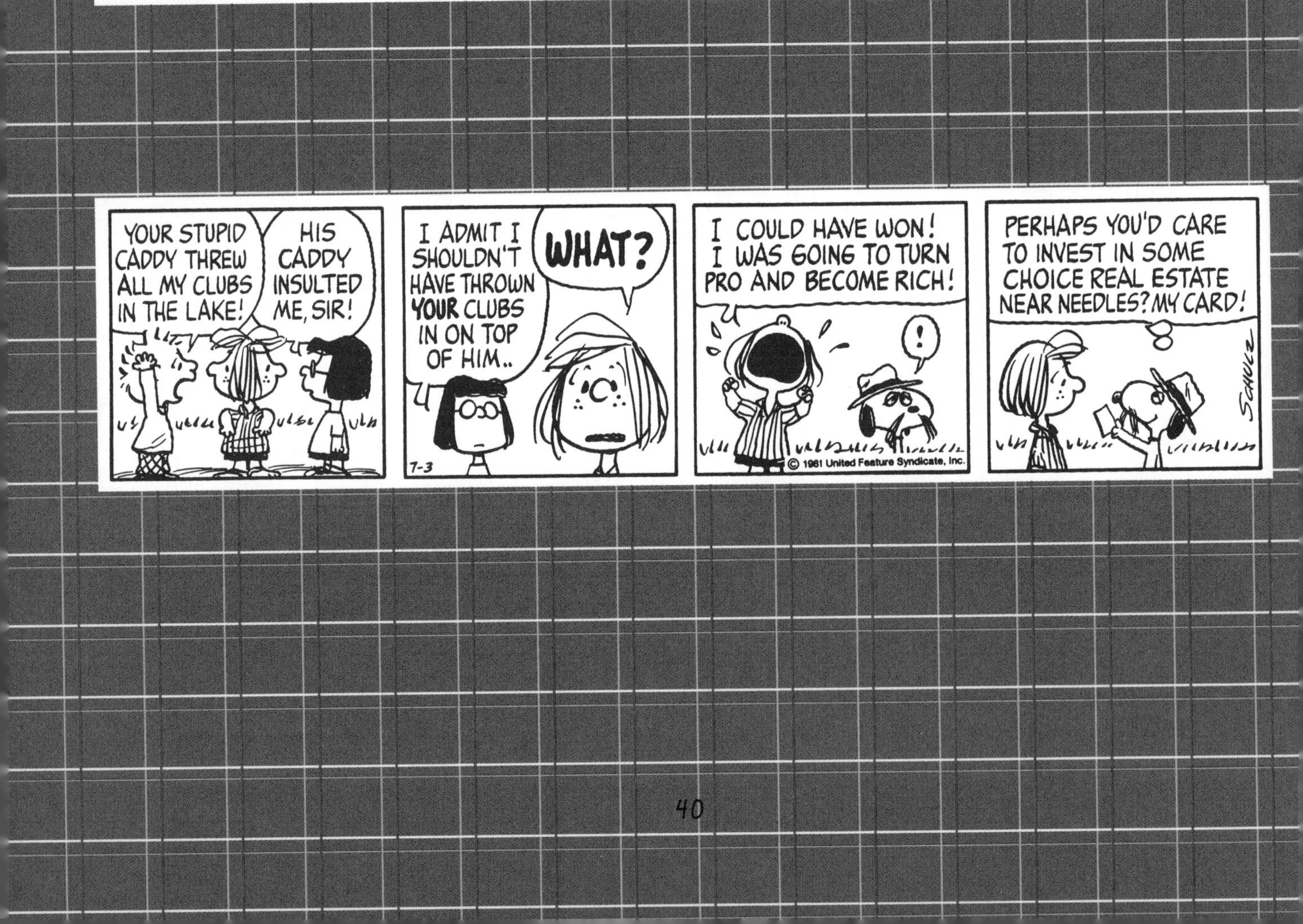
YOUR STUPID CADDY THREW ALL MY CLUBS IN THE LAKE!
HIS CADDY INSULTED ME, SIR!
7-3
I ADMIT I SHOULDN'T HAVE THROWN YOUR CLUBS IN ON TOP OF HIM..
WHAT?
I COULD HAVE WON! I WAS GOING TO TURN PRO AND BECOME RICH!
!
© 1981 United Feature Syndicate, Inc.
PERHAPS YOU'D CARE TO INVEST IN SOME CHOICE REAL ESTATE NEAR NEEDLES? MY CARD!
SCHULZ

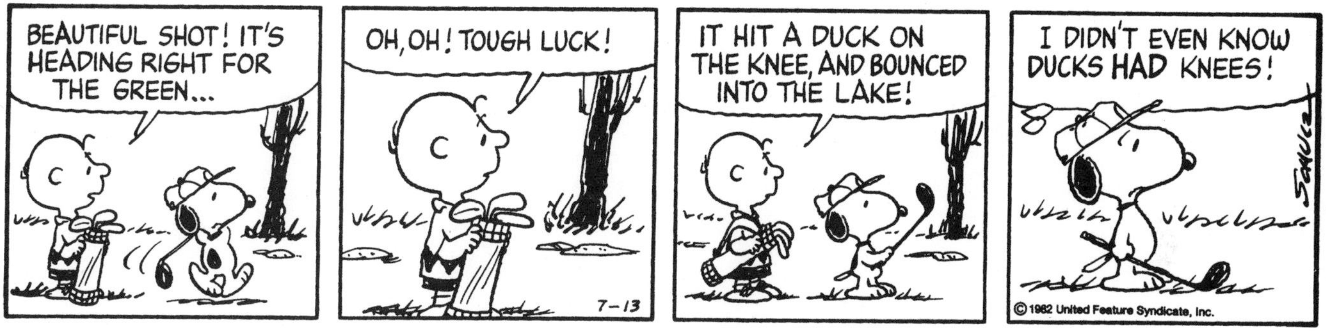
BEAUTIFUL SHOT! IT'S HEADING RIGHT FOR THE GREEN...
OH, OH! TOUGH LUCK!
7-13
IT HIT A DUCK ON THE KNEE, AND BOUNCED INTO THE LAKE!
I DIDN'T EVEN KNOW DUCKS HAD KNEES!
SCHULZ
© 1982 United Feature Syndicate, Inc.

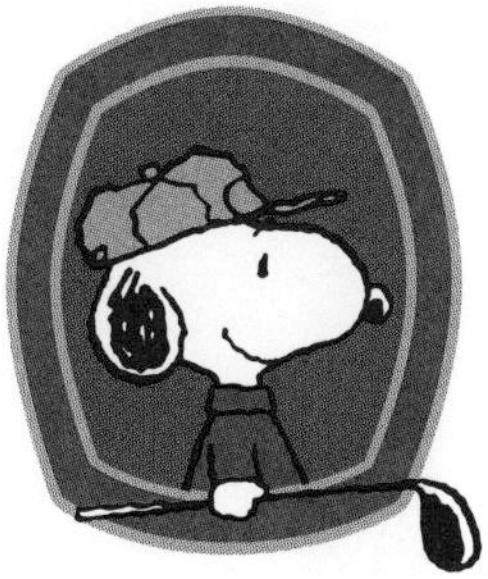

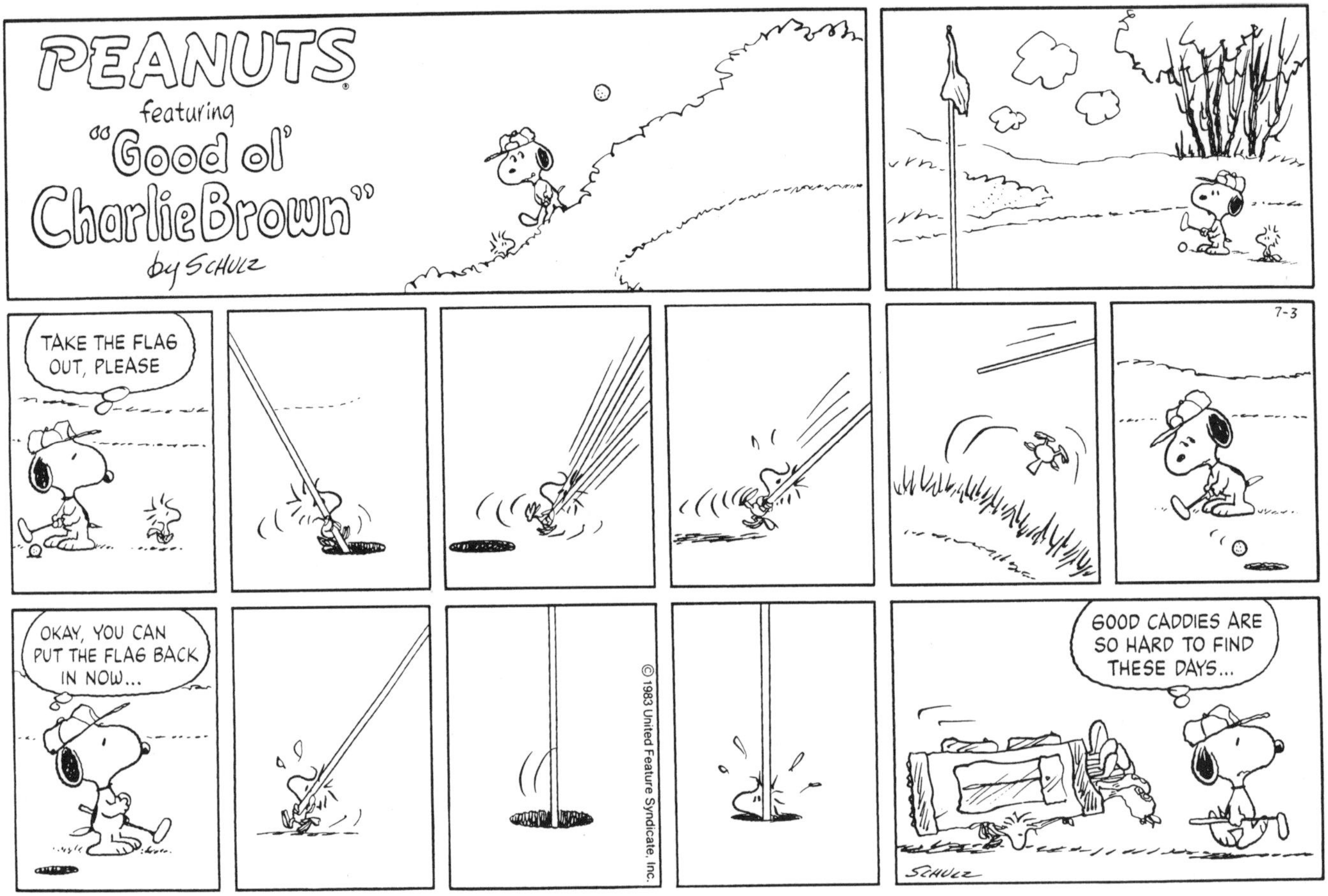
PEANUTS
featuring
"Good ol' CharlieBrown"
by SCHULZ
TAKE THE FLAG OUT, PLEASE
7-3
OKAY, YOU CAN PUT THE FLAG BACK IN NOW...
© 1983 United Feature Syndicate, Inc.
GOOD CADDIES ARE SO HARD TO FIND THESE DAYS...
SCHULZ

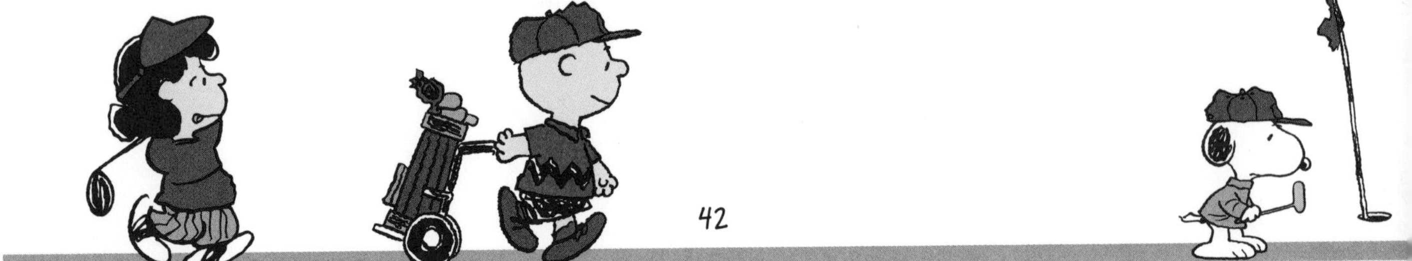

© 1983 United Feature Syndicate, Inc.   7-9

SCHULZ

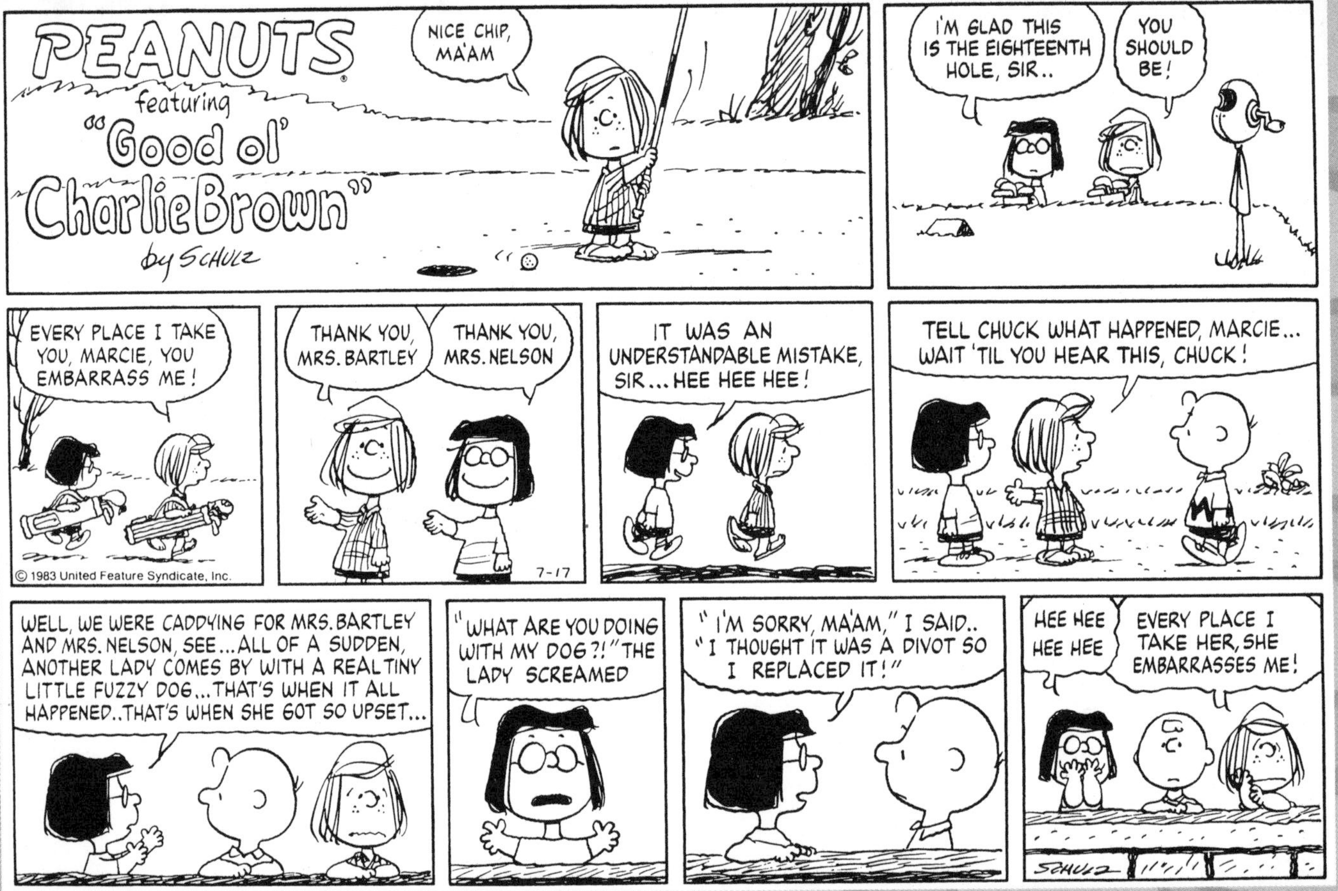
PEANUTS
featuring "Good ol' CharlieBrown"
by SCHULZ
NICE CHIP, MA'AM
I'M GLAD THIS IS THE EIGHTEENTH HOLE, SIR..
YOU SHOULD BE!
EVERY PLACE I TAKE YOU, MARCIE, YOU EMBARRASS ME!
© 1983 United Feature Syndicate, Inc.
THANK YOU, MRS. BARTLEY
THANK YOU, MRS. NELSON
7-17
IT WAS AN UNDERSTANDABLE MISTAKE, SIR... HEE HEE HEE!
TELL CHUCK WHAT HAPPENED, MARCIE... WAIT 'TIL YOU HEAR THIS, CHUCK!
WELL, WE WERE CADDYING FOR MRS. BARTLEY AND MRS. NELSON, SEE... ALL OF A SUDDEN, ANOTHER LADY COMES BY WITH A REAL TINY LITTLE FUZZY DOG... THAT'S WHEN IT ALL HAPPENED.. THAT'S WHEN SHE GOT SO UPSET...
"WHAT ARE YOU DOING WITH MY DOG?!" THE LADY SCREAMED
"I'M SORRY, MA'AM," I SAID.. "I THOUGHT IT WAS A DIVOT SO I REPLACED IT!"
HEE HEE HEE HEE
EVERY PLACE I TAKE HER, SHE EMBARRASSES ME!
SCHULZ

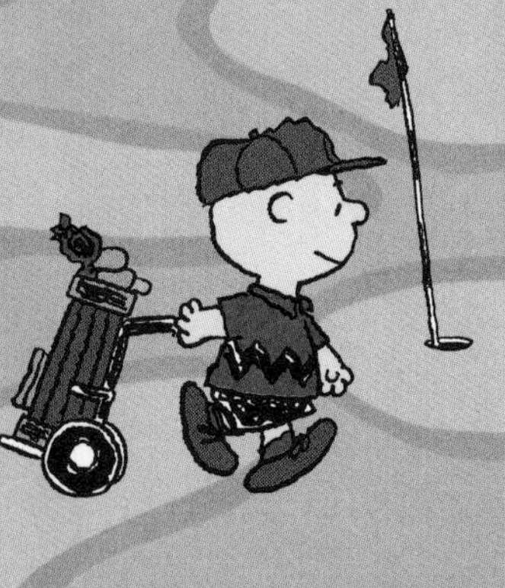

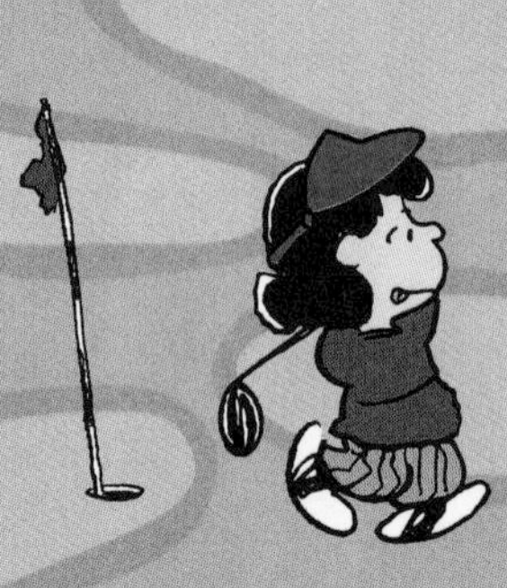

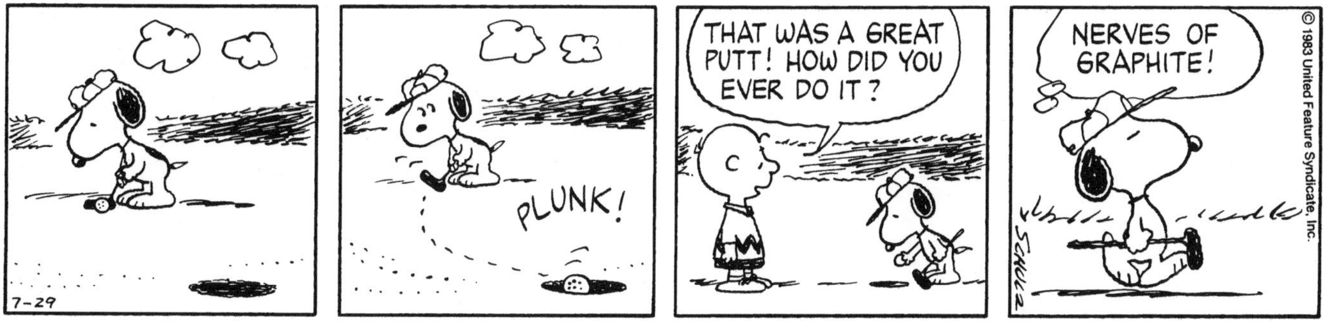
7-29
PLUNK!
THAT WAS A GREAT PUTT! HOW DID YOU EVER DO IT?
NERVES OF GRAPHITE!
© 1983 United Feature Syndicate, Inc.
SCHULZ

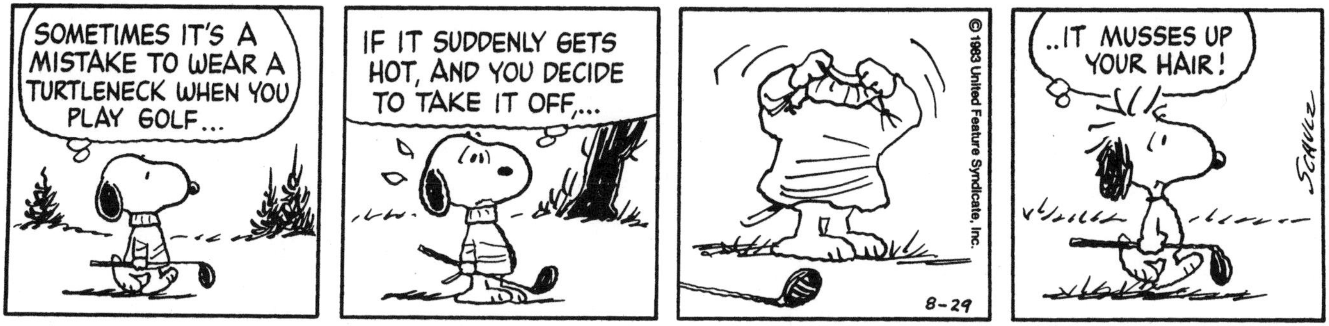
SOMETIMES IT'S A MISTAKE TO WEAR A TURTLENECK WHEN YOU PLAY GOLF...
IF IT SUDDENLY GETS HOT, AND YOU DECIDE TO TAKE IT OFF,...
© 1983 United Feature Syndicate, Inc.
8-29
..IT MUSSES UP YOUR HAIR!
SCHULZ

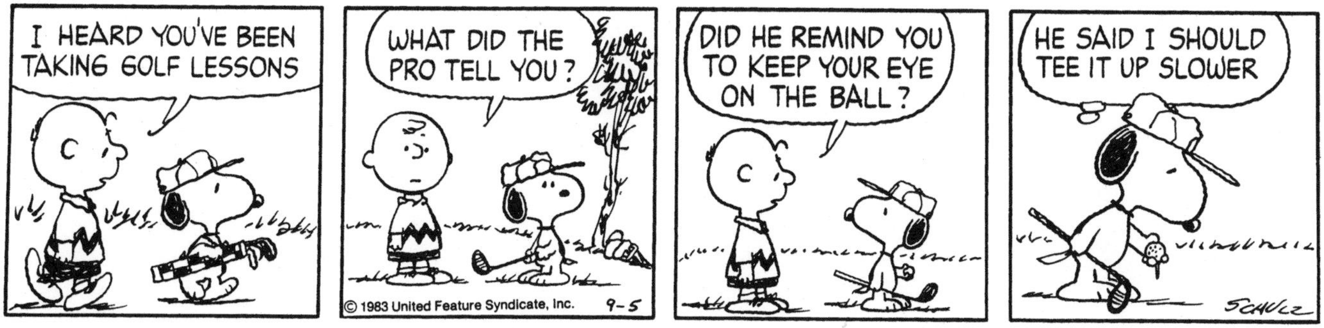
I HEARD YOU'VE BEEN TAKING GOLF LESSONS
WHAT DID THE PRO TELL YOU?
© 1983 United Feature Syndicate, Inc.
9-5
DID HE REMIND YOU TO KEEP YOUR EYE ON THE BALL?
HE SAID I SHOULD TEE IT UP SLOWER
SCHULZ

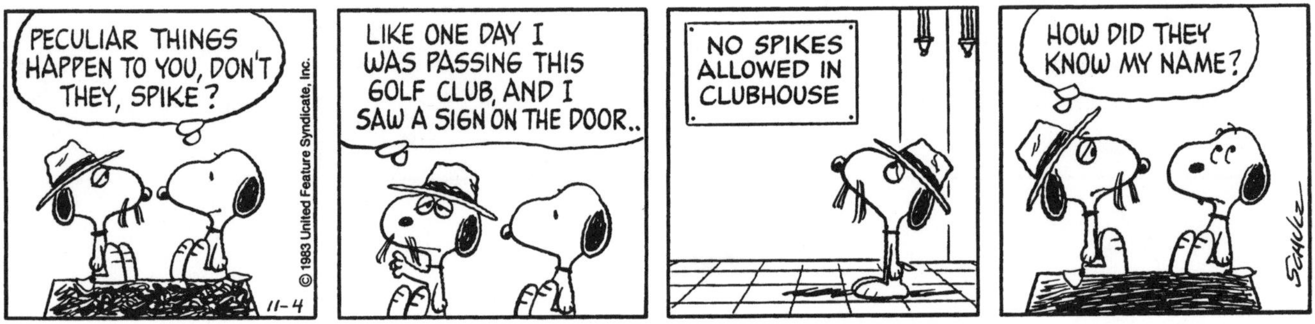
PECULIAR THINGS HAPPEN TO YOU, DON'T THEY, SPIKE?
© 1983 United Feature Syndicate, Inc.
11-4
LIKE ONE DAY I WAS PASSING THIS GOLF CLUB, AND I SAW A SIGN ON THE DOOR..
NO SPIKES ALLOWED IN CLUBHOUSE
HOW DID THEY KNOW MY NAME?
SCHULZ

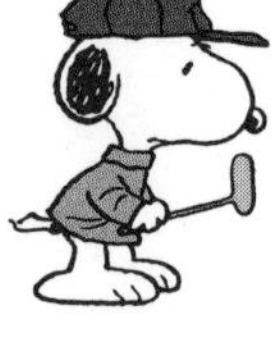

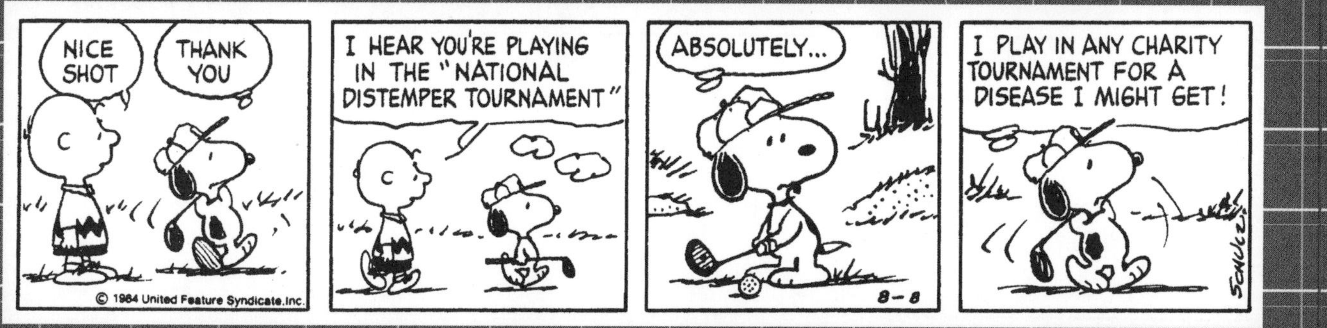
NICE SHOT
THANK YOU
I HEAR YOU'RE PLAYING IN THE "NATIONAL DISTEMPER TOURNAMENT"
ABSOLUTELY...
I PLAY IN ANY CHARITY TOURNAMENT FOR A DISEASE I MIGHT GET!
© 1984 United Feature Syndicate, Inc.
8-8
SCHULZ

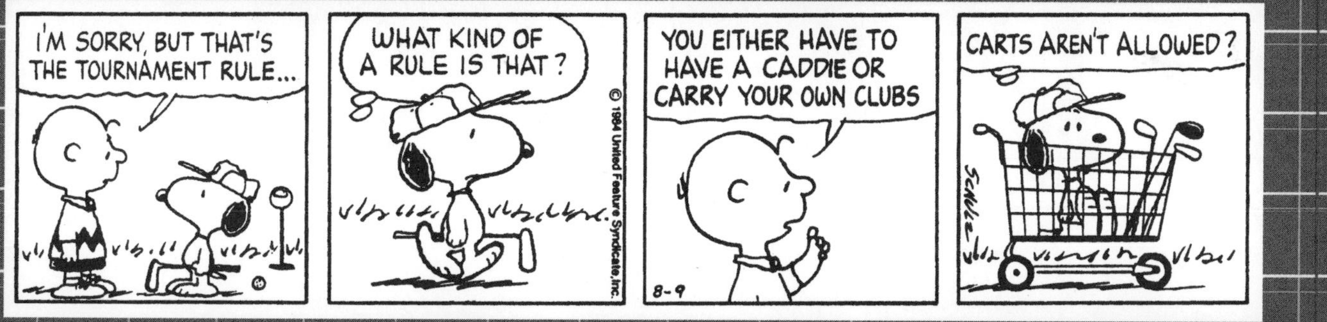
I'M SORRY, BUT THAT'S THE TOURNAMENT RULE...
WHAT KIND OF A RULE IS THAT?
© 1984 United Feature Syndicate, Inc.
YOU EITHER HAVE TO HAVE A CADDIE OR CARRY YOUR OWN CLUBS
8-9
CARTS AREN'T ALLOWED?
SCHULZ

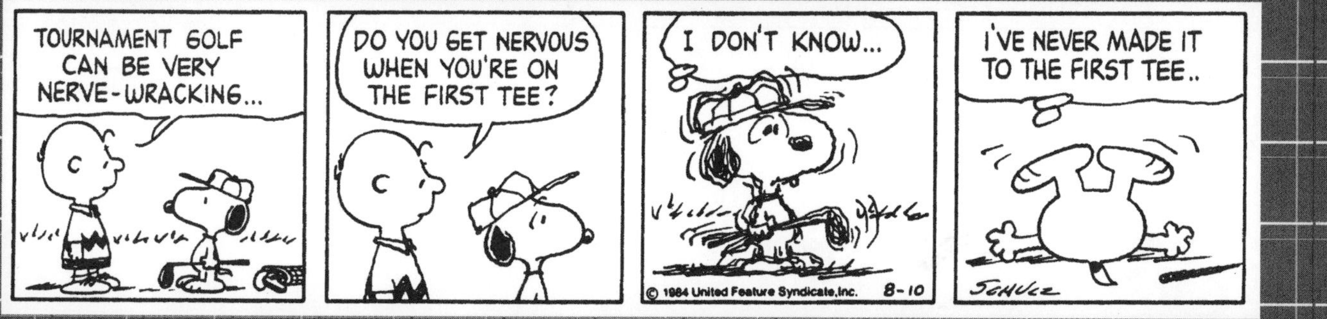
TOURNAMENT GOLF CAN BE VERY NERVE-WRACKING...
DO YOU GET NERVOUS WHEN YOU'RE ON THE FIRST TEE?
I DON'T KNOW...
© 1984 United Feature Syndicate, Inc.
8-10
I'VE NEVER MADE IT TO THE FIRST TEE..
SCHULZ

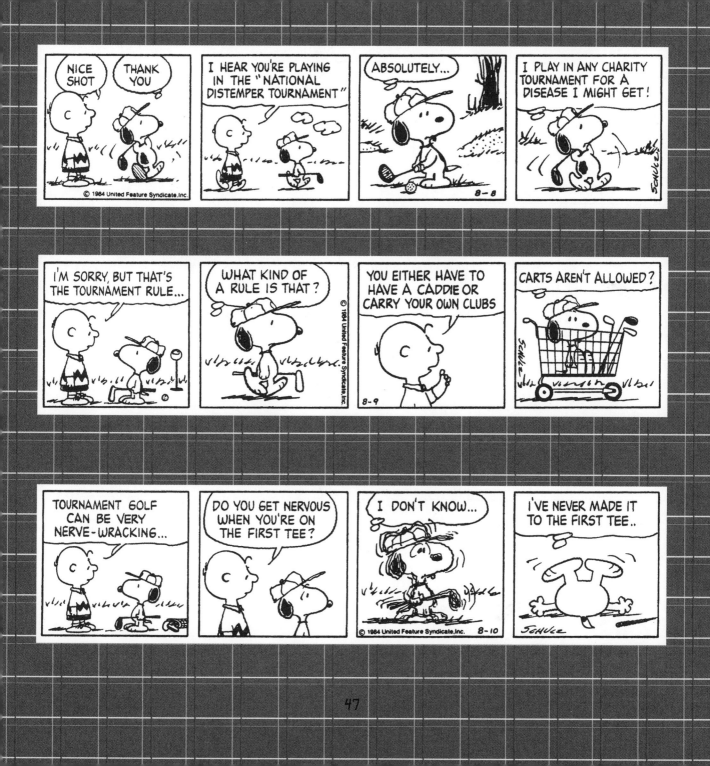

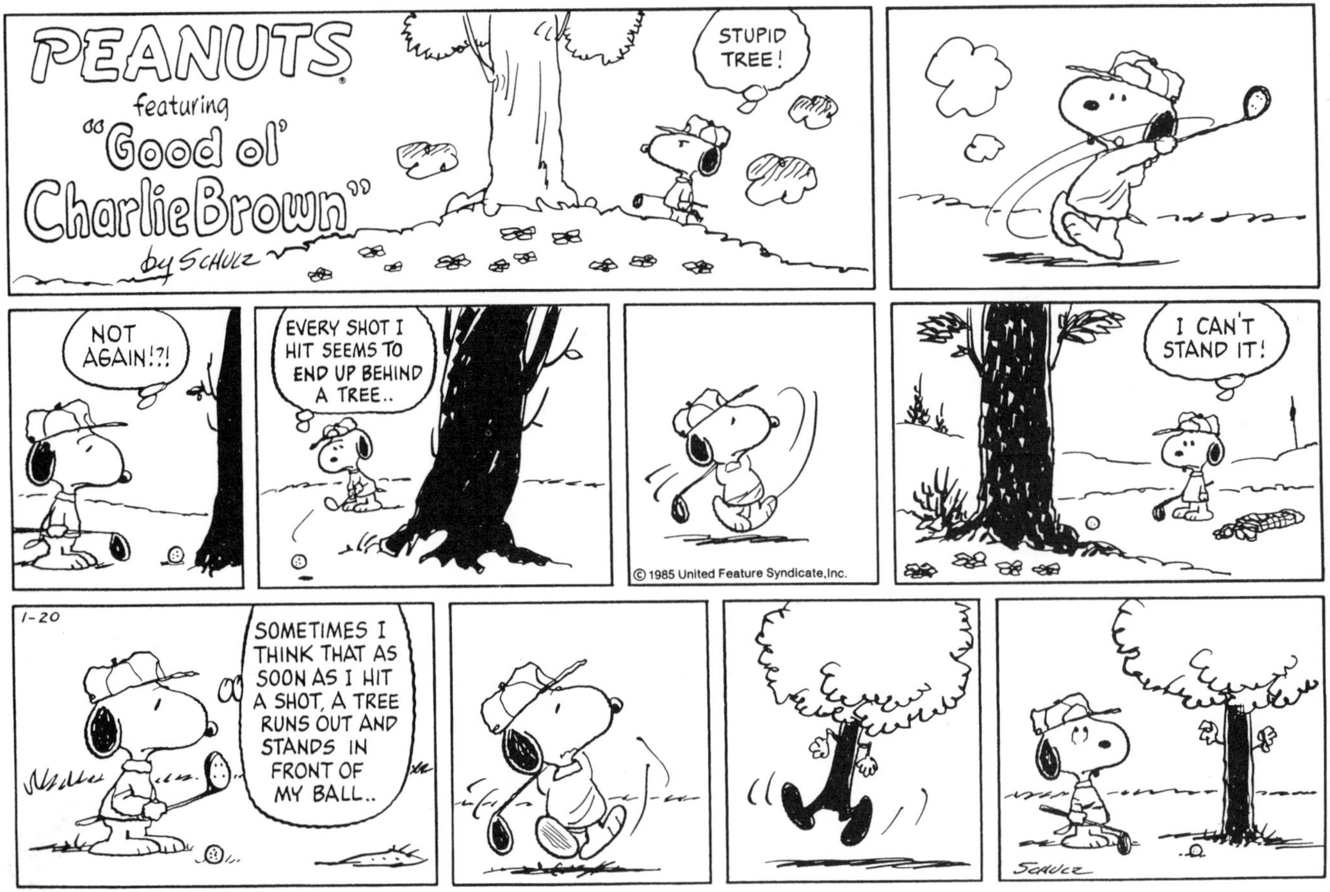
PEANUTS
featuring
"Good ol' Charlie Brown"
by SCHULZ
STUPID TREE!
NOT AGAIN!?!
EVERY SHOT I HIT SEEMS TO END UP BEHIND A TREE..
© 1985 United Feature Syndicate, Inc.
I CAN'T STAND IT!
1-20
SOMETIMES I THINK THAT AS SOON AS I HIT A SHOT, A TREE RUNS OUT AND STANDS IN FRONT OF MY BALL..
SCHULZ

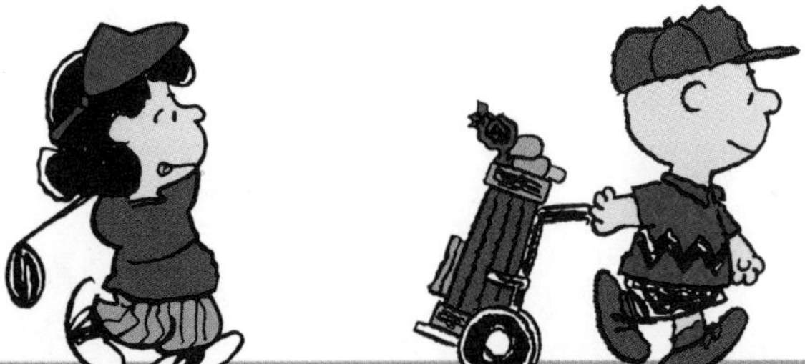

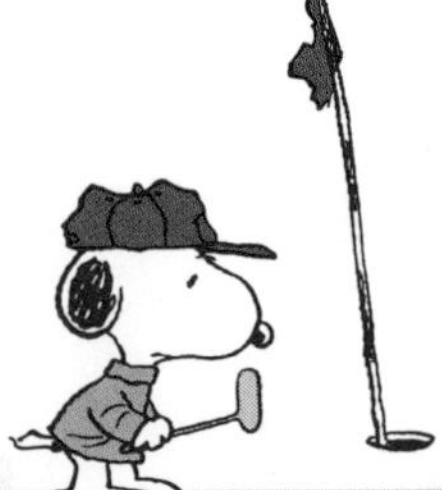

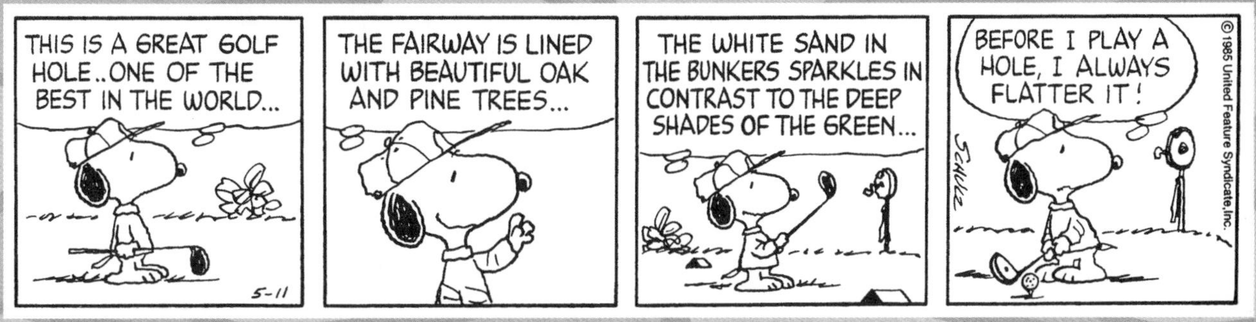
THIS IS A GREAT GOLF HOLE..ONE OF THE BEST IN THE WORLD...
5-11
THE FAIRWAY IS LINED WITH BEAUTIFUL OAK AND PINE TREES...
THE WHITE SAND IN THE BUNKERS SPARKLES IN CONTRAST TO THE DEEP SHADES OF THE GREEN...
BEFORE I PLAY A HOLE, I ALWAYS FLATTER IT!
© 1985 United Feature Syndicate, Inc.
SCHULZ

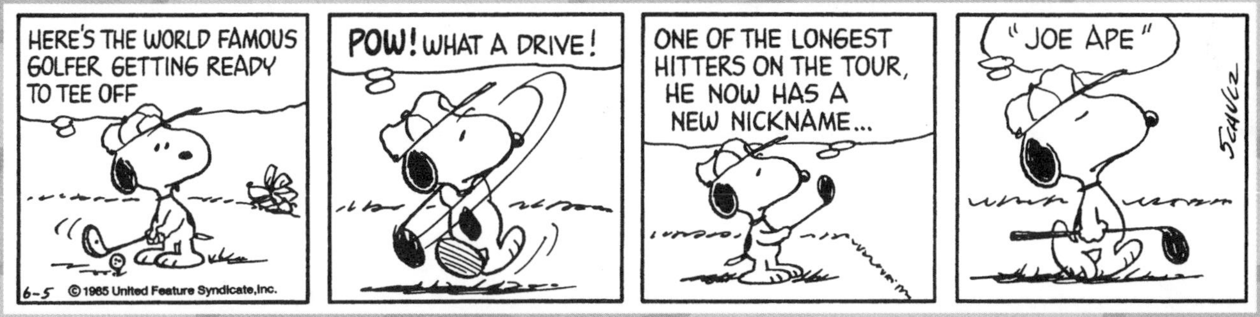
HERE'S THE WORLD FAMOUS GOLFER GETTING READY TO TEE OFF
6-5 © 1985 United Feature Syndicate, Inc.
POW! WHAT A DRIVE!
ONE OF THE LONGEST HITTERS ON THE TOUR, HE NOW HAS A NEW NICKNAME...
"JOE APE"
SCHULZ

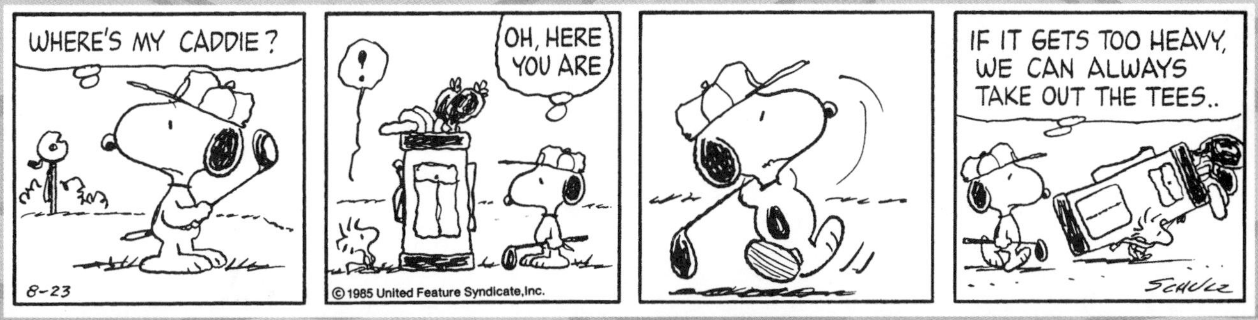
WHERE'S MY CADDIE?
8-23
!
OH, HERE YOU ARE
© 1985 United Feature Syndicate, Inc.
IF IT GETS TOO HEAVY, WE CAN ALWAYS TAKE OUT THE TEES..
SCHULZ

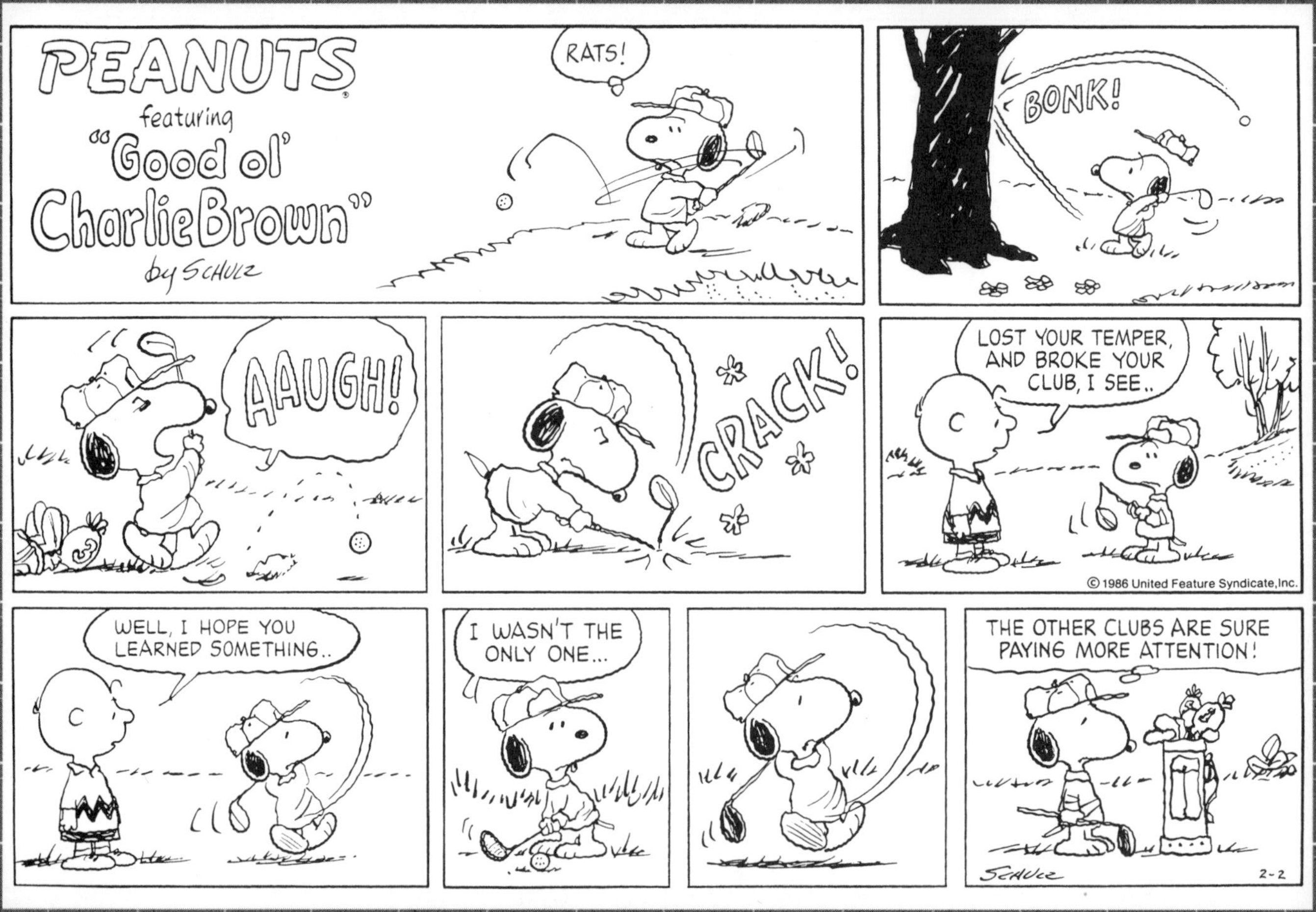
PEANUTS
featuring
"Good ol' CharlieBrown"
by SCHULZ
RATS!
BONK!
AAUGH!
CRACK!
LOST YOUR TEMPER, AND BROKE YOUR CLUB, I SEE..
© 1986 United Feature Syndicate, Inc.
WELL, I HOPE YOU LEARNED SOMETHING..
I WASN'T THE ONLY ONE...
THE OTHER CLUBS ARE SURE PAYING MORE ATTENTION!
SCHULZ
2-2

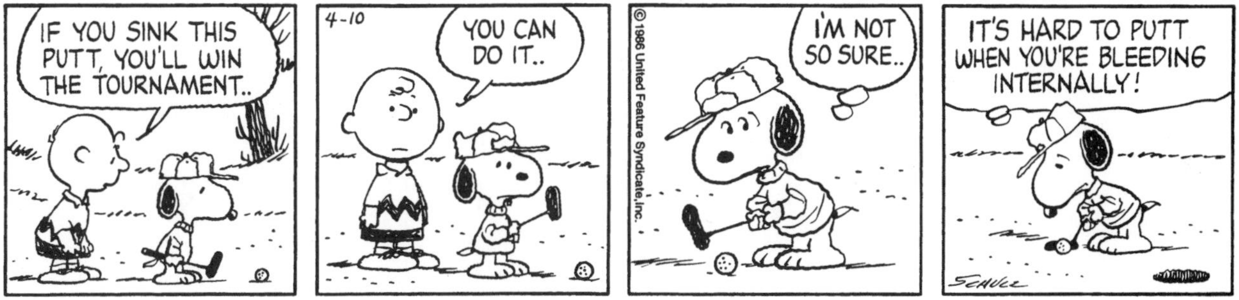
IF YOU SINK THIS PUTT, YOU'LL WIN THE TOURNAMENT..
4-10
YOU CAN DO IT..
© 1986 United Feature Syndicate, Inc.
I'M NOT SO SURE..
IT'S HARD TO PUTT WHEN YOU'RE BLEEDING INTERNALLY!
SCHULZ

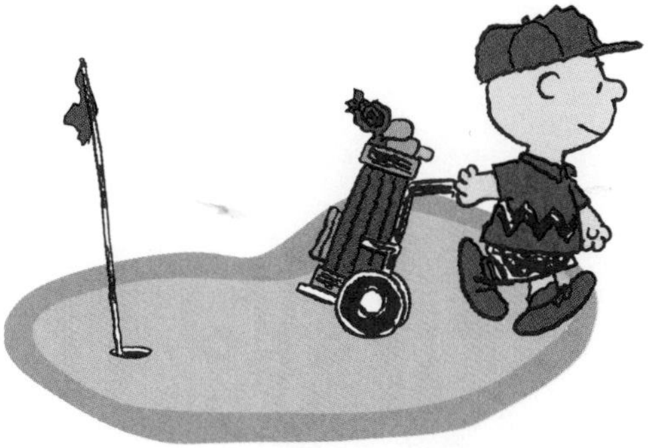

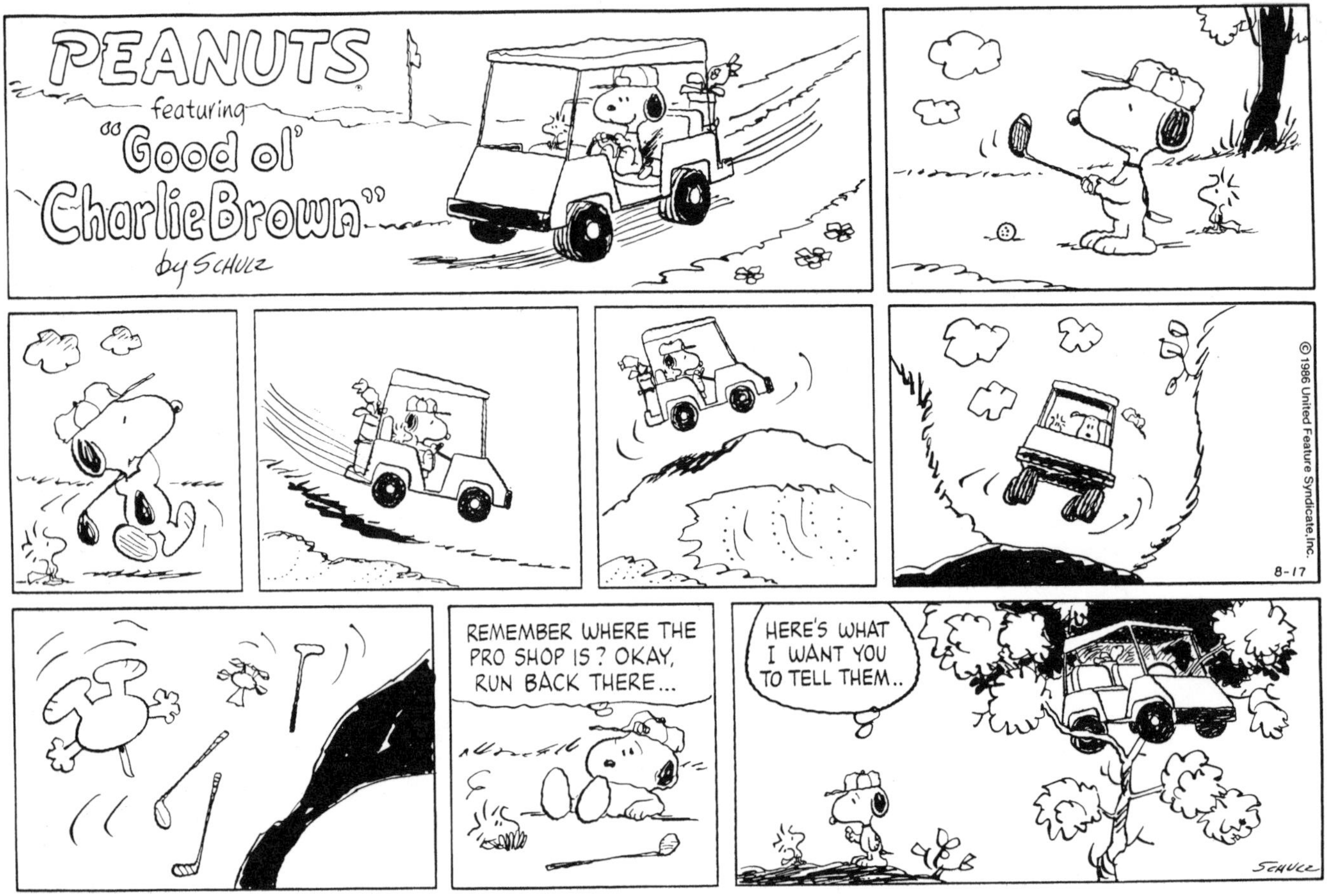
PEANUTS
featuring
"Good ol' CharlieBrown"
by SCHULZ
© 1986 United Feature Syndicate, Inc.
8-17
REMEMBER WHERE THE PRO SHOP IS? OKAY, RUN BACK THERE...
HERE'S WHAT I WANT YOU TO TELL THEM..
SCHULZ

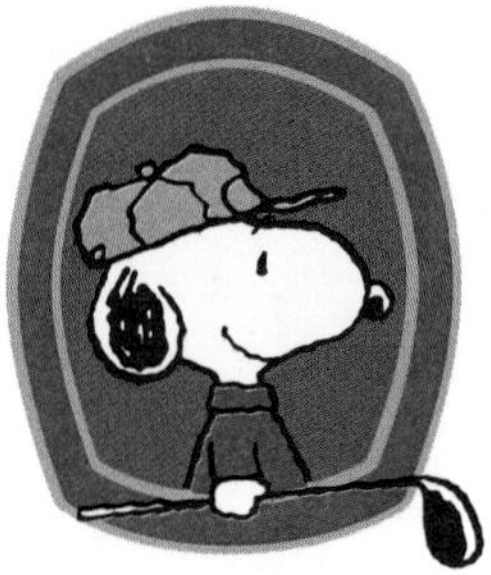

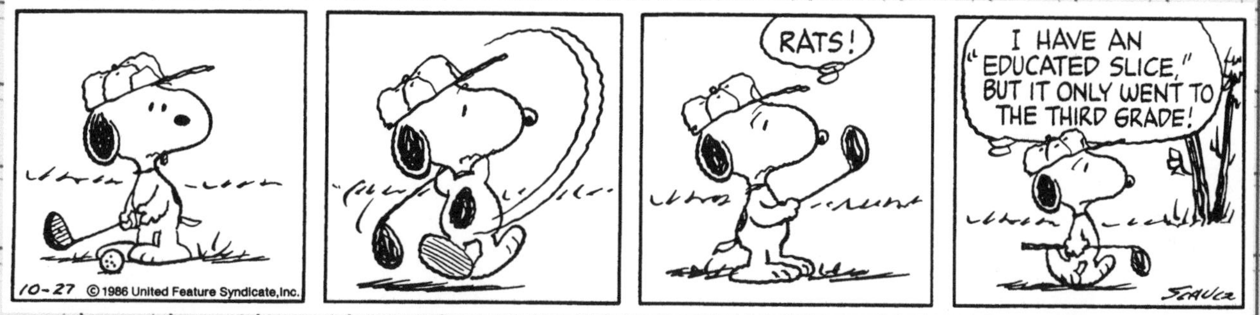
10-27
© 1986 United Feature Syndicate, Inc.
RATS!
I HAVE AN "EDUCATED SLICE," BUT IT ONLY WENT TO THE THIRD GRADE!
SCHULZ

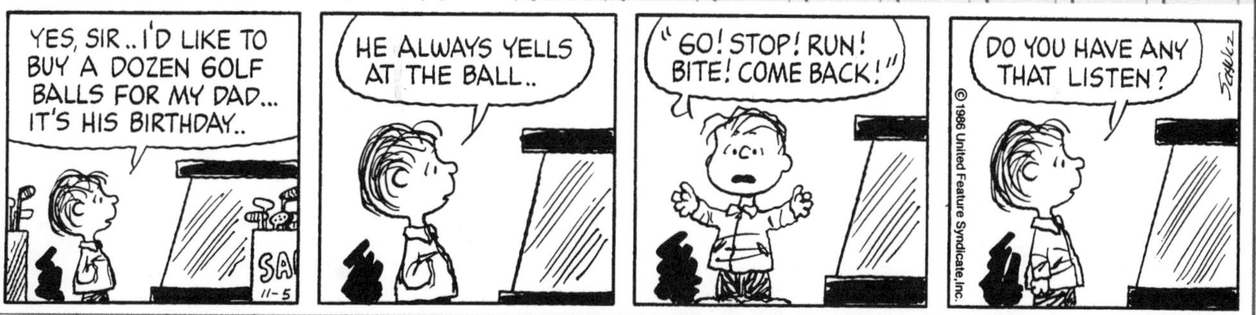
YES, SIR.. I'D LIKE TO BUY A DOZEN GOLF BALLS FOR MY DAD... IT'S HIS BIRTHDAY..
11-5
HE ALWAYS YELLS AT THE BALL..
"GO! STOP! RUN! BITE! COME BACK!"
© 1986 United Feature Syndicate, Inc.
DO YOU HAVE ANY THAT LISTEN?
SCHULZ

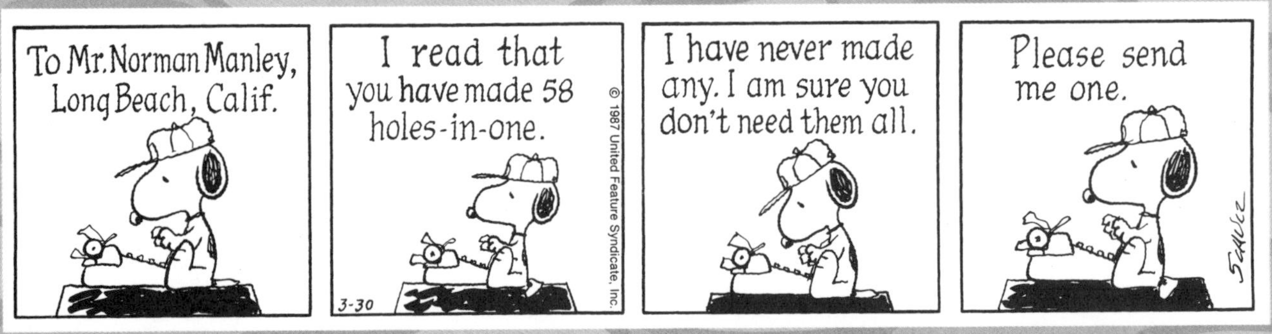

To Mr. Norman Manley, Long Beach, Calif.
I read that you have made 58 holes-in-one.
I have never made any. I am sure you don't need them all.
Please send me one.
© 1987 United Feature Syndicate, Inc.
3-30
SCHULZ

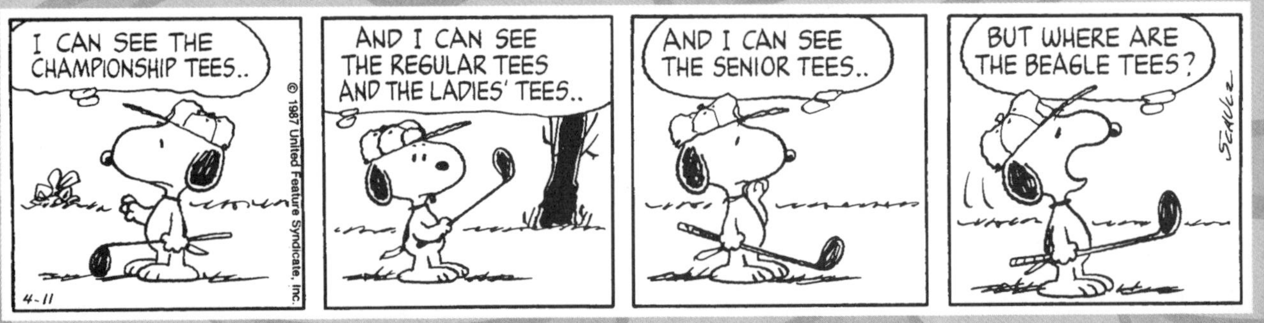

I CAN SEE THE CHAMPIONSHIP TEES..
AND I CAN SEE THE REGULAR TEES AND THE LADIES' TEES..
AND I CAN SEE THE SENIOR TEES..
BUT WHERE ARE THE BEAGLE TEES?
© 1987 United Feature Syndicate, Inc.
4-11
SCHULZ

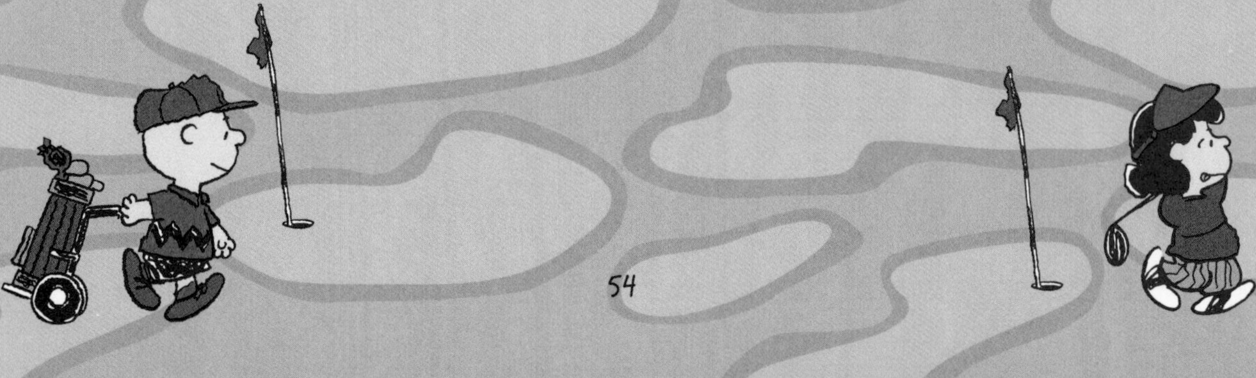

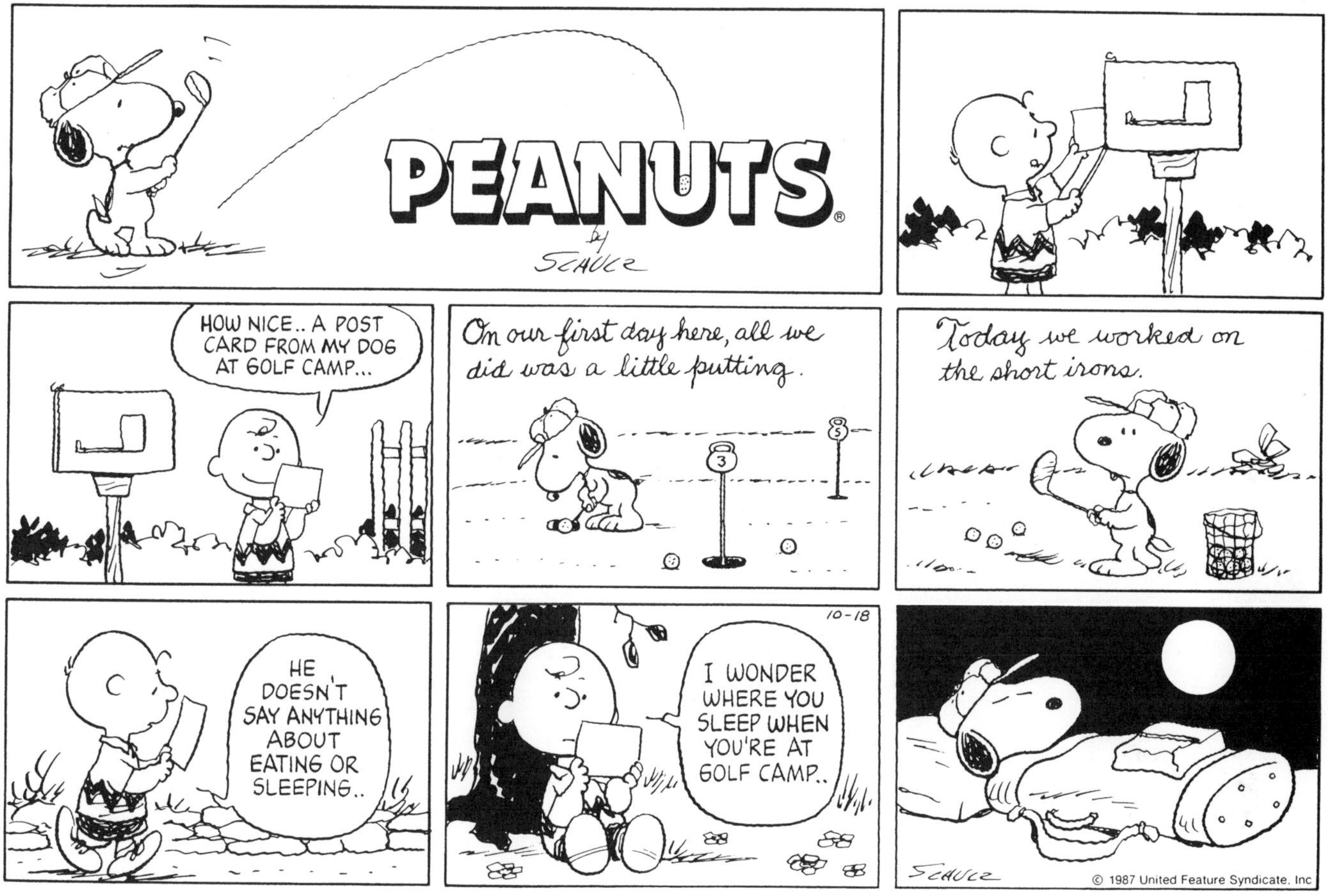
PEANUTS®
by SCHULZ
HOW NICE.. A POST CARD FROM MY DOG AT GOLF CAMP...
On our first day here, all we did was a little putting.
Today we worked on the short irons.
HE DOESN'T SAY ANYTHING ABOUT EATING OR SLEEPING..
10-18
I WONDER WHERE YOU SLEEP WHEN YOU'RE AT GOLF CAMP..
SCHULZ
© 1987 United Feature Syndicate, Inc

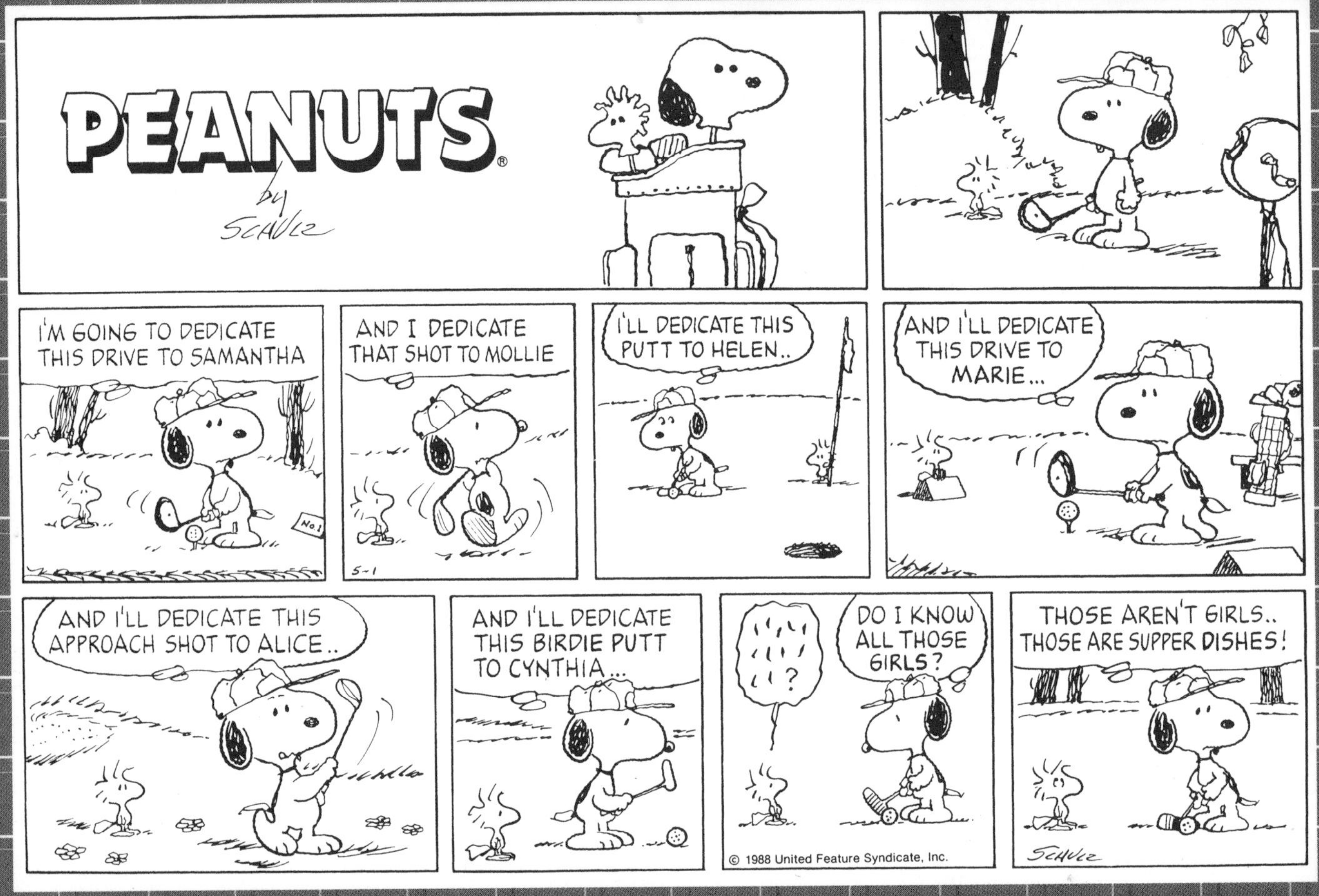
PEANUTS®
by SCHULZ
I'M GOING TO DEDICATE THIS DRIVE TO SAMANTHA
NO. 1
AND I DEDICATE THAT SHOT TO MOLLIE
5-1
I'LL DEDICATE THIS PUTT TO HELEN..
AND I'LL DEDICATE THIS DRIVE TO MARIE...
AND I'LL DEDICATE THIS APPROACH SHOT TO ALICE..
AND I'LL DEDICATE THIS BIRDIE PUTT TO CYNTHIA...
?
DO I KNOW ALL THOSE GIRLS?
© 1988 United Feature Syndicate, Inc.
THOSE AREN'T GIRLS.. THOSE ARE SUPPER DISHES!
SCHULZ

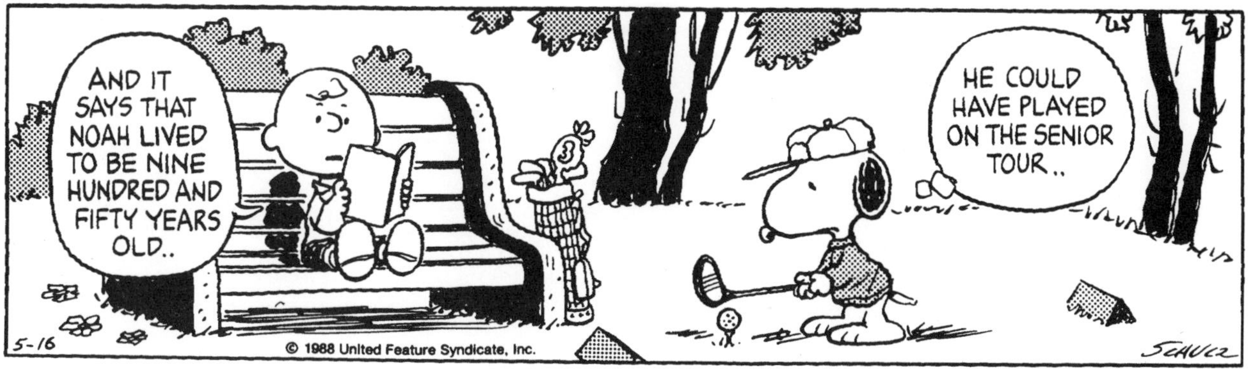
AND IT SAYS THAT NOAH LIVED TO BE NINE HUNDRED AND FIFTY YEARS OLD..
HE COULD HAVE PLAYED ON THE SENIOR TOUR..
5-16
© 1988 United Feature Syndicate, Inc.
SCHULZ

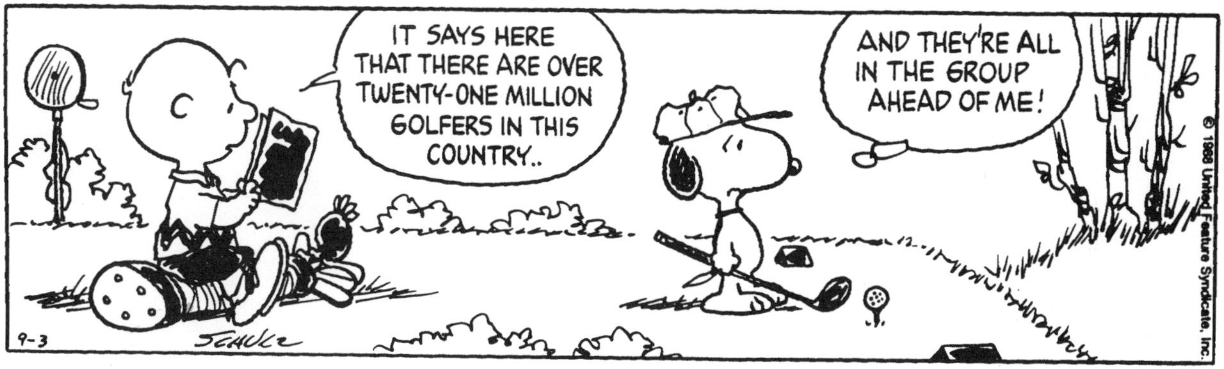
IT SAYS HERE THAT THERE ARE OVER TWENTY-ONE MILLION GOLFERS IN THIS COUNTRY..
AND THEY'RE ALL IN THE GROUP AHEAD OF ME!
9-3
SCHULZ
© 1988 United Feature Syndicate, Inc.

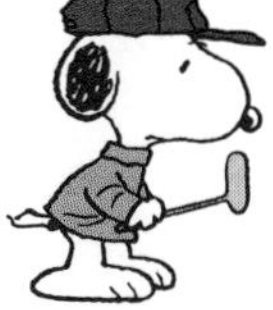

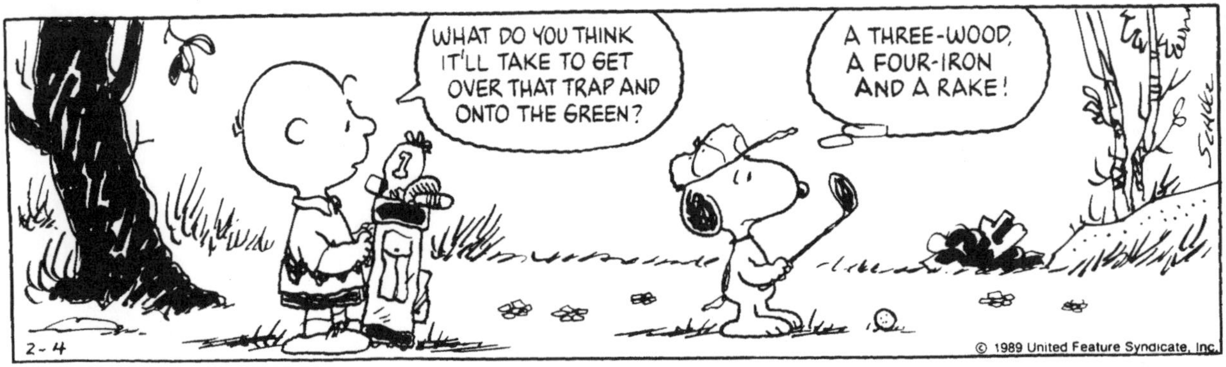
2-4
WHAT DO YOU THINK IT'LL TAKE TO GET OVER THAT TRAP AND ONTO THE GREEN?
A THREE-WOOD, A FOUR-IRON AND A RAKE!
© 1989 United Feature Syndicate, Inc.

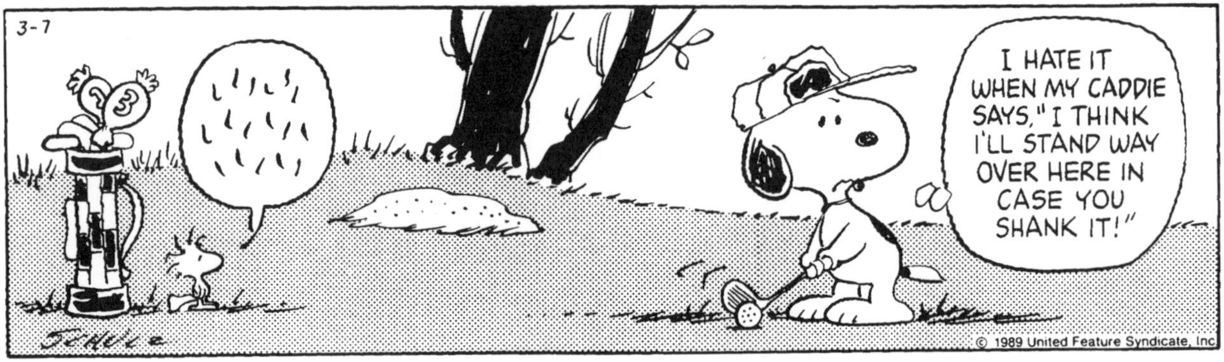
3-7
I HATE IT WHEN MY CADDIE SAYS, "I THINK I'LL STAND WAY OVER HERE IN CASE YOU SHANK IT!"
© 1989 United Feature Syndicate, Inc.

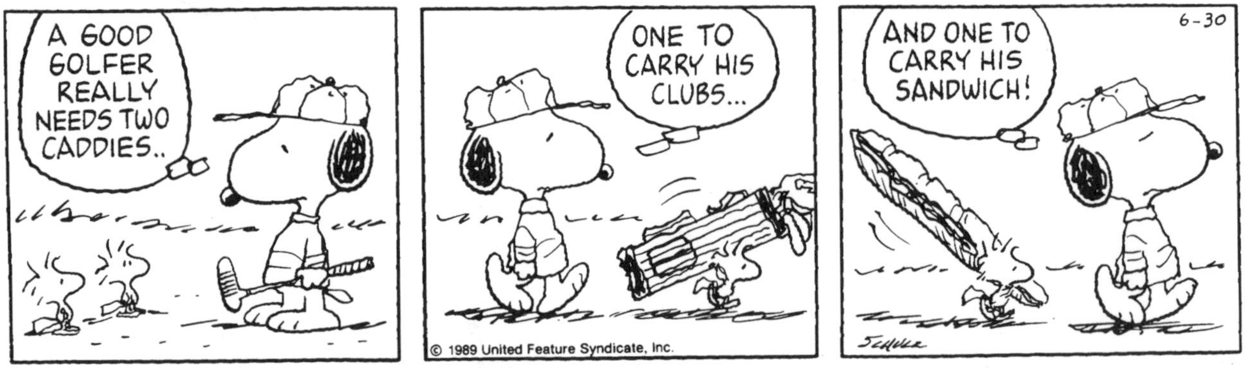
A GOOD GOLFER REALLY NEEDS TWO CADDIES..
ONE TO CARRY HIS CLUBS...
© 1989 United Feature Syndicate, Inc.
6-30
AND ONE TO CARRY HIS SANDWICH!

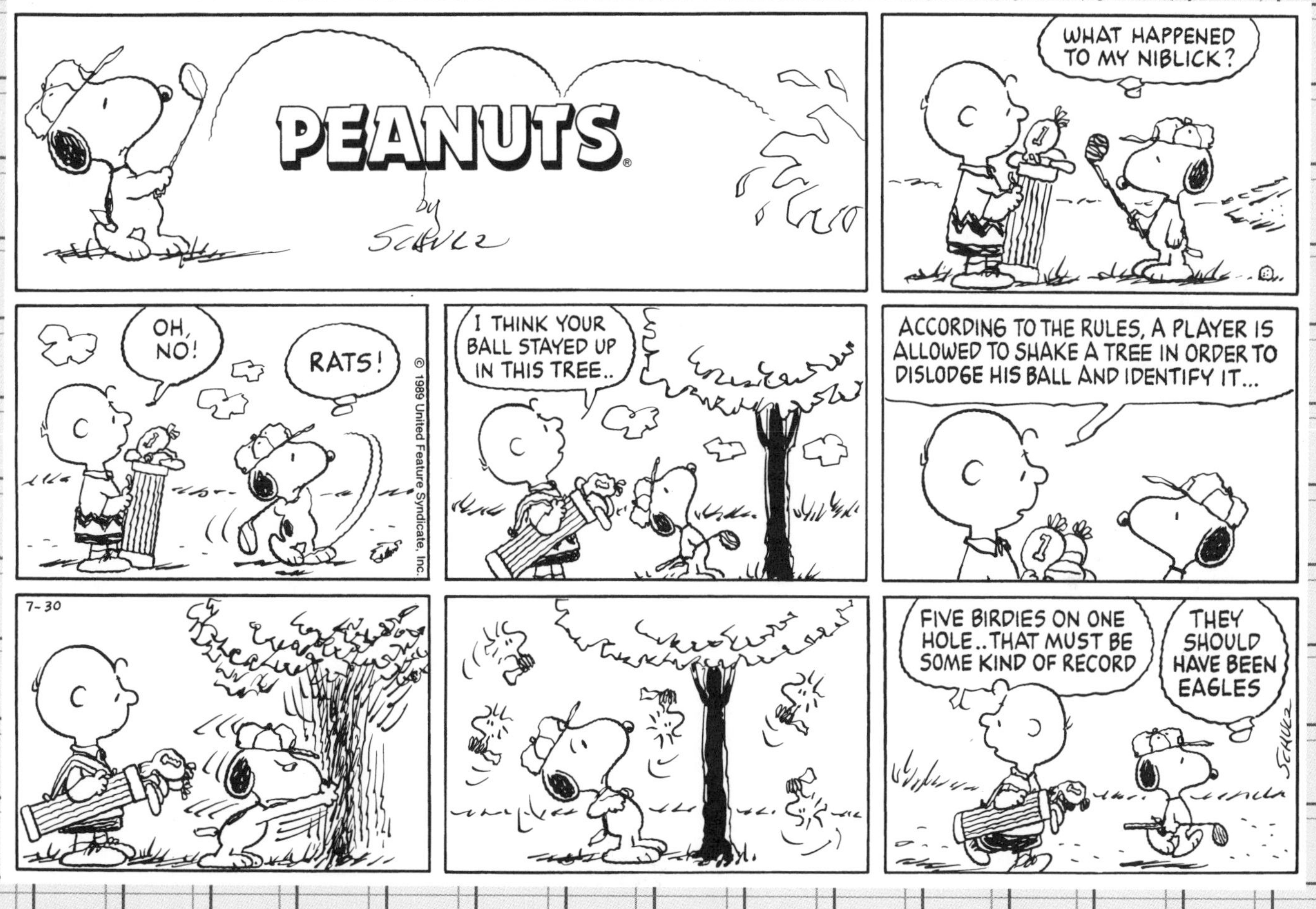
PEANUTS
by
SCHULZ
WHAT HAPPENED TO MY NIBLICK?
OH, NO!
RATS!
© 1989 United Feature Syndicate, Inc.
I THINK YOUR BALL STAYED UP IN THIS TREE..
ACCORDING TO THE RULES, A PLAYER IS ALLOWED TO SHAKE A TREE IN ORDER TO DISLODGE HIS BALL AND IDENTIFY IT...
7-30
FIVE BIRDIES ON ONE HOLE..THAT MUST BE SOME KIND OF RECORD
THEY SHOULD HAVE BEEN EAGLES
SCHULZ

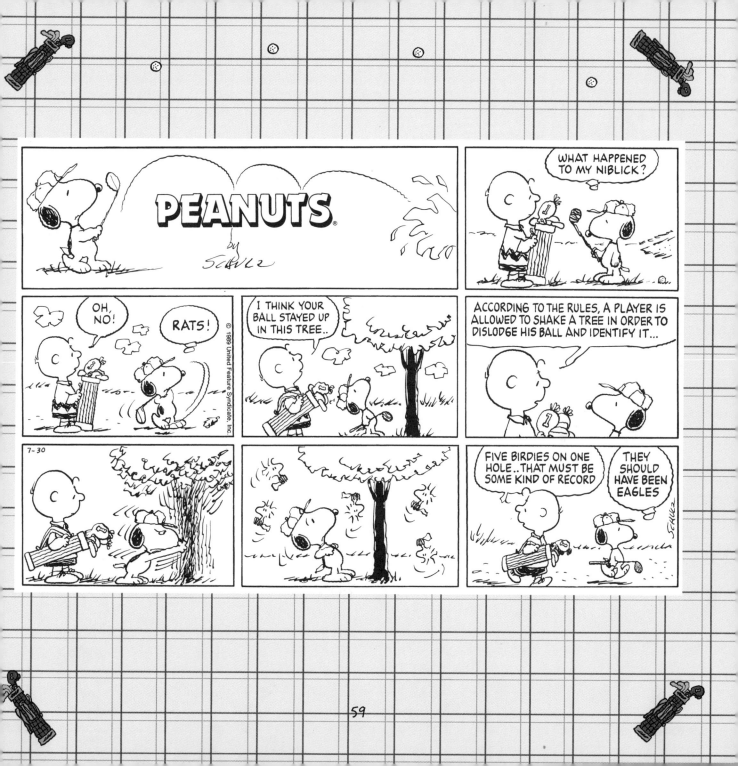

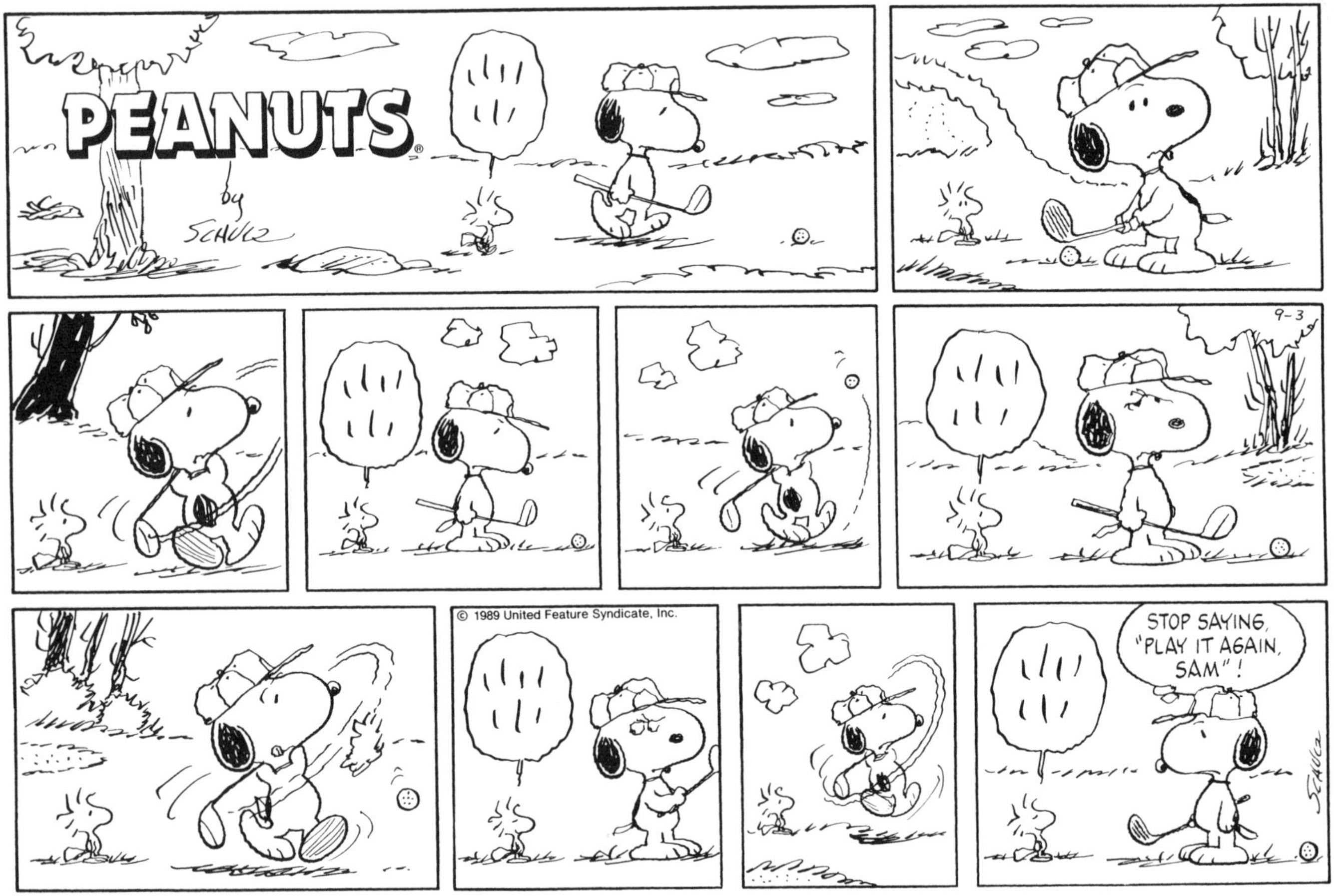
PEANUTS
by SCHULZ
9-3
© 1989 United Feature Syndicate, Inc.
STOP SAYING, "PLAY IT AGAIN, SAM"!
SCHULZ

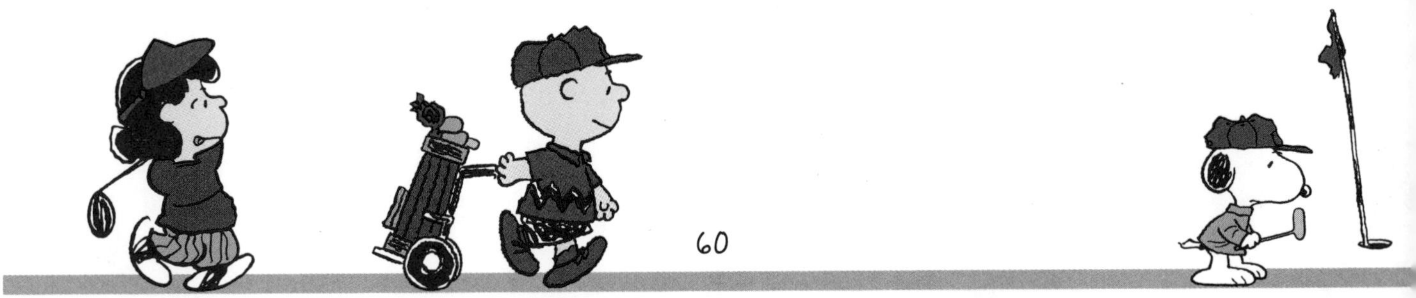

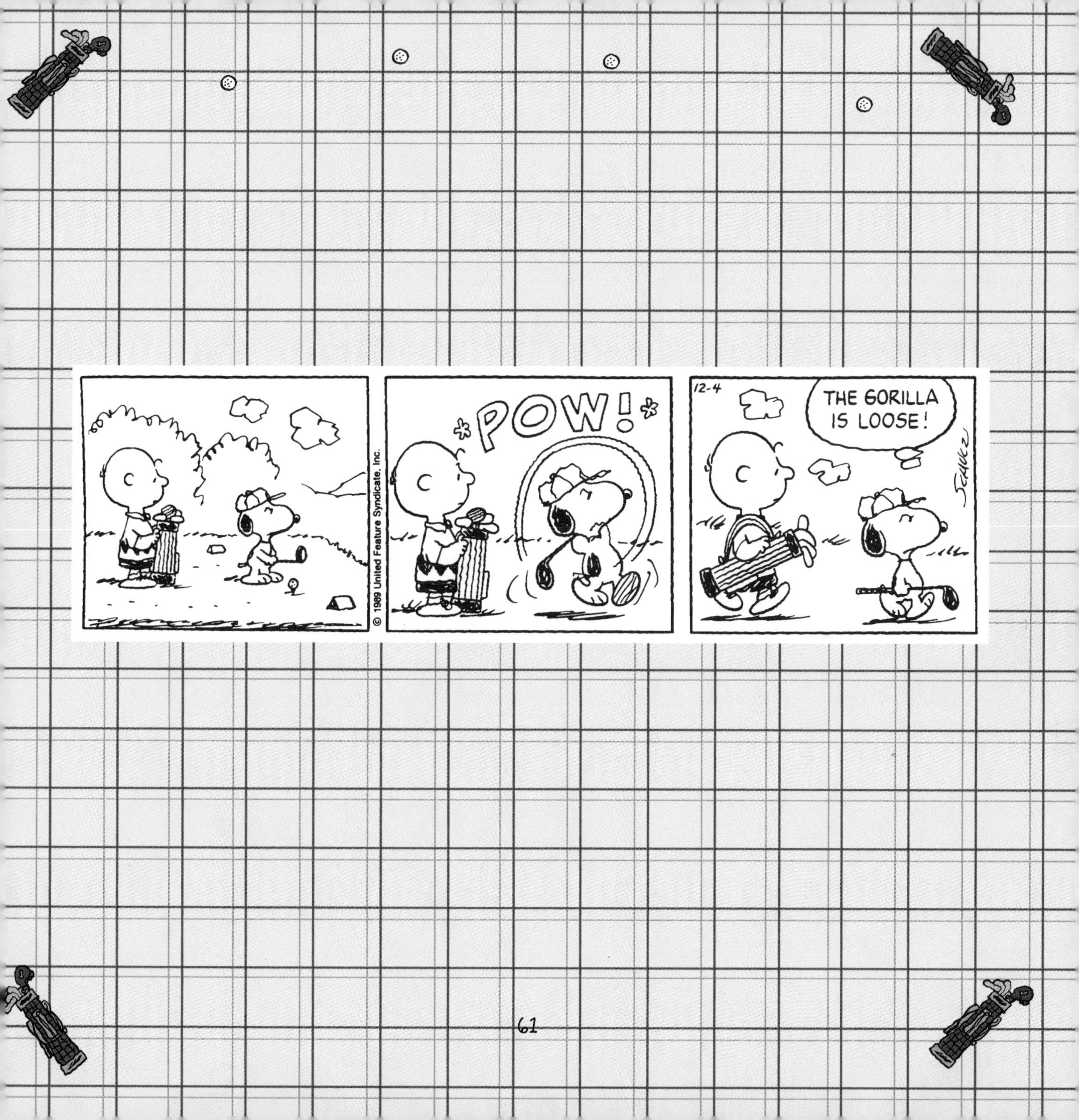

© 1989 United Feature Syndicate, Inc.
POW!
12-4
THE GORILLA IS LOOSE!
SCHULZ

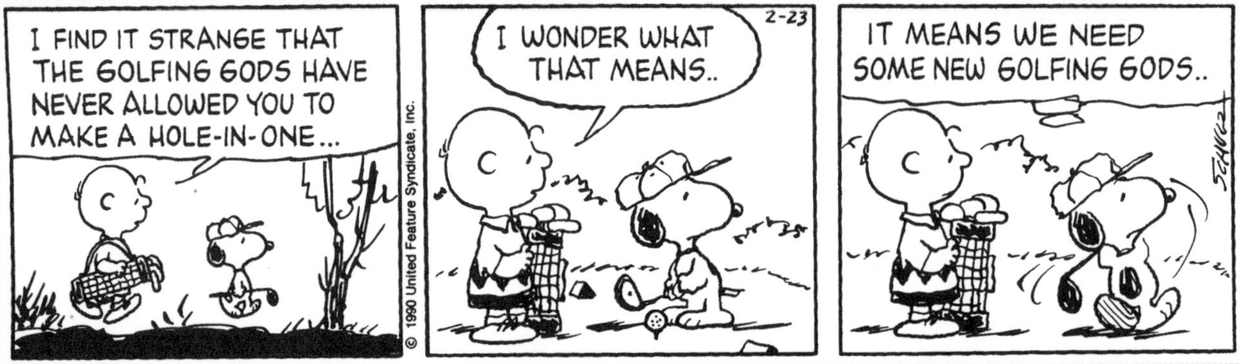
I FIND IT STRANGE THAT THE GOLFING GODS HAVE NEVER ALLOWED YOU TO MAKE A HOLE-IN-ONE...
© 1990 United Feature Syndicate, Inc.
2-23
I WONDER WHAT THAT MEANS..
IT MEANS WE NEED SOME NEW GOLFING GODS..
SCHULZ

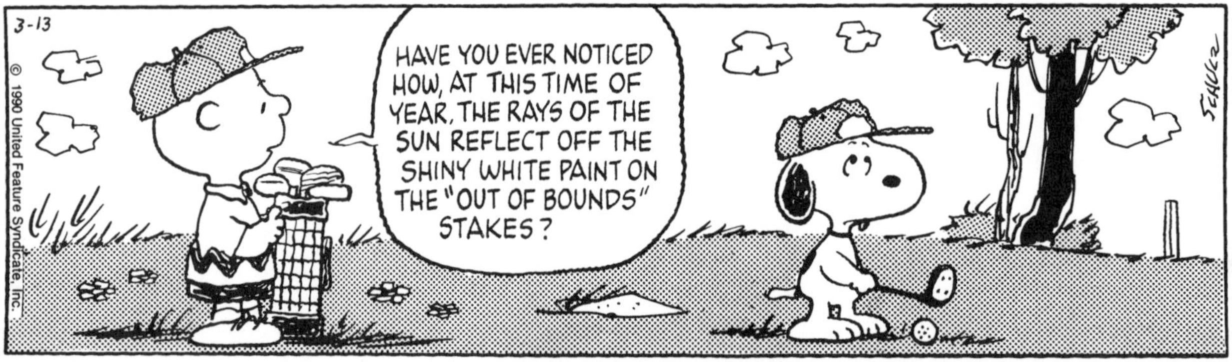
3-13
© 1990 United Feature Syndicate, Inc.
HAVE YOU EVER NOTICED HOW, AT THIS TIME OF YEAR, THE RAYS OF THE SUN REFLECT OFF THE SHINY WHITE PAINT ON THE "OUT OF BOUNDS" STAKES?
SCHULZ

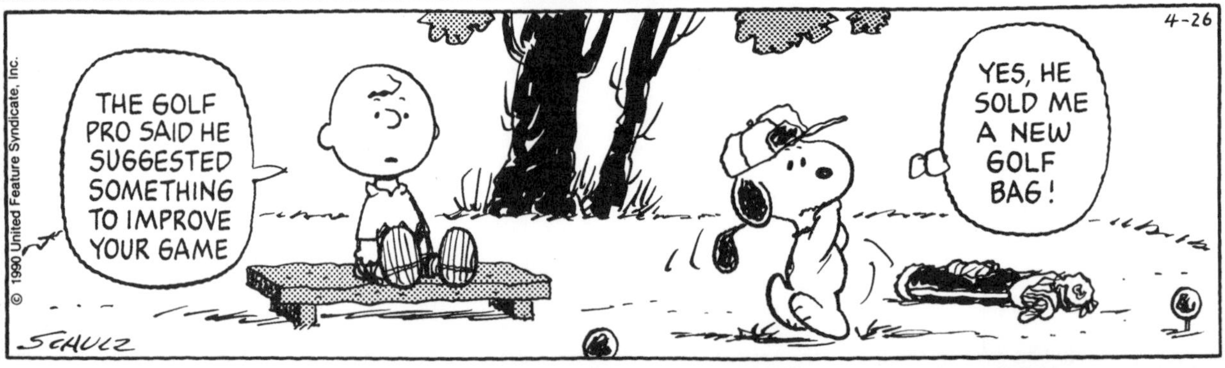
© 1990 United Feature Syndicate, Inc.
4-26
THE GOLF PRO SAID HE SUGGESTED SOMETHING TO IMPROVE YOUR GAME
YES, HE SOLD ME A NEW GOLF BAG!
SCHULZ

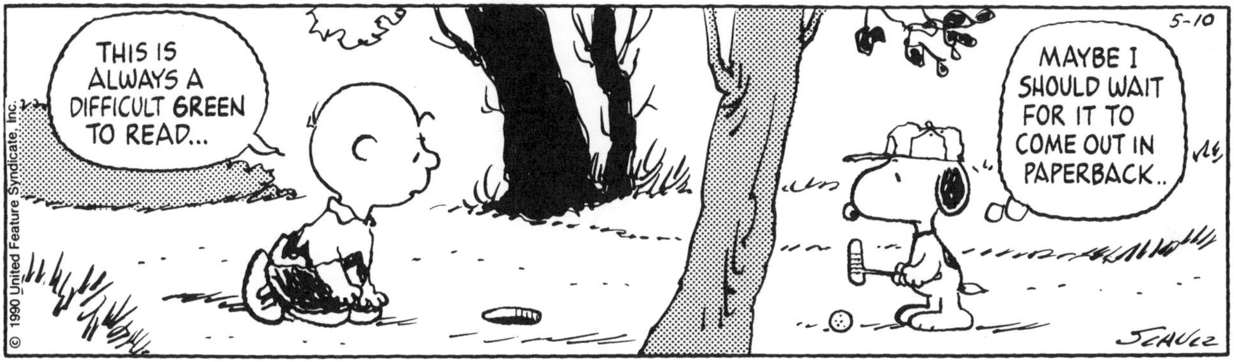
5-10
THIS IS ALWAYS A DIFFICULT GREEN TO READ...
MAYBE I SHOULD WAIT FOR IT TO COME OUT IN PAPERBACK..
© 1990 United Feature Syndicate, Inc.
SCHULZ

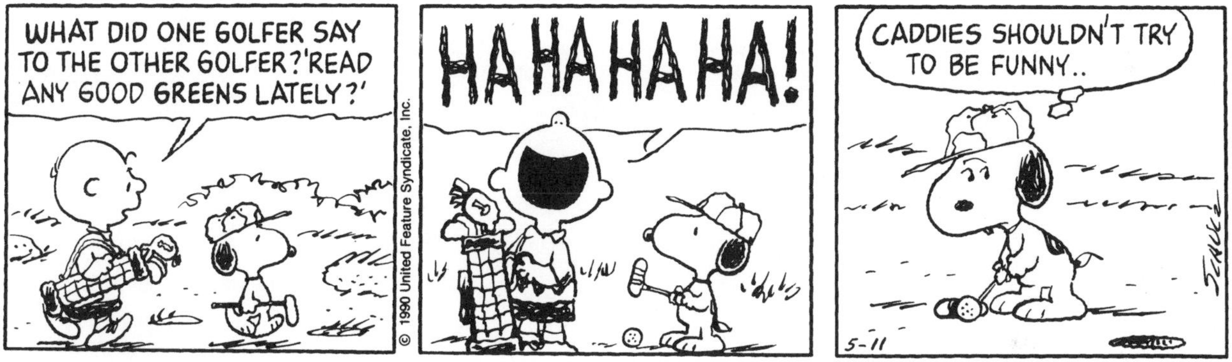
WHAT DID ONE GOLFER SAY TO THE OTHER GOLFER? 'READ ANY GOOD GREENS LATELY?'
HAHAHAHA!
© 1990 United Feature Syndicate, Inc.
CADDIES SHOULDN'T TRY TO BE FUNNY..
SCHULZ
5-11

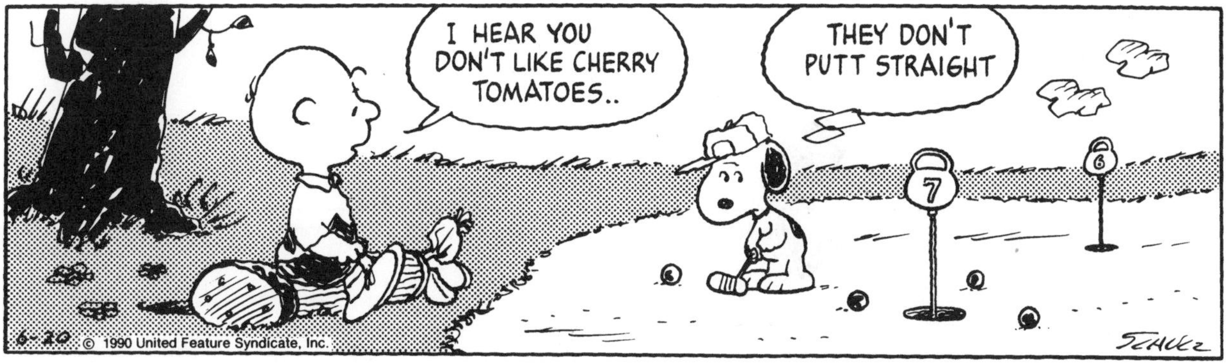
I HEAR YOU DON'T LIKE CHERRY TOMATOES..
THEY DON'T PUTT STRAIGHT
7
6
6-20 © 1990 United Feature Syndicate, Inc.
SCHULZ

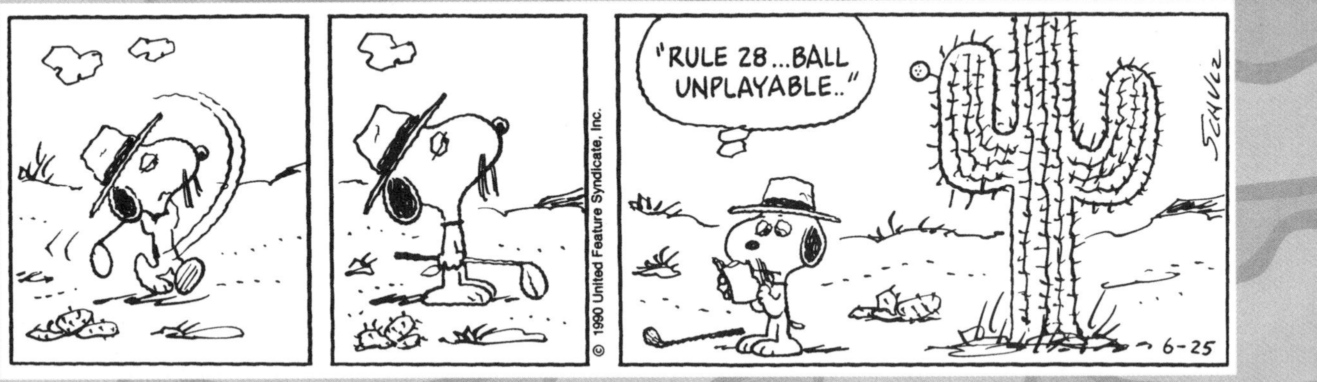
© 1990 United Feature Syndicate, Inc.
"RULE 28...BALL UNPLAYABLE.."
SCHULZ
6-25

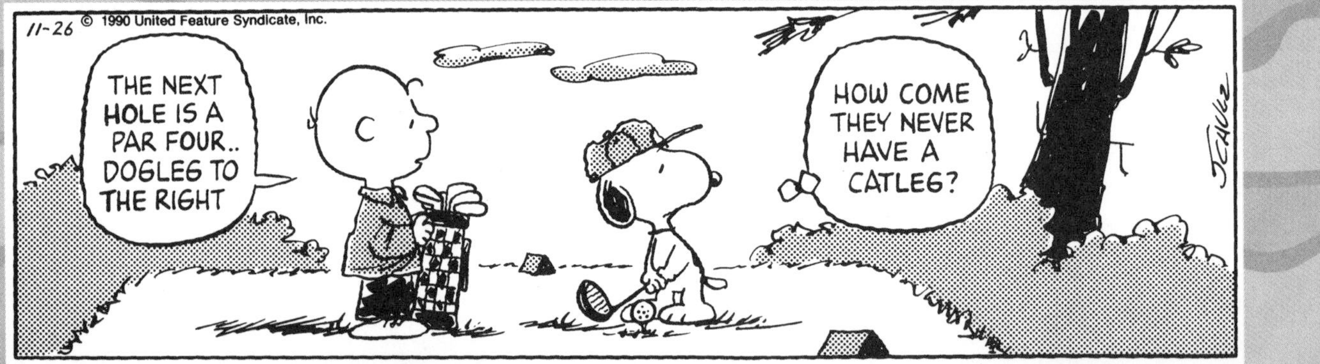
11-26 © 1990 United Feature Syndicate, Inc.
THE NEXT HOLE IS A PAR FOUR.. DOGLEG TO THE RIGHT
HOW COME THEY NEVER HAVE A CATLEG?
SCHULZ

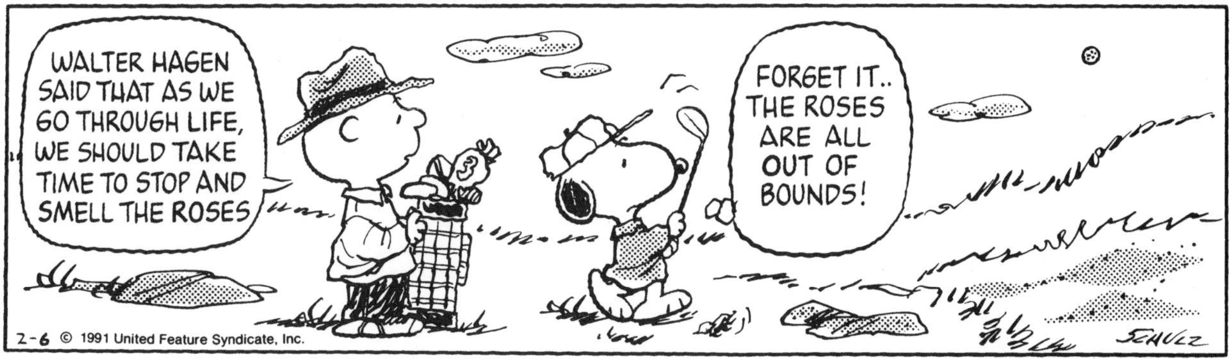
WALTER HAGEN SAID THAT AS WE GO THROUGH LIFE, WE SHOULD TAKE TIME TO STOP AND SMELL THE ROSES
FORGET IT.. THE ROSES ARE ALL OUT OF BOUNDS!
2-6 © 1991 United Feature Syndicate, Inc.
SCHULZ

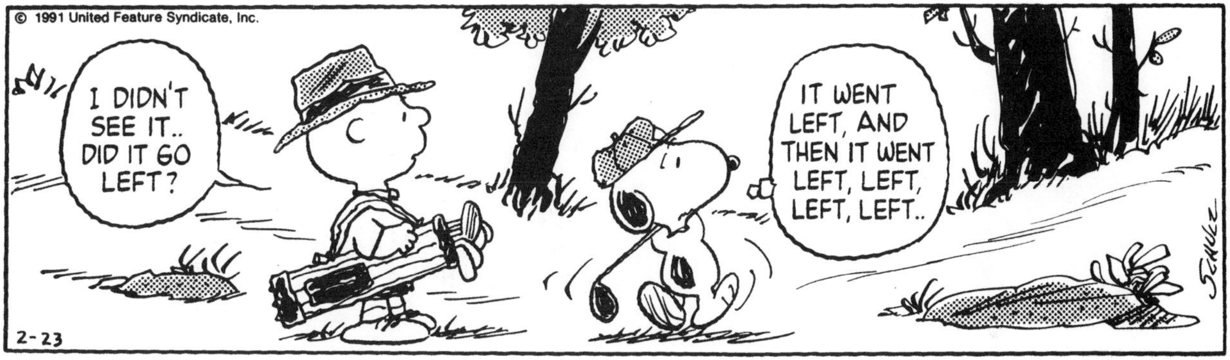
© 1991 United Feature Syndicate, Inc.
I DIDN'T SEE IT.. DID IT GO LEFT?
IT WENT LEFT, AND THEN IT WENT LEFT, LEFT, LEFT, LEFT..
SCHULZ
2-23

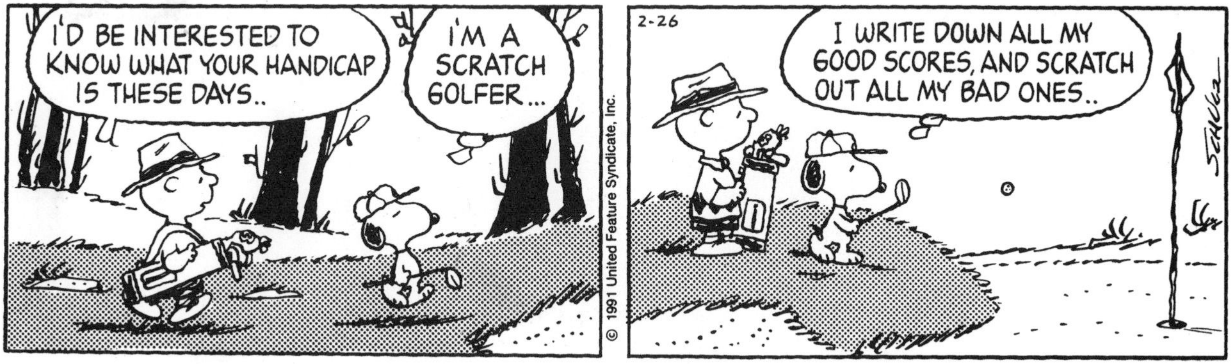
I'D BE INTERESTED TO KNOW WHAT YOUR HANDICAP IS THESE DAYS..
I'M A SCRATCH GOLFER...
© 1991 United Feature Syndicate, Inc.
2-26
I WRITE DOWN ALL MY GOOD SCORES, AND SCRATCH OUT ALL MY BAD ONES..
SCHULZ

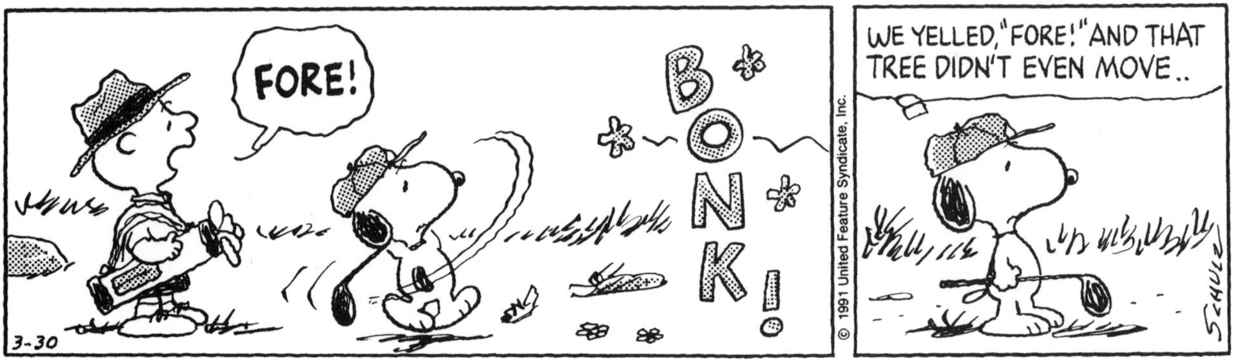
3-30
FORE!
BONK!
© 1991 United Feature Syndicate, Inc.
WE YELLED, "FORE!" AND THAT TREE DIDN'T EVEN MOVE..
SCHULZ

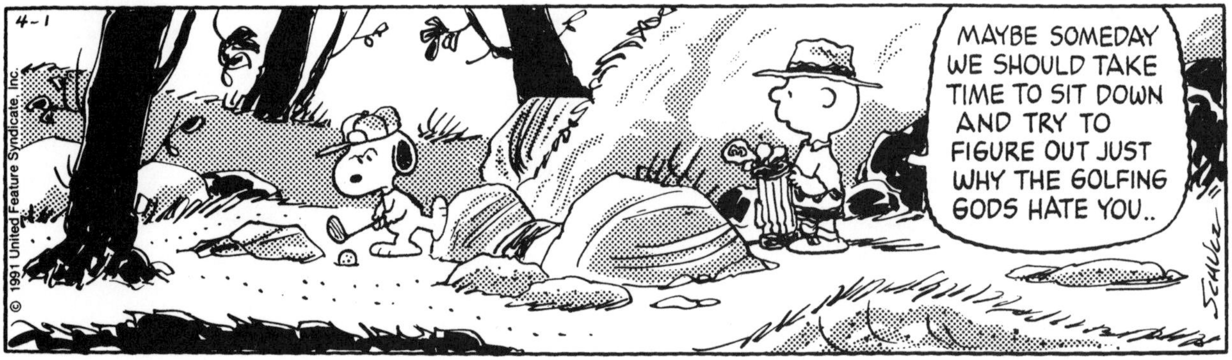
4-1
© 1991 United Feature Syndicate, Inc.
MAYBE SOMEDAY WE SHOULD TAKE TIME TO SIT DOWN AND TRY TO FIGURE OUT JUST WHY THE GOLFING GODS HATE YOU..
SCHULZ

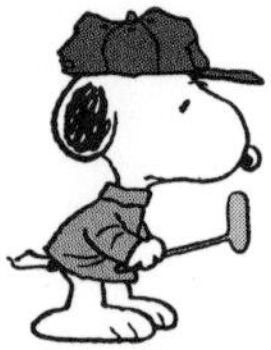

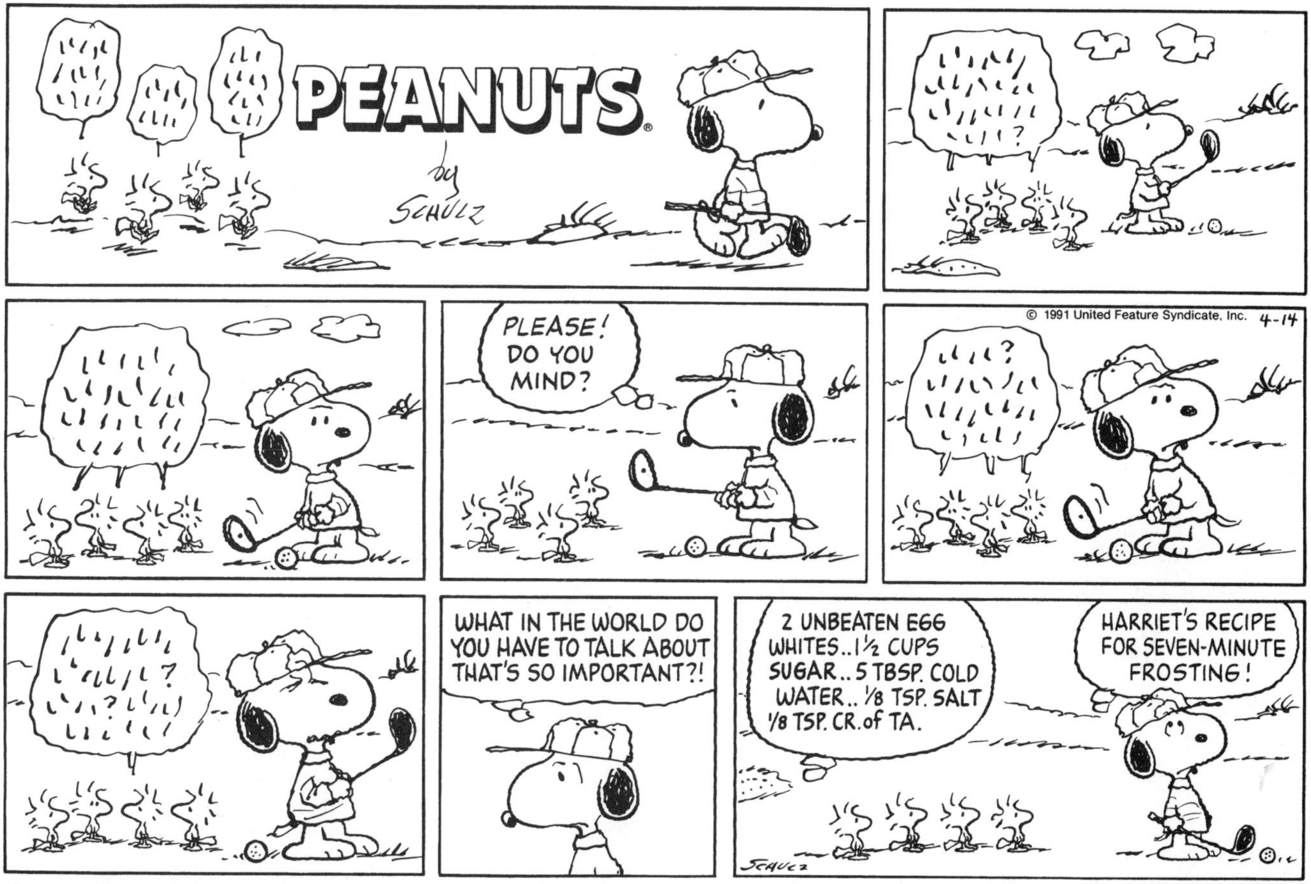
PEANUTS
by SCHULZ
PLEASE! DO YOU MIND?
© 1991 United Feature Syndicate, Inc. 4-14
WHAT IN THE WORLD DO YOU HAVE TO TALK ABOUT THAT'S SO IMPORTANT?!
2 UNBEATEN EGG WHITES..1½ CUPS SUGAR..5 TBSP. COLD WATER..⅛ TSP. SALT ⅛ TSP. CR. of TA.
HARRIET'S RECIPE FOR SEVEN-MINUTE FROSTING!
SCHULZ

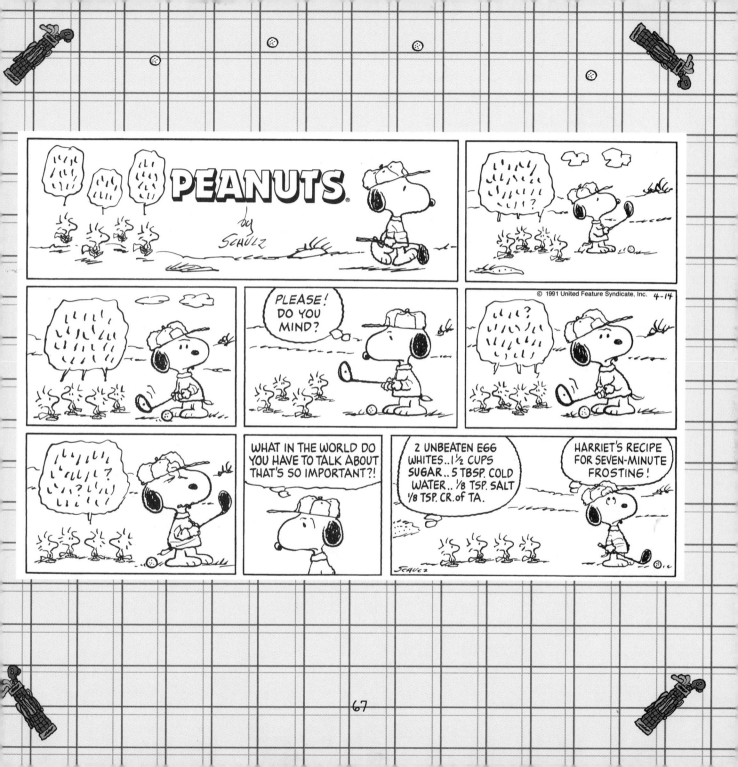

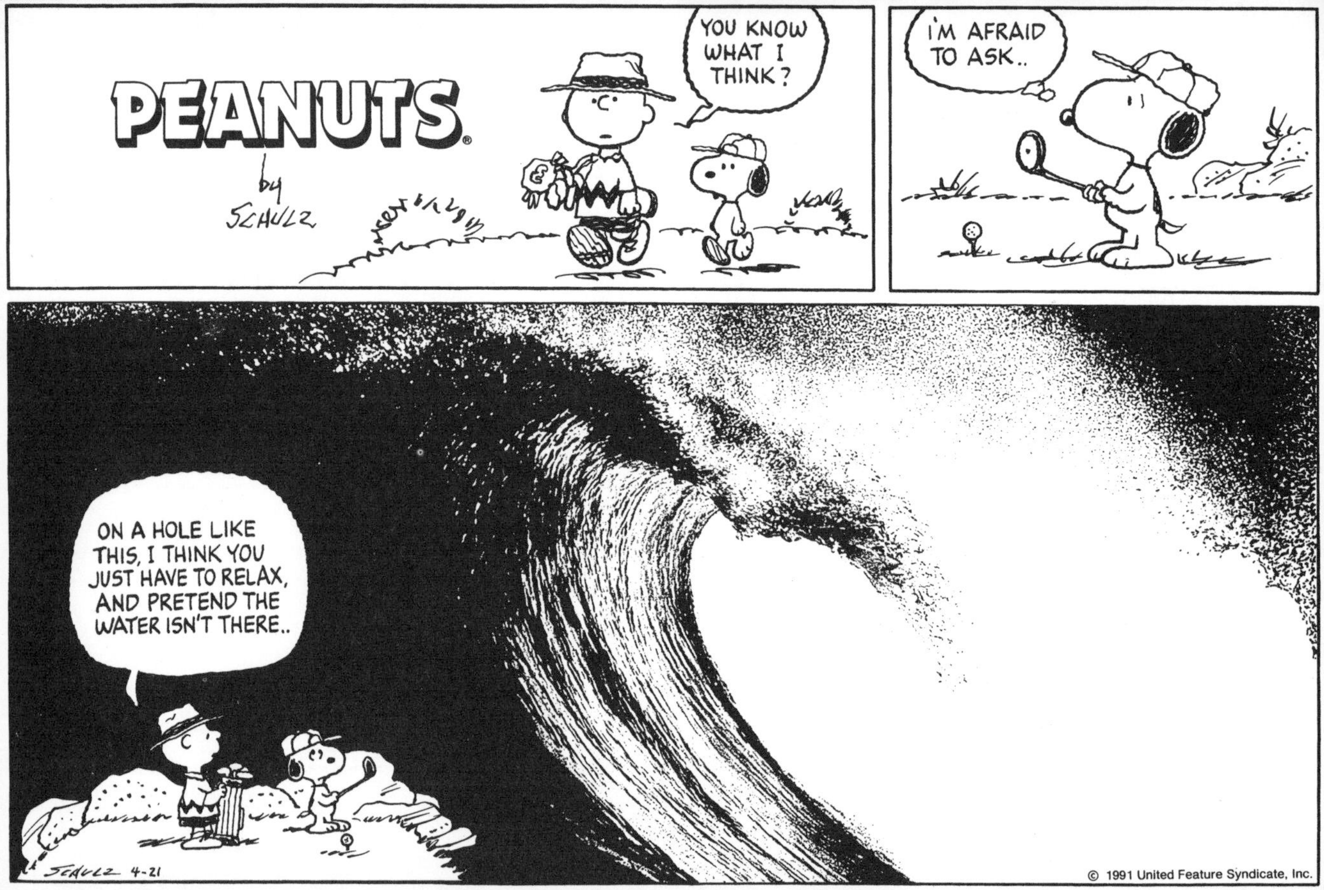
PEANUTS
by SCHULZ
YOU KNOW WHAT I THINK?
I'M AFRAID TO ASK..
ON A HOLE LIKE THIS, I THINK YOU JUST HAVE TO RELAX, AND PRETEND THE WATER ISN'T THERE..
SCHULZ 4-21
© 1991 United Feature Syndicate, Inc.

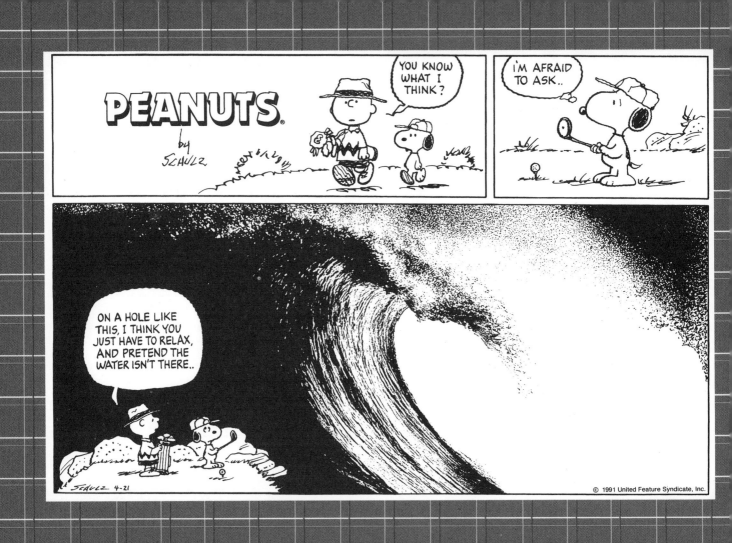

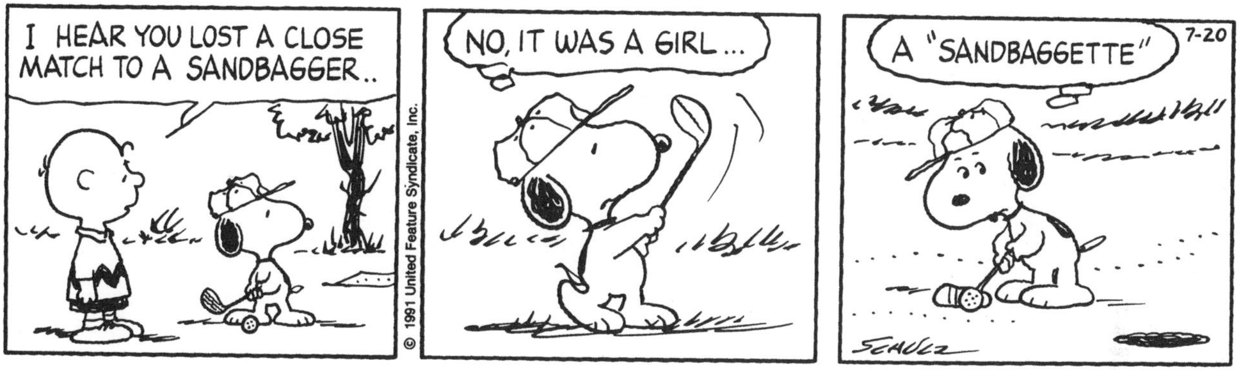
I HEAR YOU LOST A CLOSE MATCH TO A SANDBAGGER..
© 1991 United Feature Syndicate, Inc.
NO, IT WAS A GIRL...
7-20
A "SANDBAGGETTE"
SCHULZ

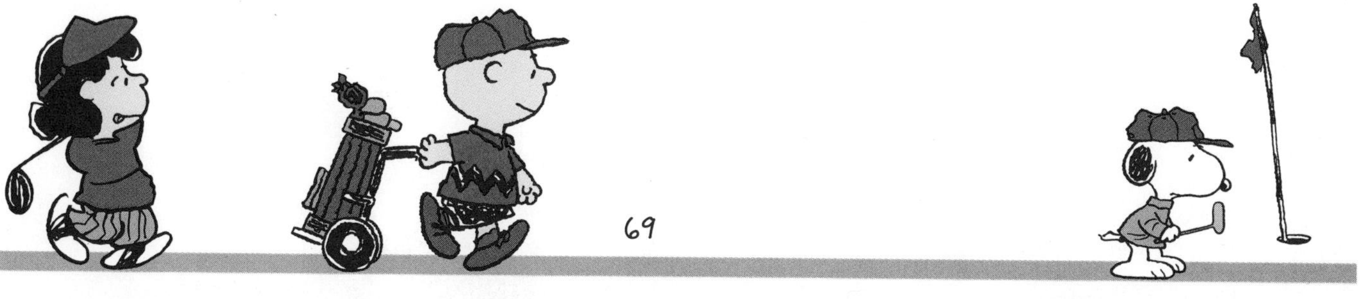

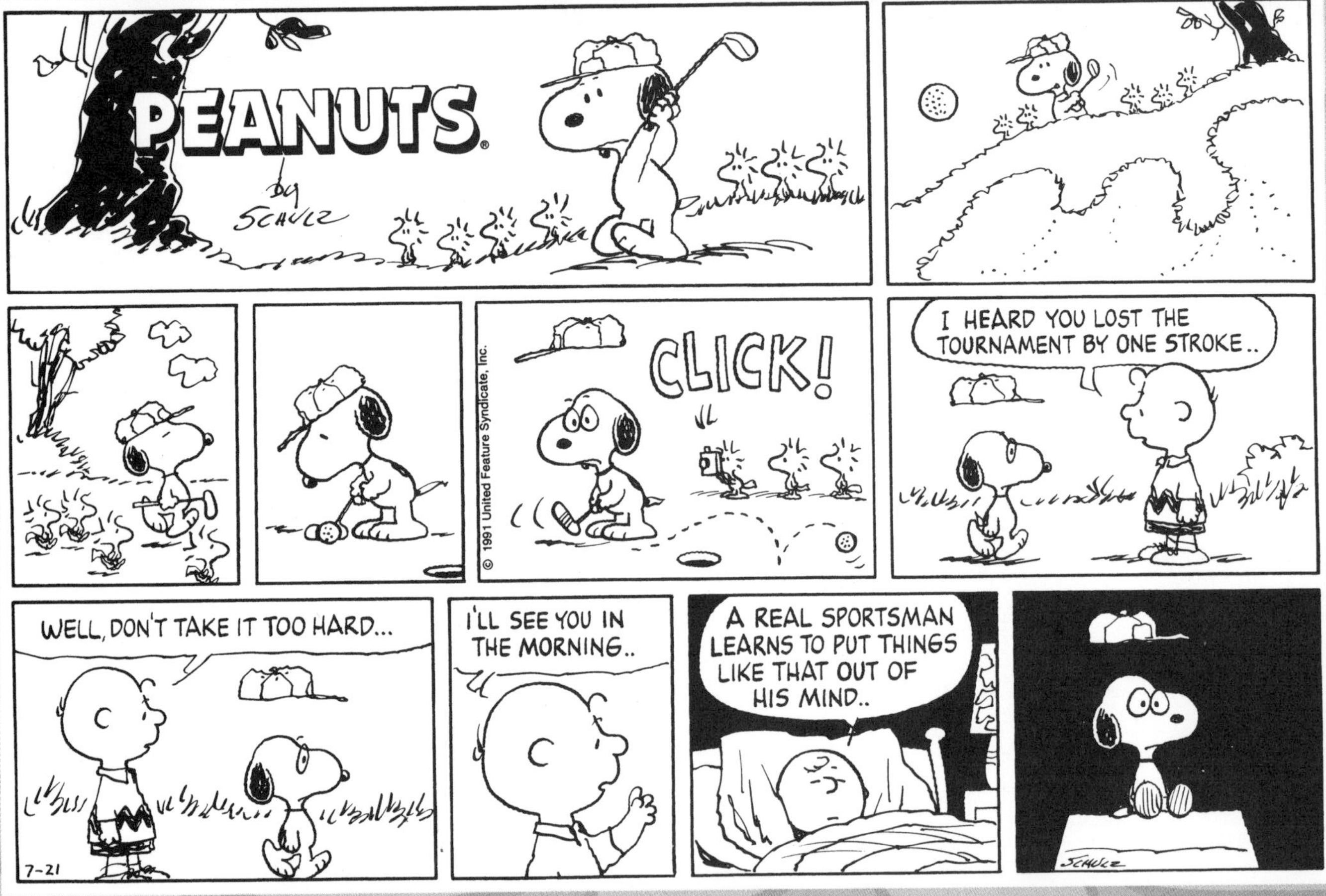
PEANUTS
by SCHULZ
© 1991 United Feature Syndicate, Inc.
CLICK!
I HEARD YOU LOST THE TOURNAMENT BY ONE STROKE..
WELL, DON'T TAKE IT TOO HARD...
7-21
I'LL SEE YOU IN THE MORNING..
A REAL SPORTSMAN LEARNS TO PUT THINGS LIKE THAT OUT OF HIS MIND..
SCHULZ

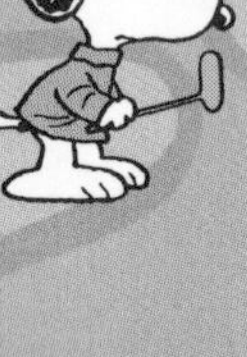

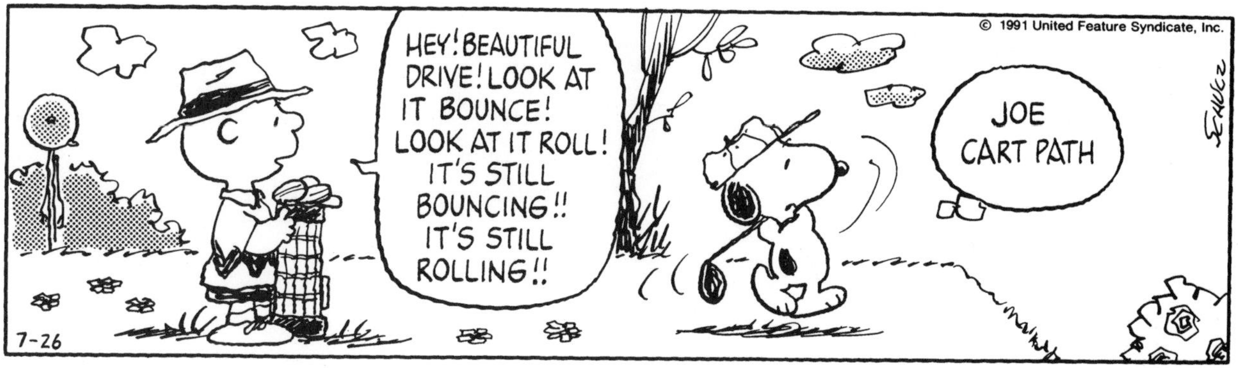

HEY! BEAUTIFUL DRIVE! LOOK AT IT BOUNCE! LOOK AT IT ROLL! IT'S STILL BOUNCING!! IT'S STILL ROLLING!!
JOE CART PATH
7-26
© 1991 United Feature Syndicate, Inc.
SCHULZ

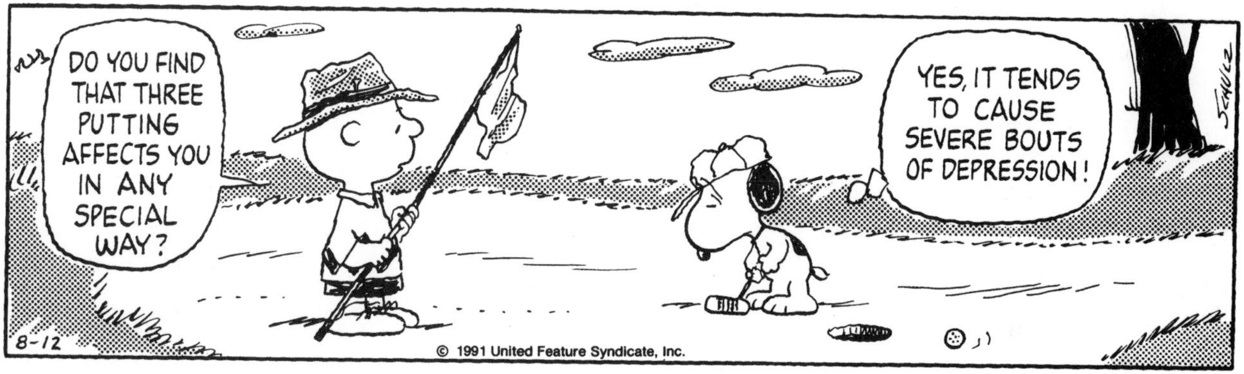

DO YOU FIND THAT THREE PUTTING AFFECTS YOU IN ANY SPECIAL WAY?
YES, IT TENDS TO CAUSE SEVERE BOUTS OF DEPRESSION!
8-12
© 1991 United Feature Syndicate, Inc.
SCHULZ

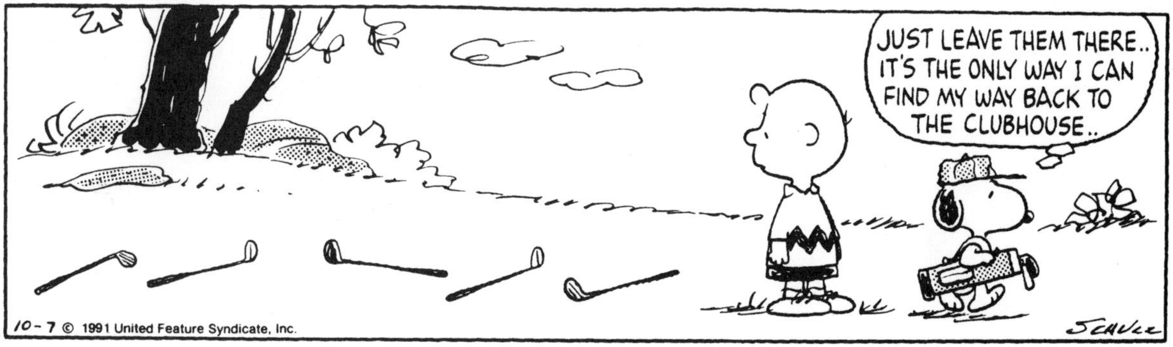

JUST LEAVE THEM THERE.. IT'S THE ONLY WAY I CAN FIND MY WAY BACK TO THE CLUBHOUSE..
10-7 © 1991 United Feature Syndicate, Inc.
SCHULZ

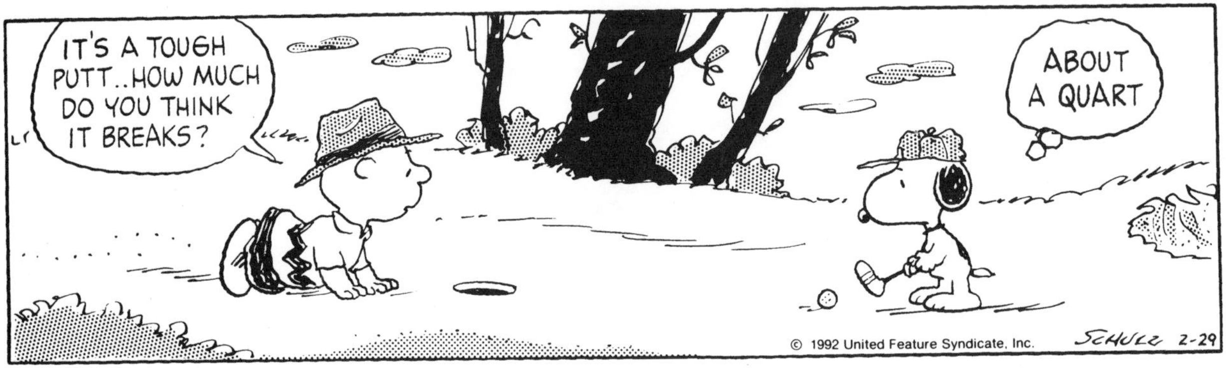
IT'S A TOUGH PUTT..HOW MUCH DO YOU THINK IT BREAKS?
ABOUT A QUART
© 1992 United Feature Syndicate, Inc.
SCHULZ 2-29

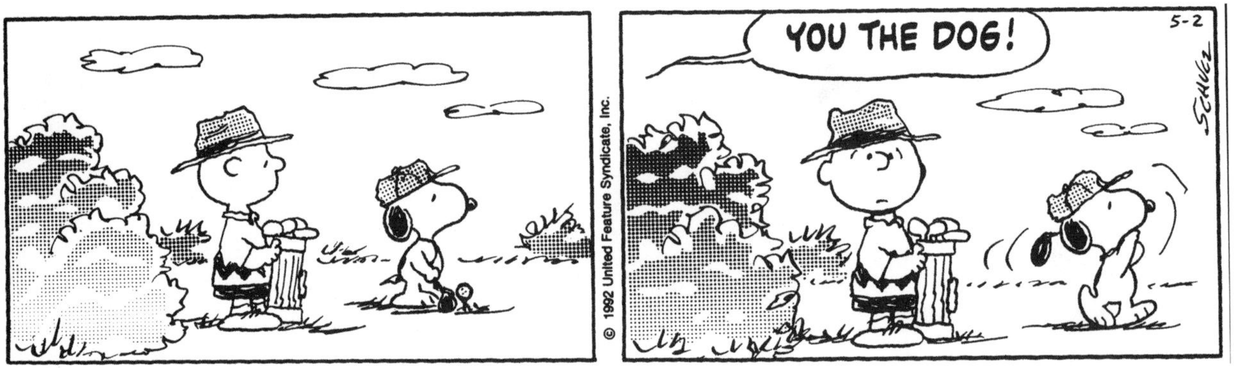
© 1992 United Feature Syndicate, Inc.
YOU THE DOG!
5-2
SCHULZ

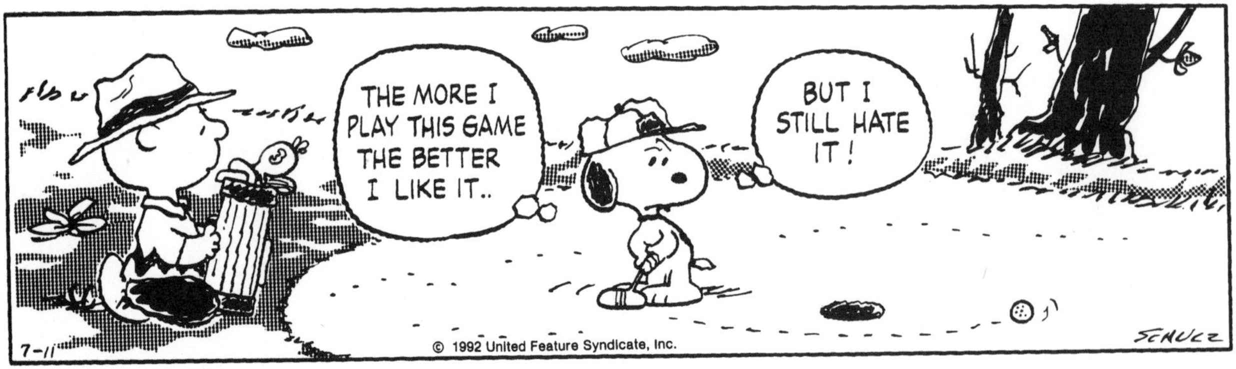
THE MORE I PLAY THIS GAME THE BETTER I LIKE IT..
BUT I STILL HATE IT!
7-11
© 1992 United Feature Syndicate, Inc.
SCHULZ

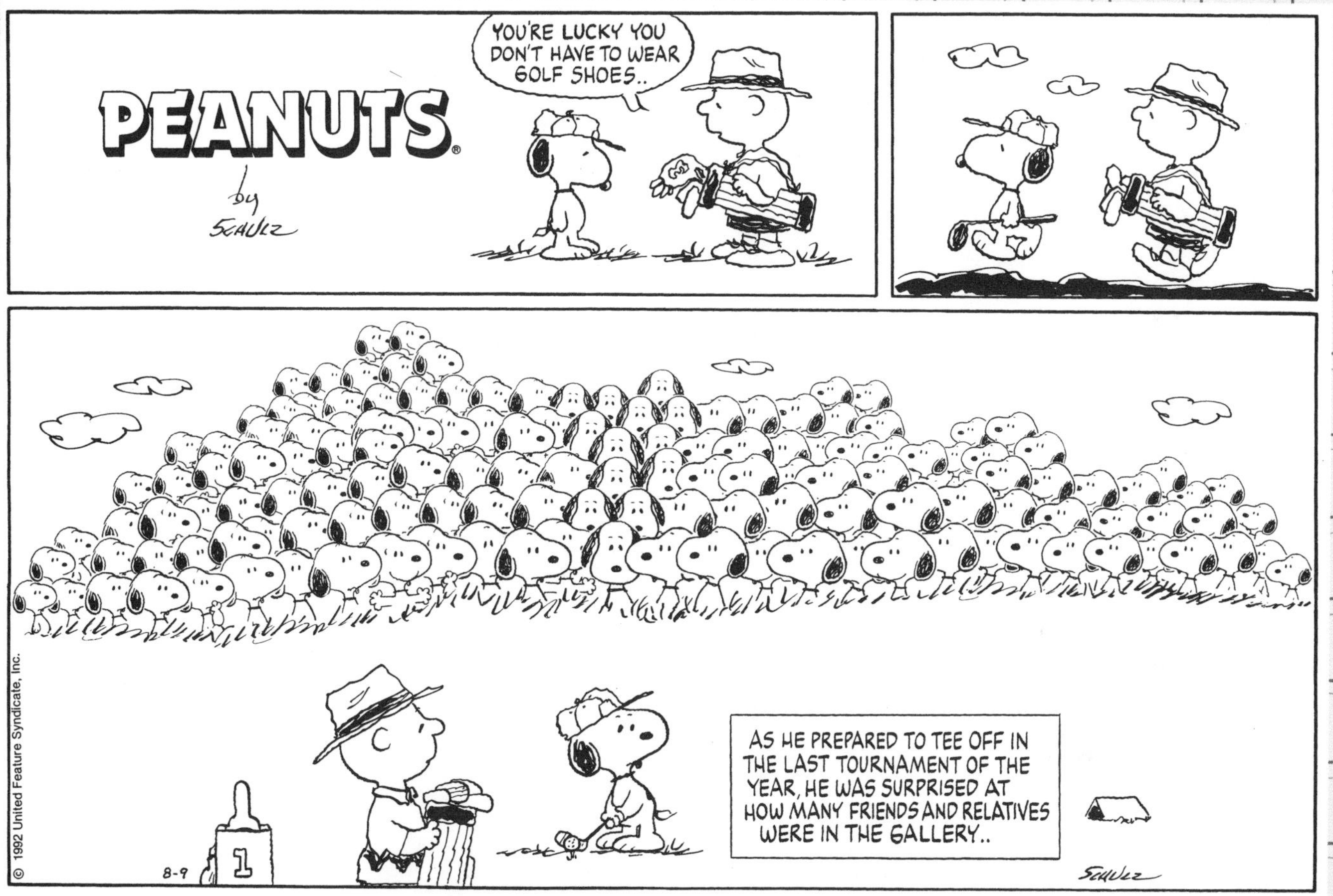
PEANUTS
by SCHULZ
YOU'RE LUCKY YOU DON'T HAVE TO WEAR GOLF SHOES..
AS HE PREPARED TO TEE OFF IN THE LAST TOURNAMENT OF THE YEAR, HE WAS SURPRISED AT HOW MANY FRIENDS AND RELATIVES WERE IN THE GALLERY..
1
8-9
SCHULZ
© 1992 United Feature Syndicate, Inc.

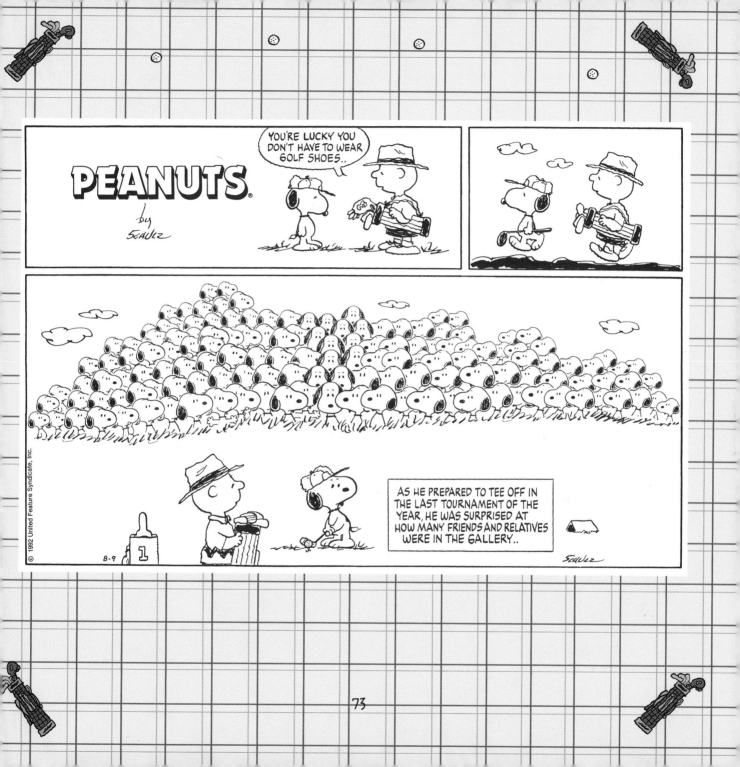

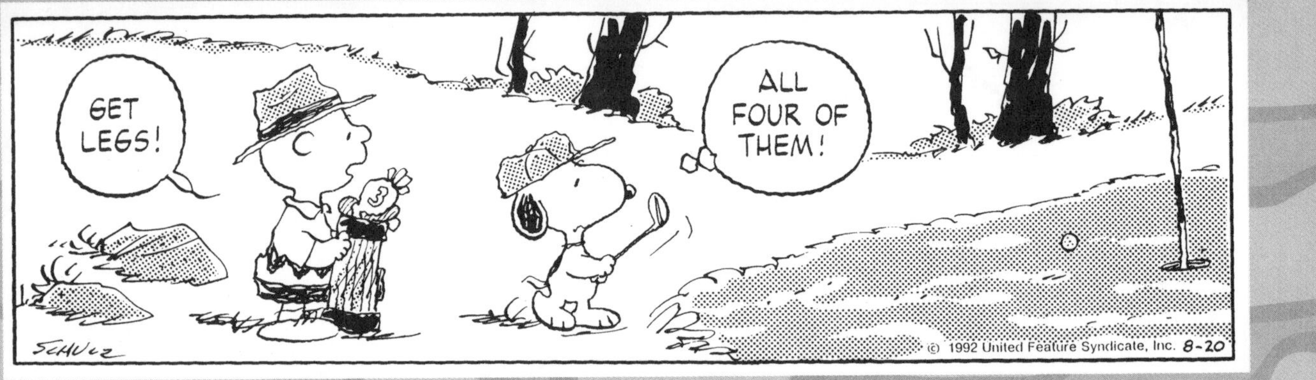
GET LEGS!
ALL FOUR OF THEM!
SCHULZ
© 1992 United Feature Syndicate, Inc. 8-20

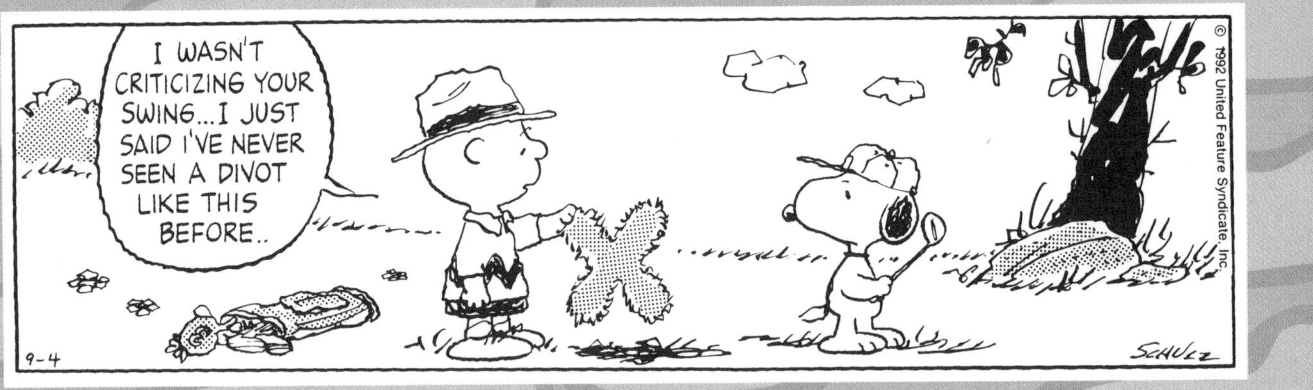
I WASN'T CRITICIZING YOUR SWING...I JUST SAID I'VE NEVER SEEN A DIVOT LIKE THIS BEFORE..
© 1992 United Feature Syndicate, Inc.
9-4
SCHULZ

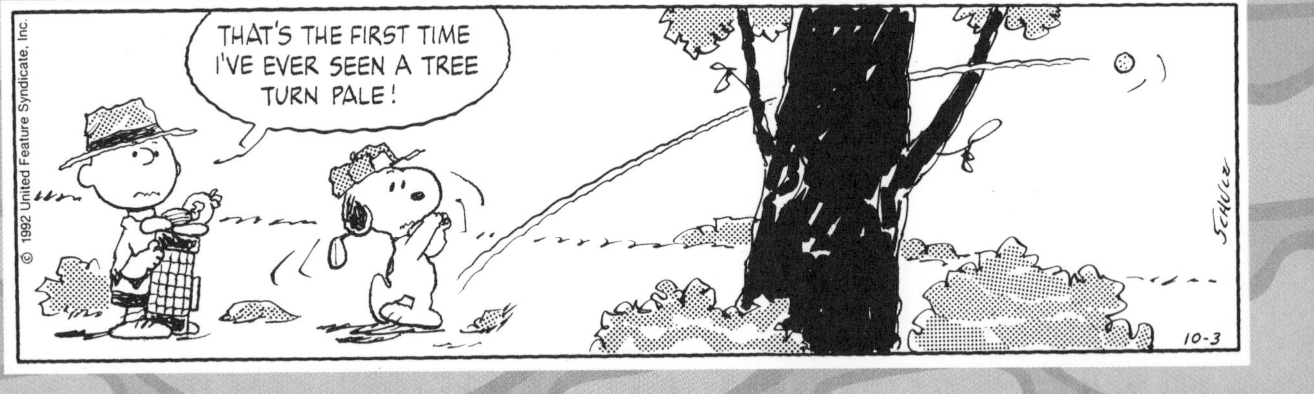
THAT'S THE FIRST TIME I'VE EVER SEEN A TREE TURN PALE!
© 1992 United Feature Syndicate, Inc.
SCHULZ
10-3

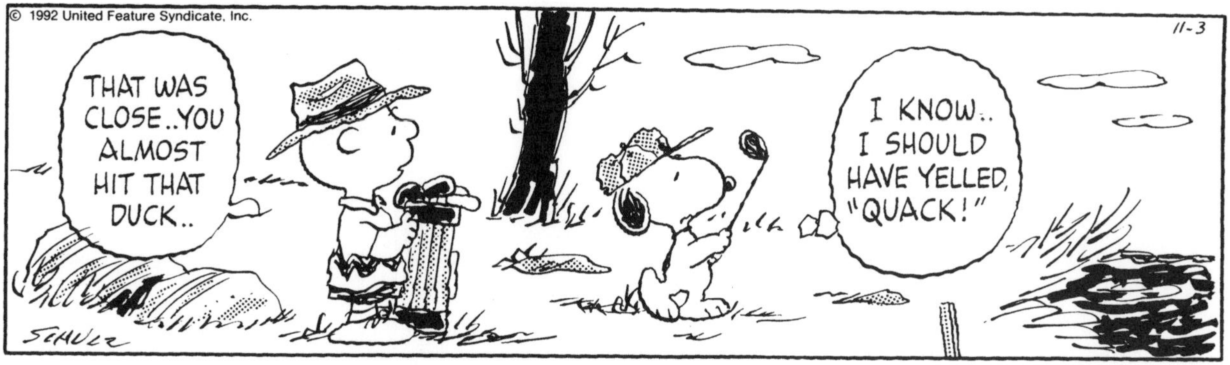
© 1992 United Feature Syndicate, Inc.
11-3
THAT WAS CLOSE..YOU ALMOST HIT THAT DUCK..
I KNOW.. I SHOULD HAVE YELLED, "QUACK!"
SCHULZ

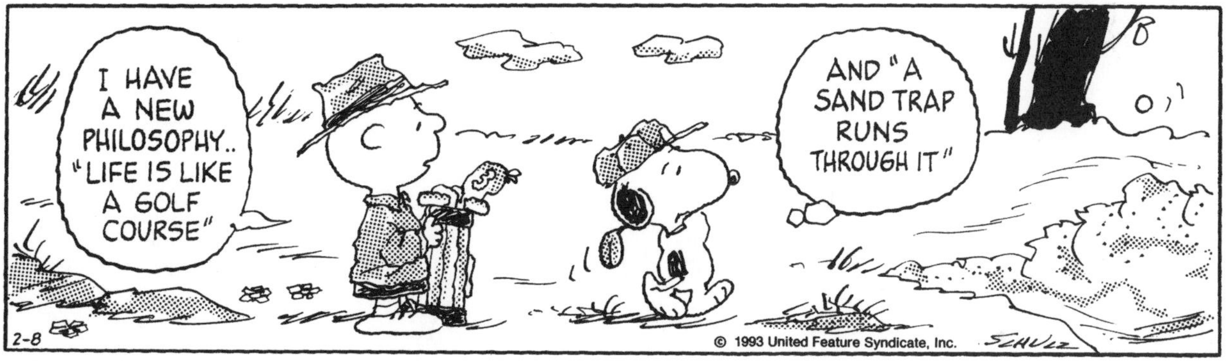
I HAVE A NEW PHILOSOPHY.. "LIFE IS LIKE A GOLF COURSE"
AND "A SAND TRAP RUNS THROUGH IT"
2-8
© 1993 United Feature Syndicate, Inc.
SCHULZ

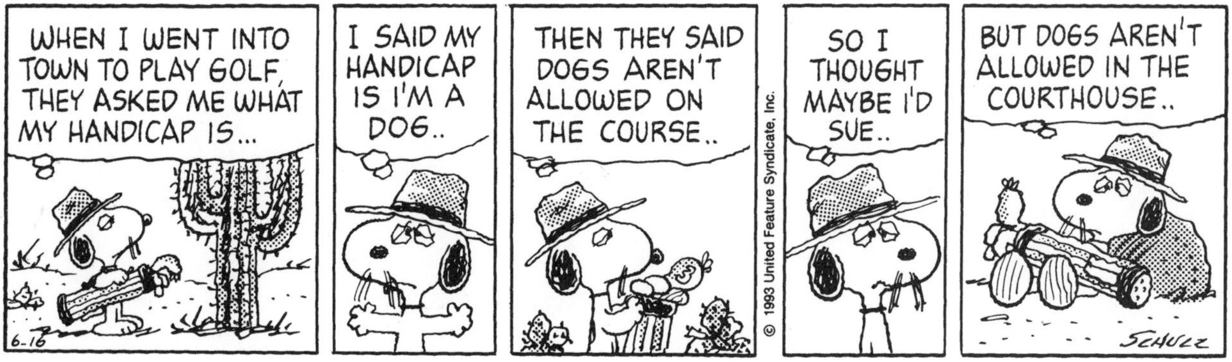
WHEN I WENT INTO TOWN TO PLAY GOLF, THEY ASKED ME WHAT MY HANDICAP IS...
6-16
I SAID MY HANDICAP IS I'M A DOG..
THEN THEY SAID DOGS AREN'T ALLOWED ON THE COURSE..
© 1993 United Feature Syndicate, Inc.
SO I THOUGHT MAYBE I'D SUE..
BUT DOGS AREN'T ALLOWED IN THE COURTHOUSE..
SCHULZ

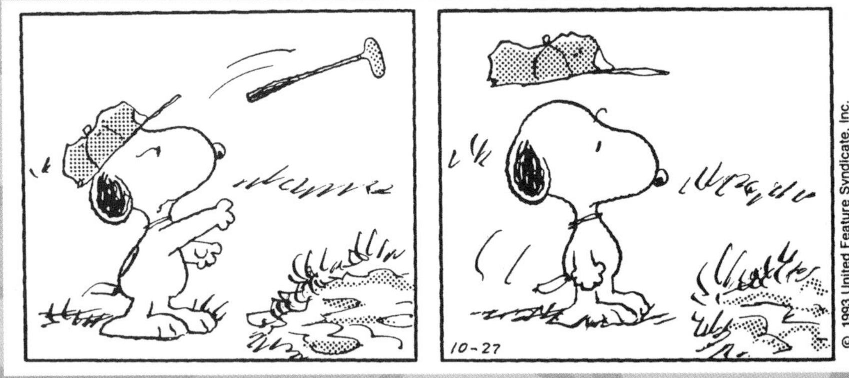
10-27
© 1993 United Feature Syndicate, Inc.
THE LOCH NESS PUTTER!
SCHULZ

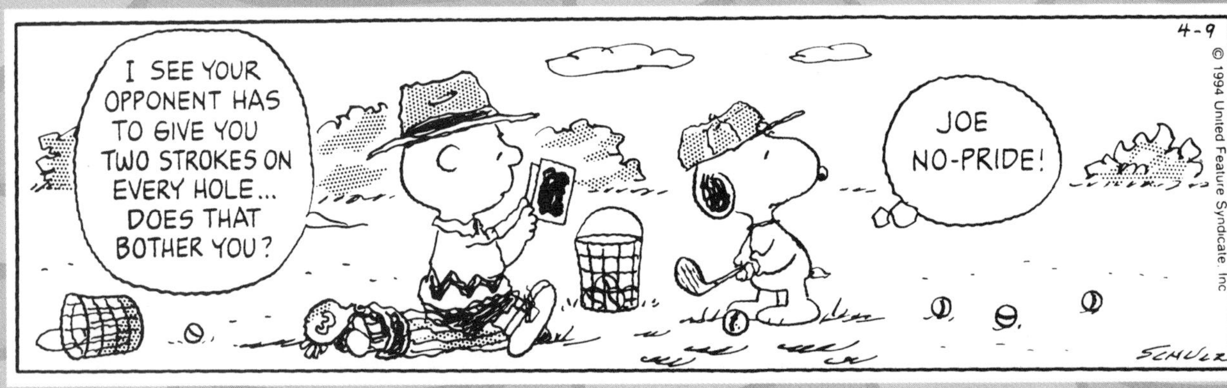
4-9
© 1994 United Feature Syndicate, Inc
I SEE YOUR OPPONENT HAS TO GIVE YOU TWO STROKES ON EVERY HOLE... DOES THAT BOTHER YOU?
JOE NO-PRIDE!
SCHULZ

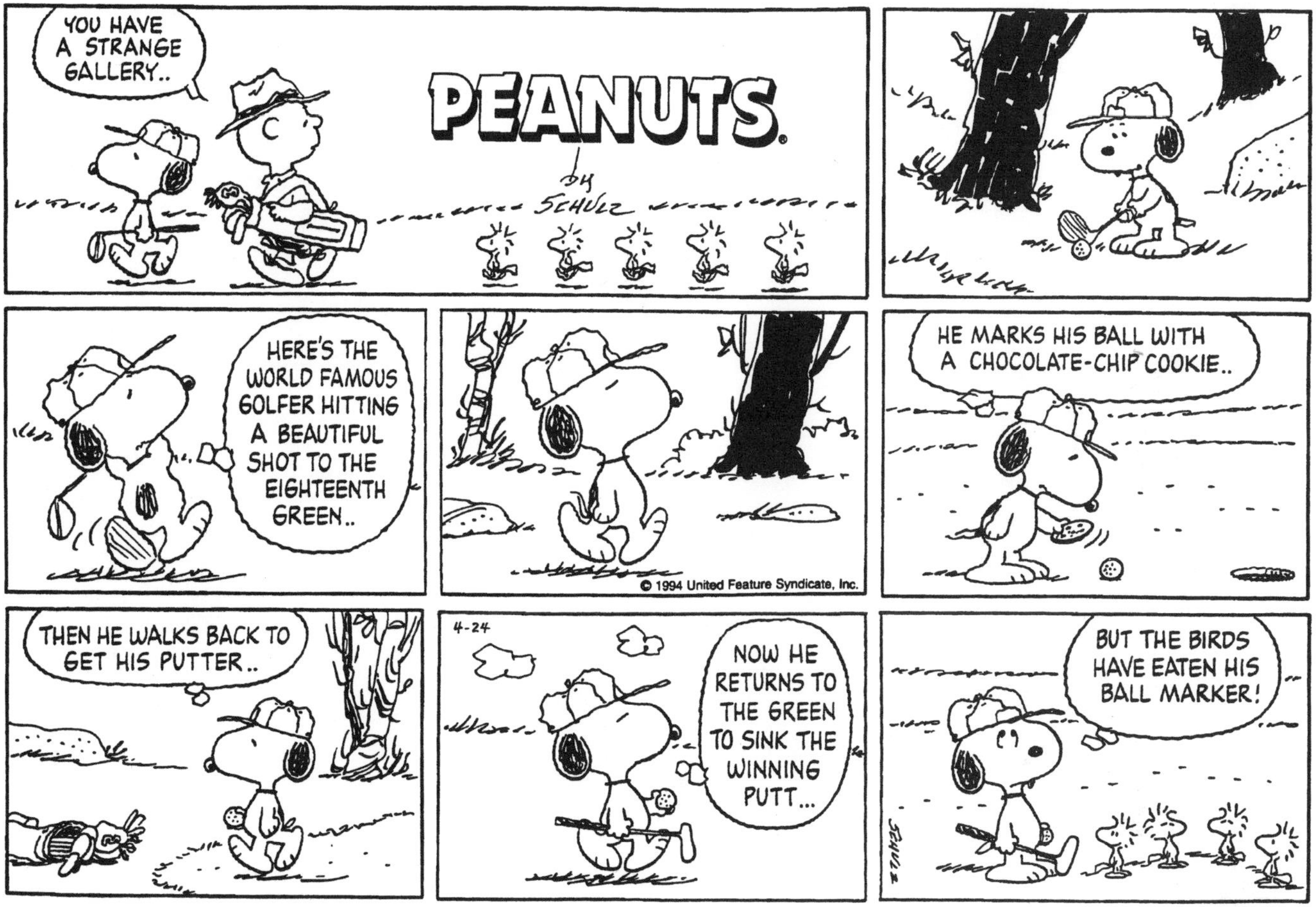
YOU HAVE A STRANGE GALLERY..
PEANUTS
by SCHULZ
HERE'S THE WORLD FAMOUS GOLFER HITTING A BEAUTIFUL SHOT TO THE EIGHTEENTH GREEN..
© 1994 United Feature Syndicate, Inc.
HE MARKS HIS BALL WITH A CHOCOLATE-CHIP COOKIE..
THEN HE WALKS BACK TO GET HIS PUTTER..
4-24
NOW HE RETURNS TO THE GREEN TO SINK THE WINNING PUTT...
BUT THE BIRDS HAVE EATEN HIS BALL MARKER!
SCHULZ

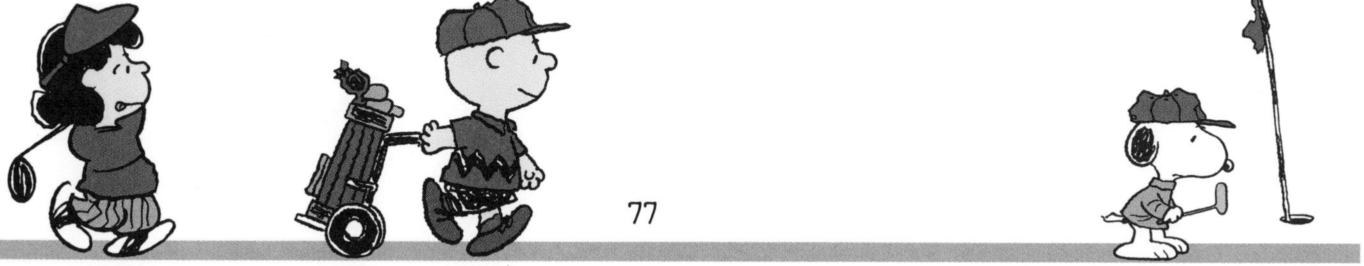

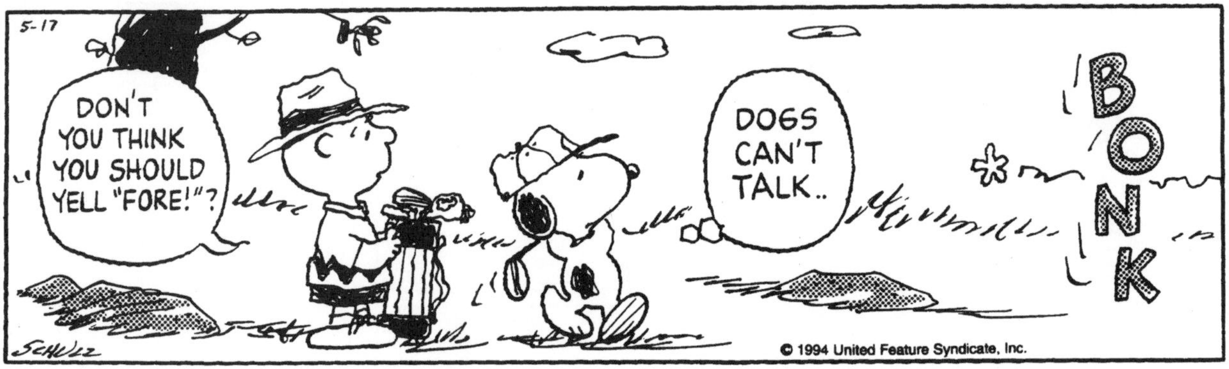
5-17
DON'T YOU THINK YOU SHOULD YELL "FORE!"?
DOGS CAN'T TALK..
BONK
SCHULZ
© 1994 United Feature Syndicate, Inc.

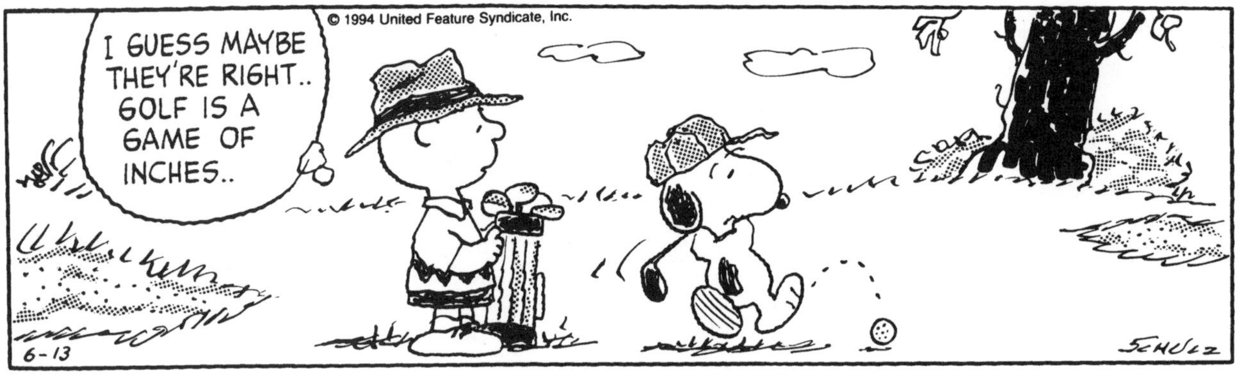
© 1994 United Feature Syndicate, Inc.
I GUESS MAYBE THEY'RE RIGHT.. GOLF IS A GAME OF INCHES..
6-13
SCHULZ

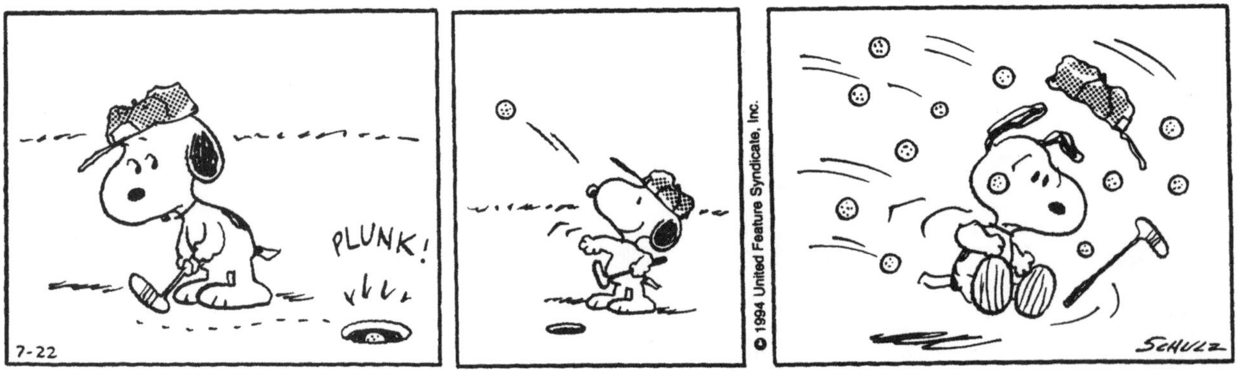
PLUNK!
7-22
© 1994 United Feature Syndicate, Inc.
SCHULZ

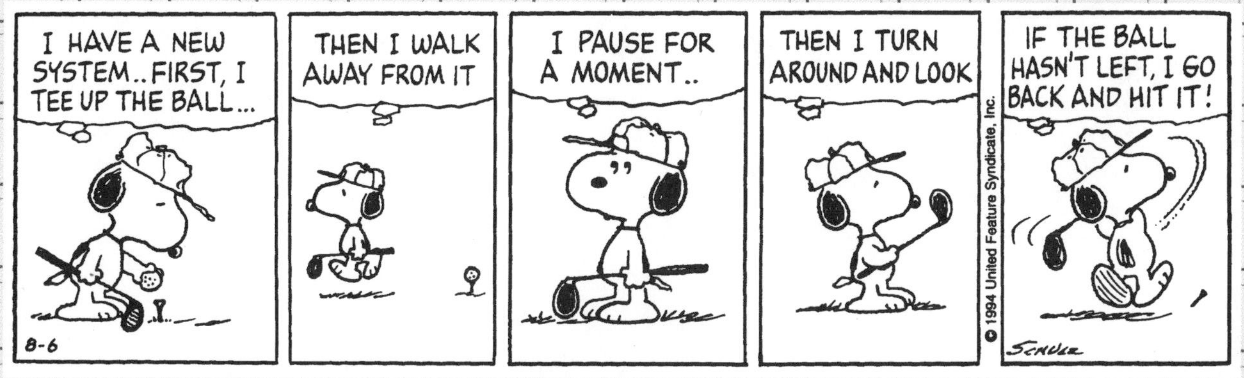
I HAVE A NEW SYSTEM.. FIRST, I TEE UP THE BALL...
8-6
THEN I WALK AWAY FROM IT
I PAUSE FOR A MOMENT..
THEN I TURN AROUND AND LOOK
IF THE BALL HASN'T LEFT, I GO BACK AND HIT IT!
© 1994 United Feature Syndicate, Inc.

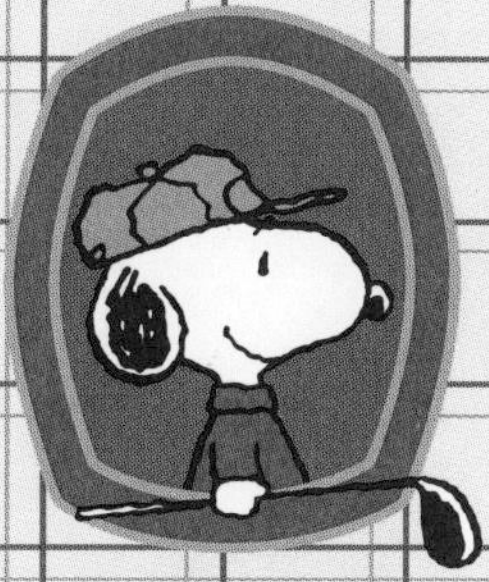

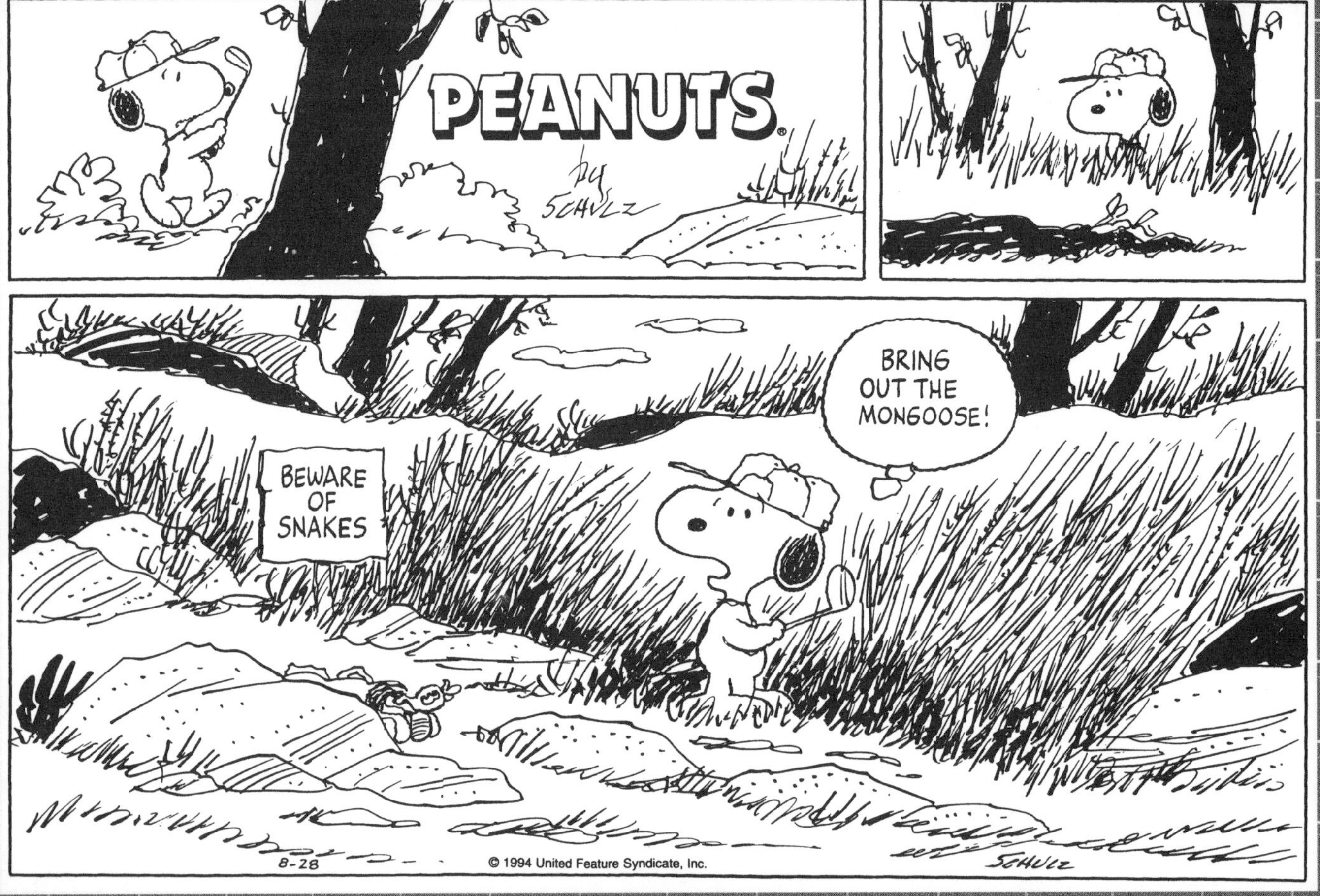
PEANUTS
by SCHULZ
BEWARE OF SNAKES
BRING OUT THE MONGOOSE!
8-28
© 1994 United Feature Syndicate, Inc.
SCHULZ

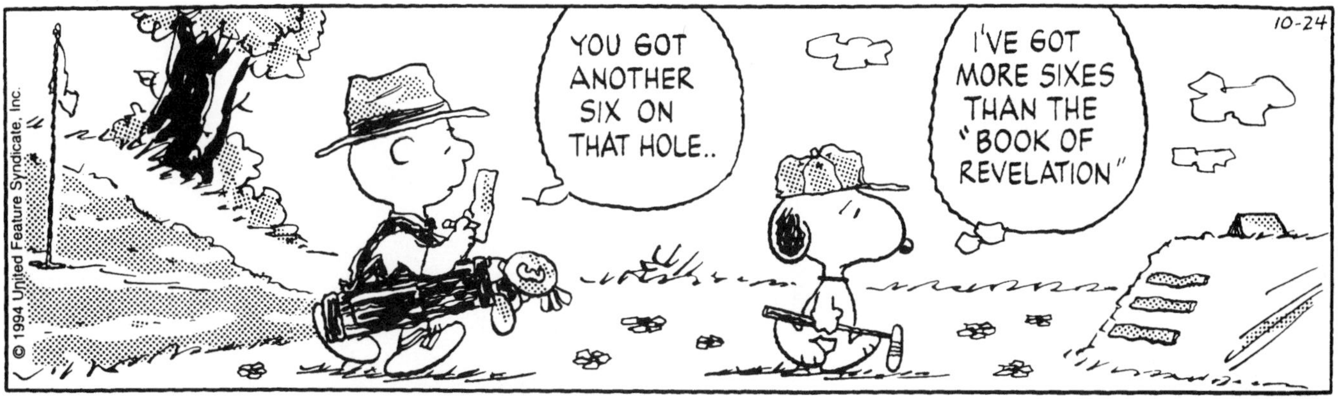
10-24
YOU GOT ANOTHER SIX ON THAT HOLE..
I'VE GOT MORE SIXES THAN THE "BOOK OF REVELATION"
© 1994 United Feature Syndicate, Inc.

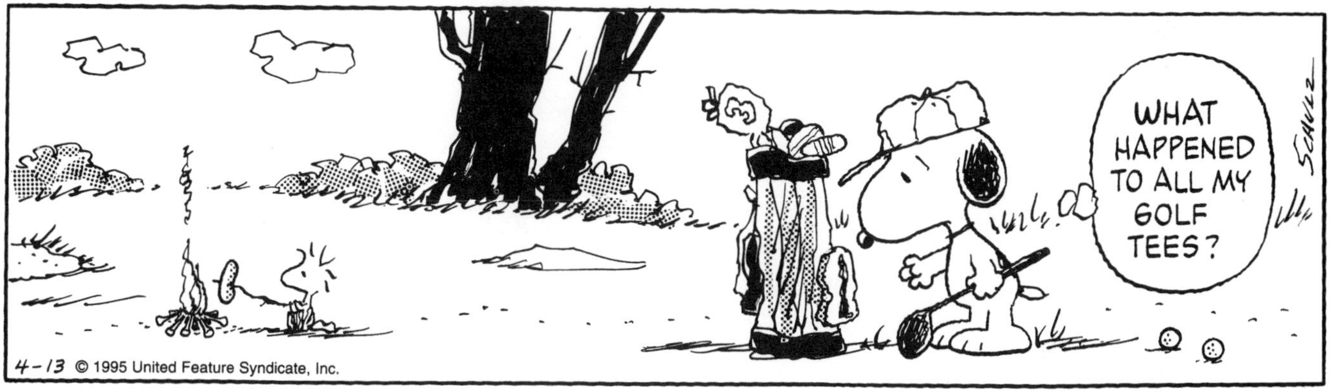
WHAT HAPPENED TO ALL MY GOLF TEES?
SCHULZ
4-13 © 1995 United Feature Syndicate, Inc.

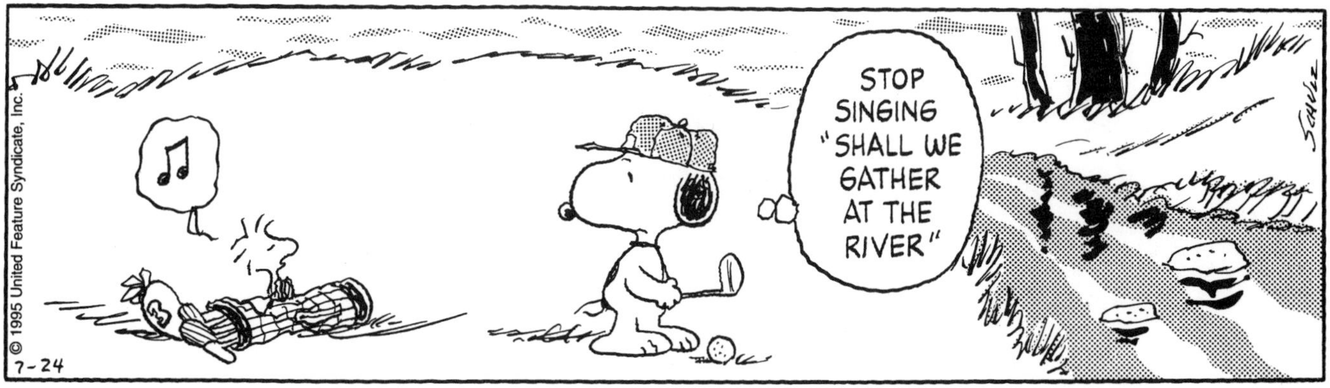
STOP SINGING "SHALL WE GATHER AT THE RIVER"
SCHULZ
© 1995 United Feature Syndicate, Inc.
7-24

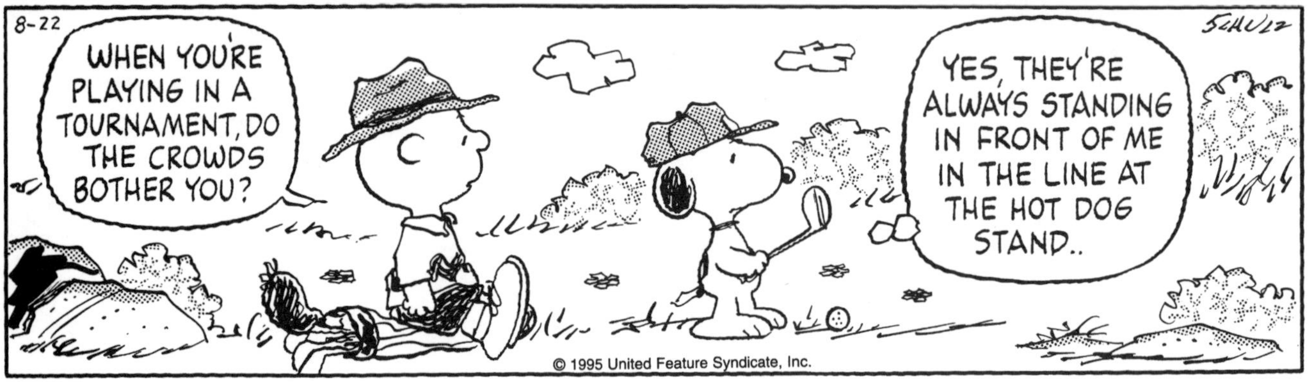
8-22
WHEN YOU'RE PLAYING IN A TOURNAMENT, DO THE CROWDS BOTHER YOU?
YES, THEY'RE ALWAYS STANDING IN FRONT OF ME IN THE LINE AT THE HOT DOG STAND..
SCHULZ
© 1995 United Feature Syndicate, Inc.

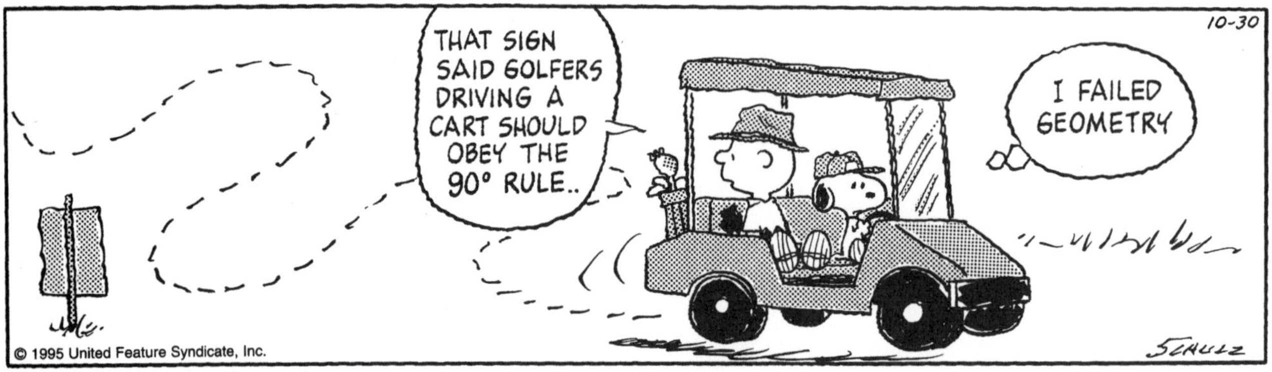
10-30
THAT SIGN SAID GOLFERS DRIVING A CART SHOULD OBEY THE 90° RULE..
I FAILED GEOMETRY
SCHULZ
© 1995 United Feature Syndicate, Inc.

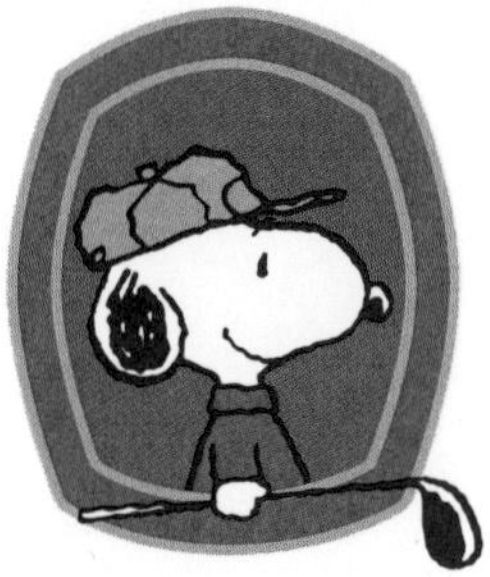

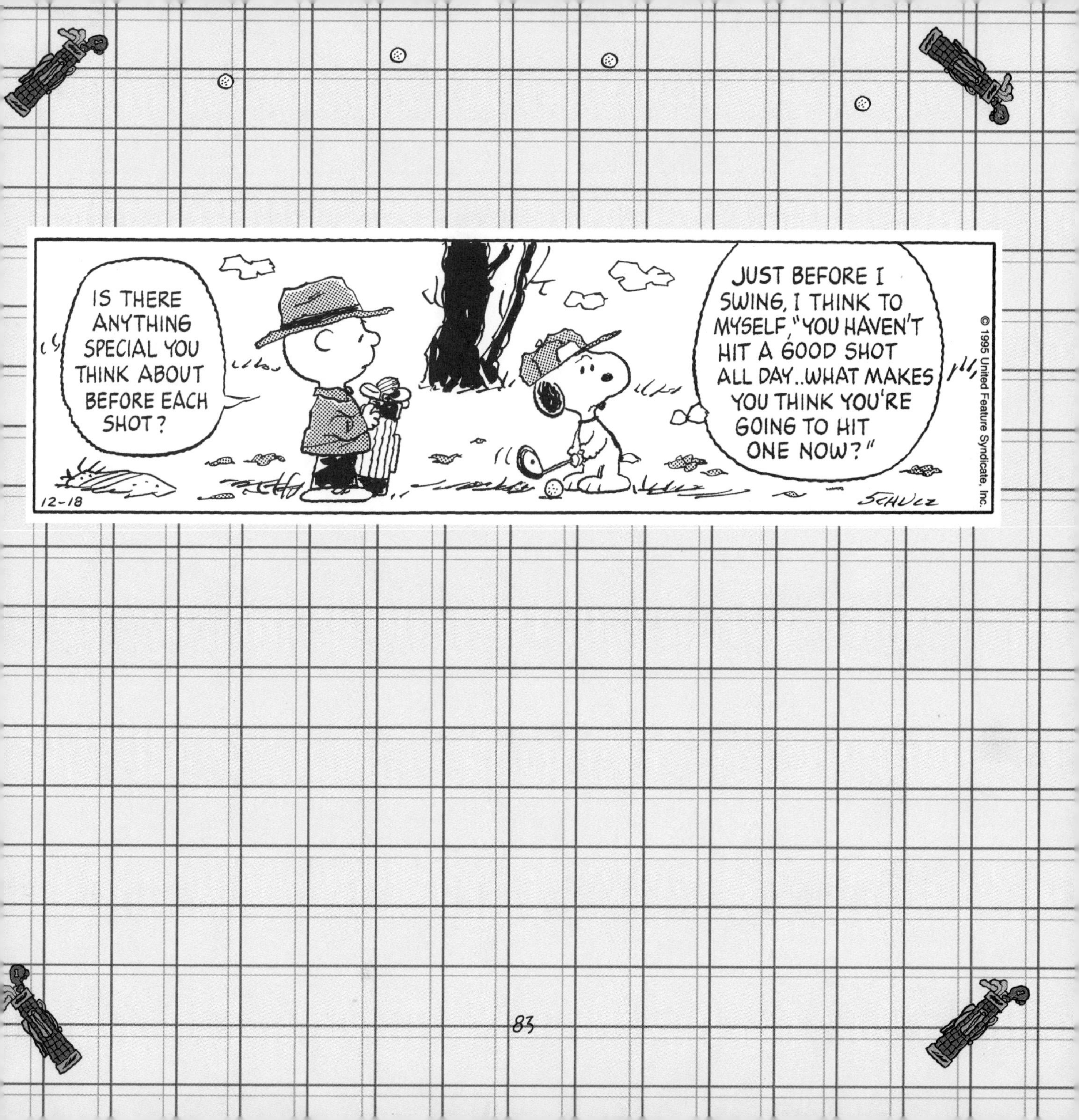
IS THERE ANYTHING SPECIAL YOU THINK ABOUT BEFORE EACH SHOT?
JUST BEFORE I SWING, I THINK TO MYSELF, "YOU HAVEN'T HIT A GOOD SHOT ALL DAY..WHAT MAKES YOU THINK YOU'RE GOING TO HIT ONE NOW?"
12-18
SCHULZ

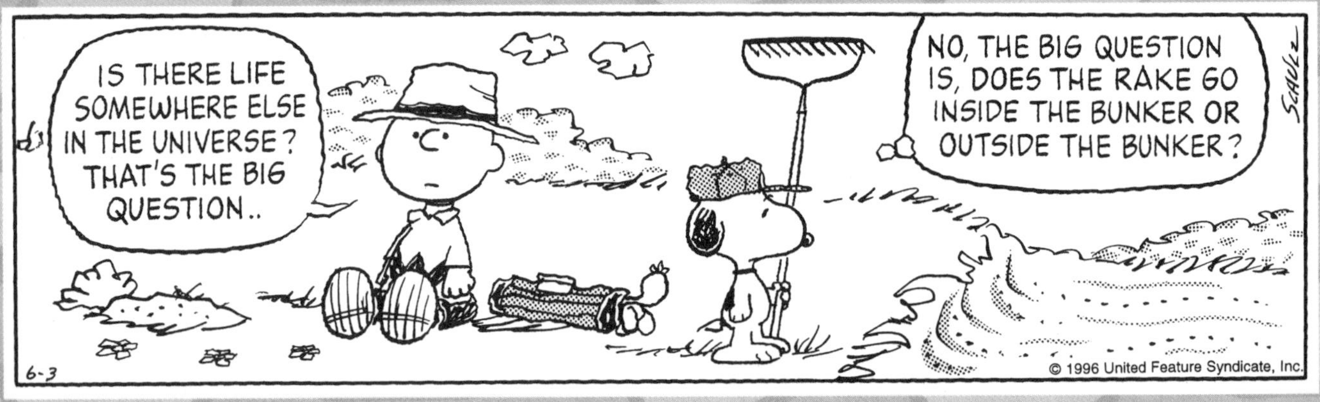
IS THERE LIFE SOMEWHERE ELSE IN THE UNIVERSE? THAT'S THE BIG QUESTION..
NO, THE BIG QUESTION IS, DOES THE RAKE GO INSIDE THE BUNKER OR OUTSIDE THE BUNKER?
SCHULZ
6-3
© 1996 United Feature Syndicate, Inc.

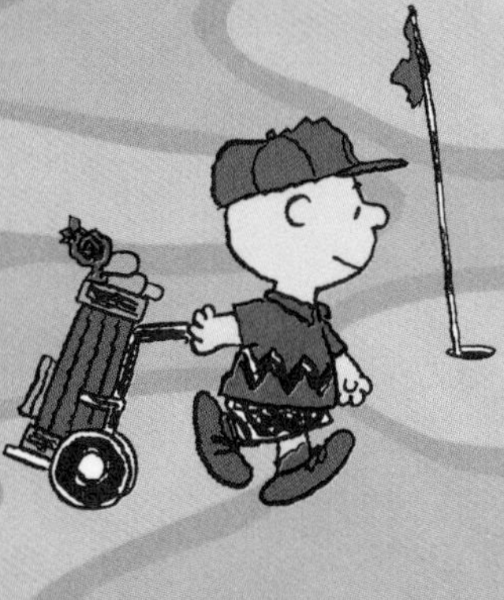

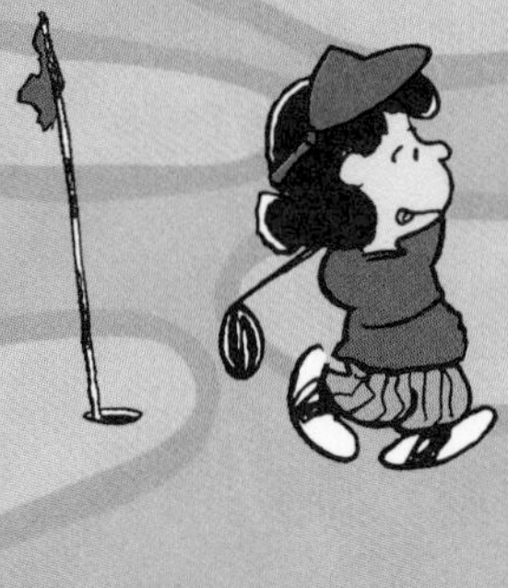

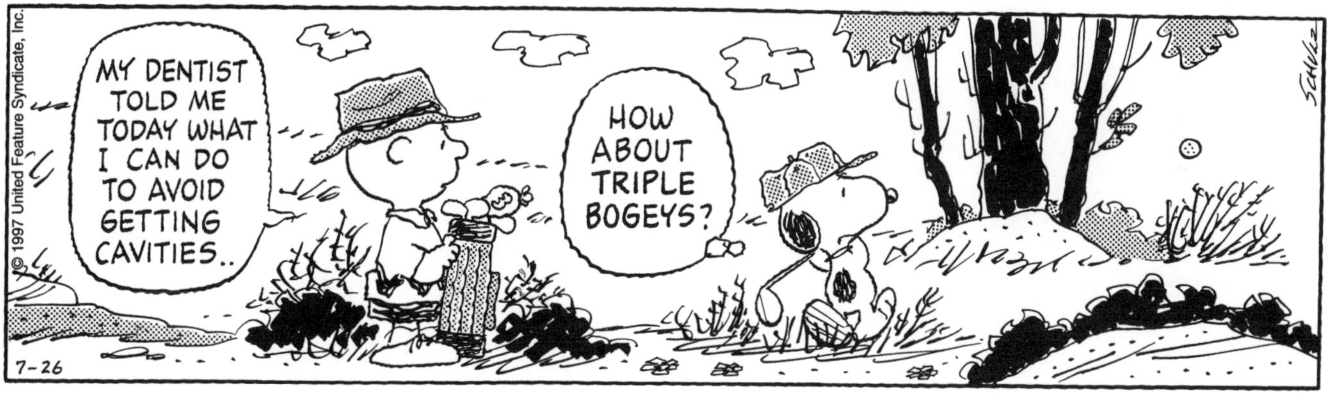
© 1997 United Feature Syndicate, Inc.
MY DENTIST TOLD ME TODAY WHAT I CAN DO TO AVOID GETTING CAVITIES..
HOW ABOUT TRIPLE BOGEYS?
SCHULZ
7-26

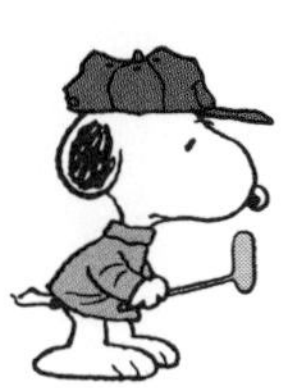

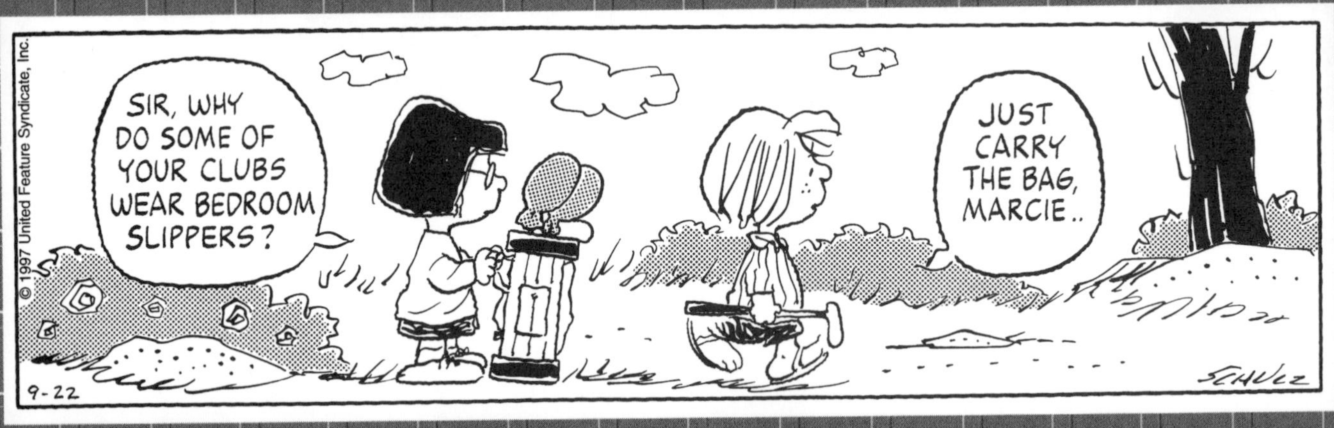
© 1997 United Feature Syndicate, Inc.
SIR, WHY DO SOME OF YOUR CLUBS WEAR BEDROOM SLIPPERS?
JUST CARRY THE BAG, MARCIE..
9-22
SCHULZ

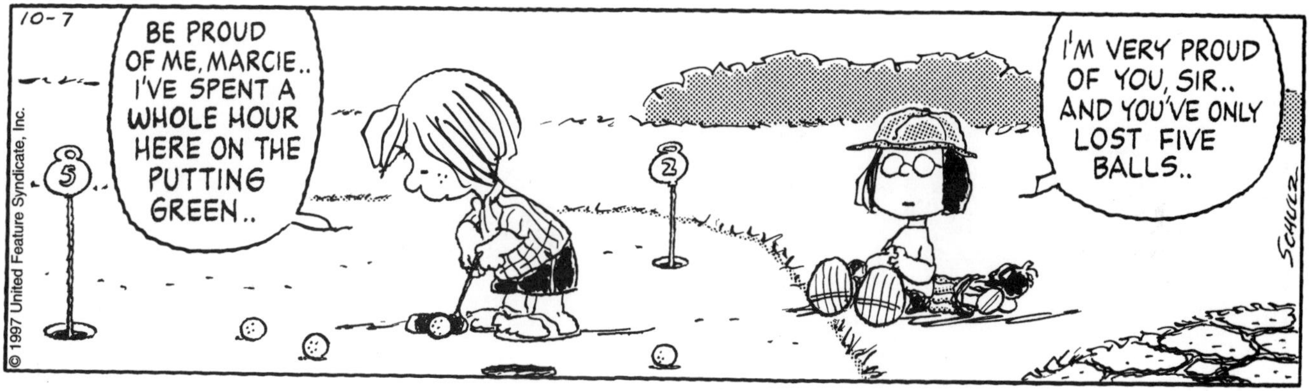
10-7
© 1997 United Feature Syndicate, Inc.
BE PROUD OF ME, MARCIE.. I'VE SPENT A WHOLE HOUR HERE ON THE PUTTING GREEN..
I'M VERY PROUD OF YOU, SIR.. AND YOU'VE ONLY LOST FIVE BALLS..
SCHULZ

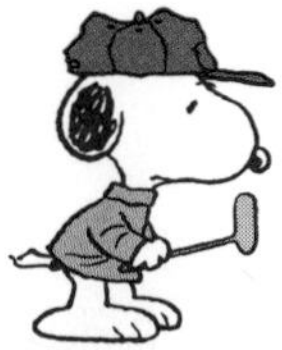

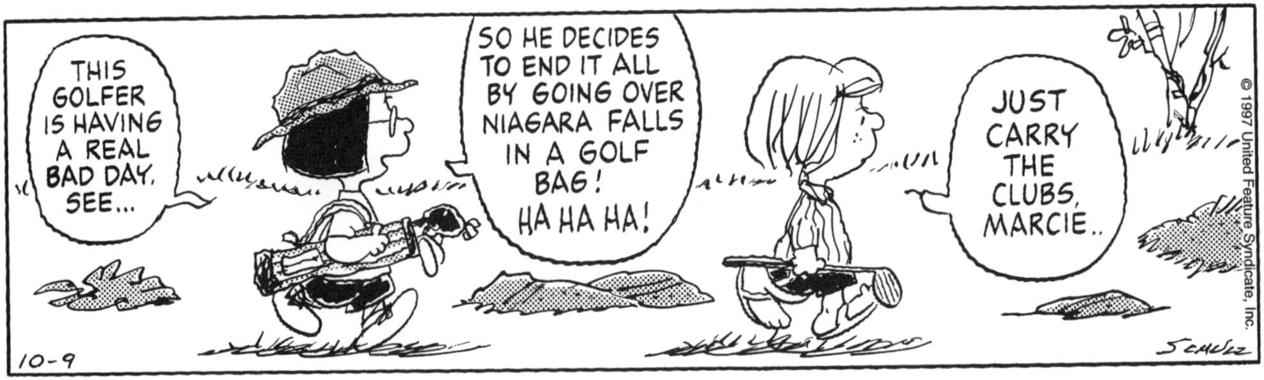
THIS GOLFER IS HAVING A REAL BAD DAY. SEE...
SO HE DECIDES TO END IT ALL BY GOING OVER NIAGARA FALLS IN A GOLF BAG! HA HA HA!
JUST CARRY THE CLUBS, MARCIE..
10-9
© 1997 United Feature Syndicate, Inc.

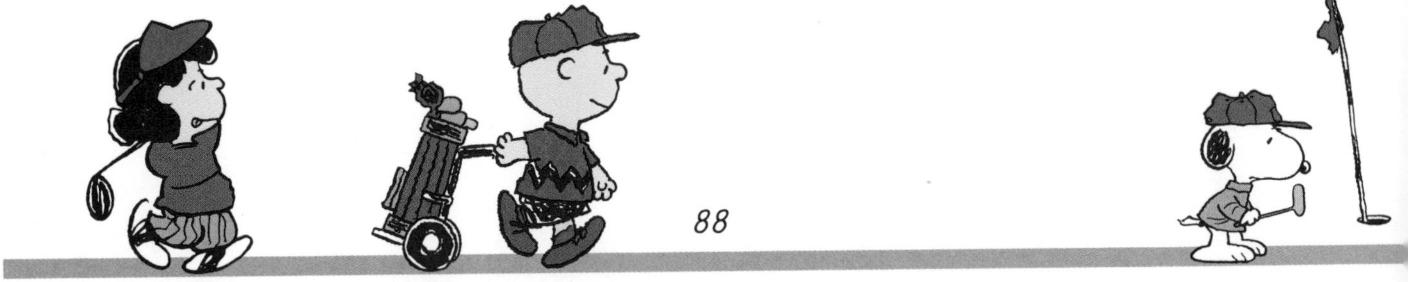

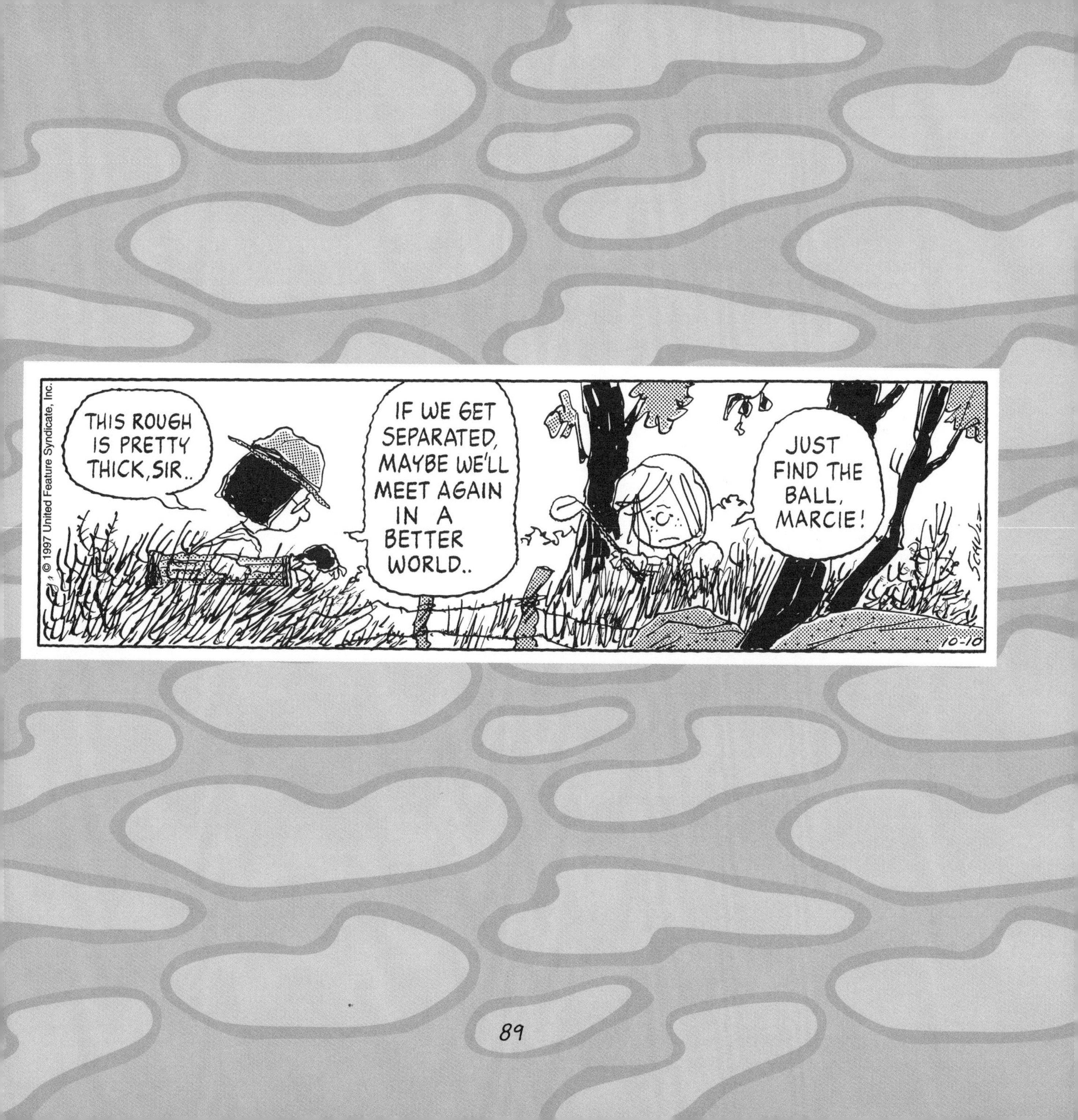
© 1997 United Feature Syndicate, Inc.
THIS ROUGH IS PRETTY THICK, SIR..
IF WE GET SEPARATED, MAYBE WE'LL MEET AGAIN IN A BETTER WORLD..
JUST FIND THE BALL, MARCIE!
SCHULZ
10-10

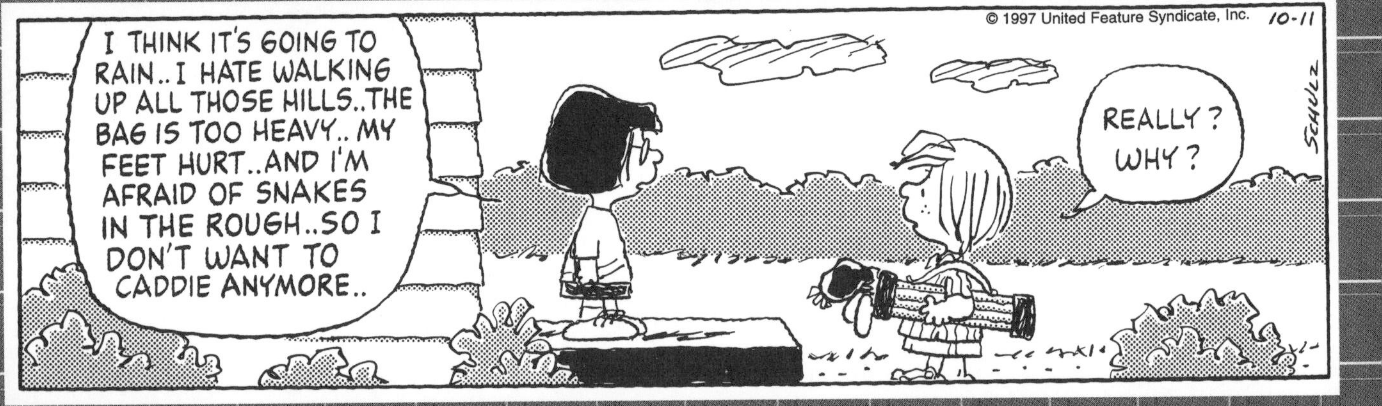
© 1997 United Feature Syndicate, Inc.
10-11
SCHULZ
I THINK IT'S GOING TO RAIN..I HATE WALKING UP ALL THOSE HILLS..THE BAG IS TOO HEAVY.. MY FEET HURT..AND I'M AFRAID OF SNAKES IN THE ROUGH..SO I DON'T WANT TO CADDIE ANYMORE..
REALLY? WHY?

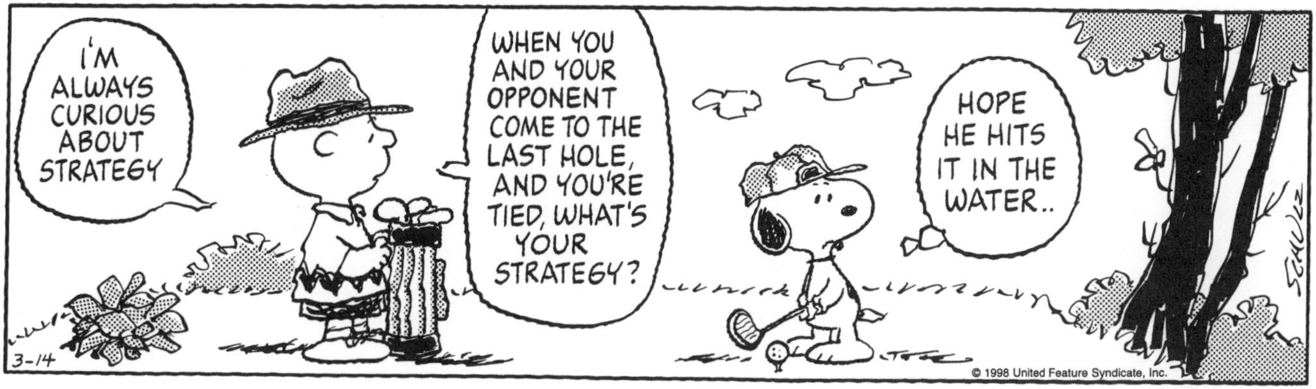
I'M ALWAYS CURIOUS ABOUT STRATEGY
WHEN YOU AND YOUR OPPONENT COME TO THE LAST HOLE, AND YOU'RE TIED, WHAT'S YOUR STRATEGY?
HOPE HE HITS IT IN THE WATER..
3-14
SCHULZ
© 1998 United Feature Syndicate, Inc.

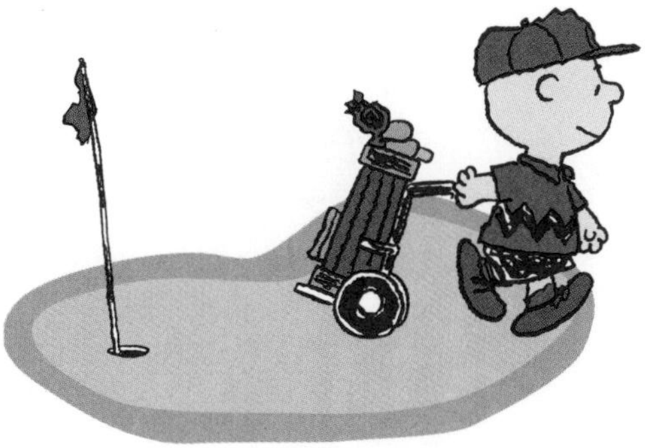

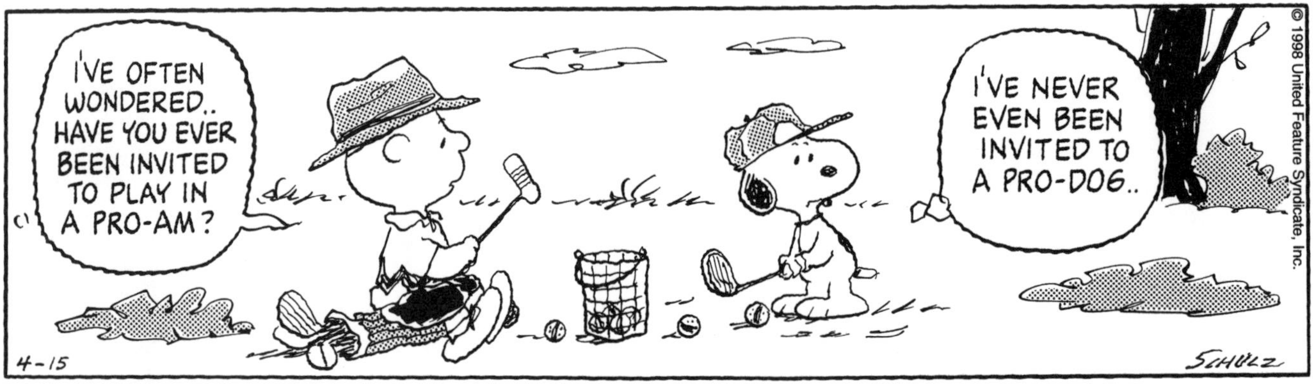
I'VE OFTEN WONDERED.. HAVE YOU EVER BEEN INVITED TO PLAY IN A PRO-AM?
I'VE NEVER EVEN BEEN INVITED TO A PRO-DOG..
4-15
SCHULZ
© 1998 United Feature Syndicate, Inc.

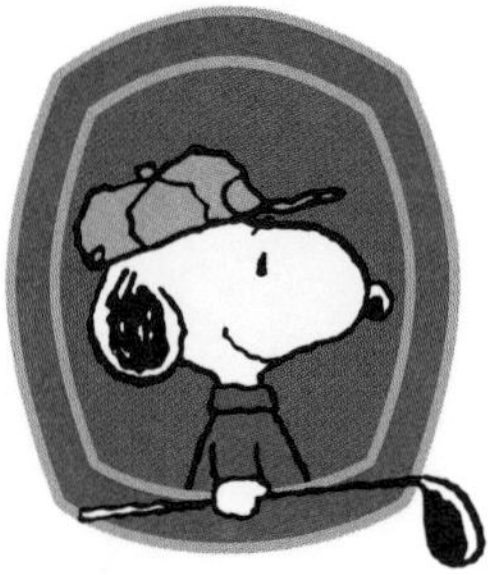

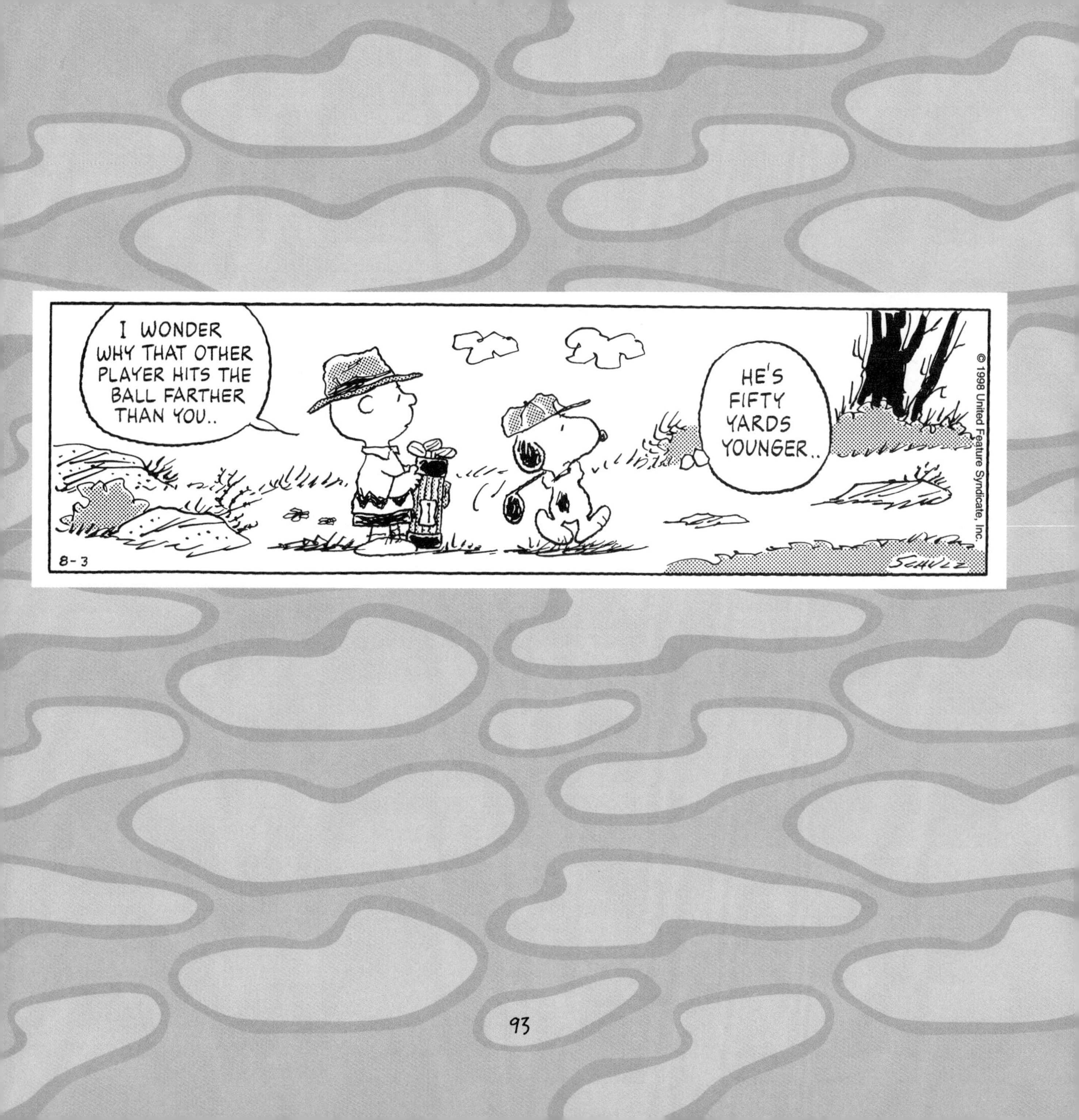
I WONDER WHY THAT OTHER PLAYER HITS THE BALL FARTHER THAN YOU..
HE'S FIFTY YARDS YOUNGER..
© 1998 United Feature Syndicate, Inc.
8-3
SCHULZ

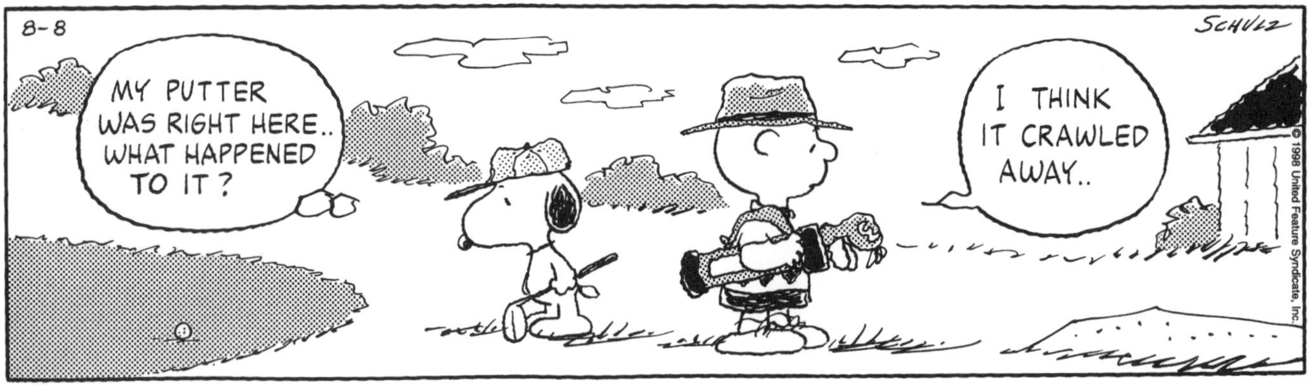
8-8
SCHULZ
MY PUTTER WAS RIGHT HERE.. WHAT HAPPENED TO IT?
I THINK IT CRAWLED AWAY..
© 1998 United Feature Syndicate, Inc.

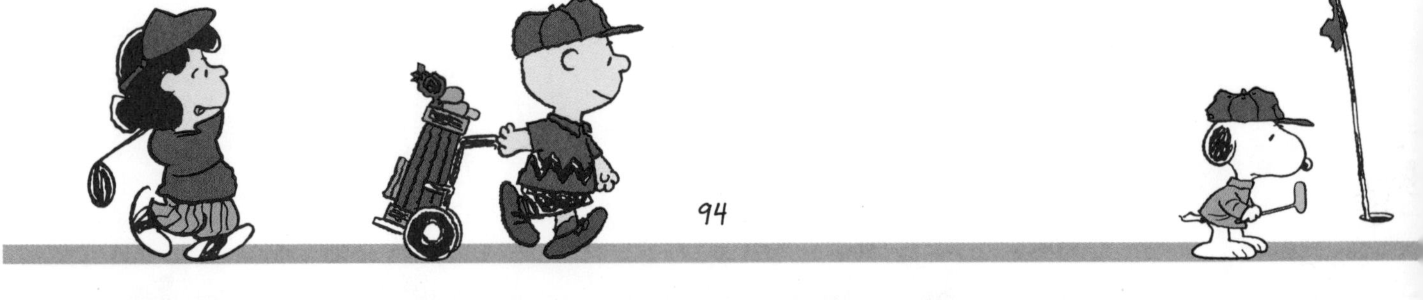

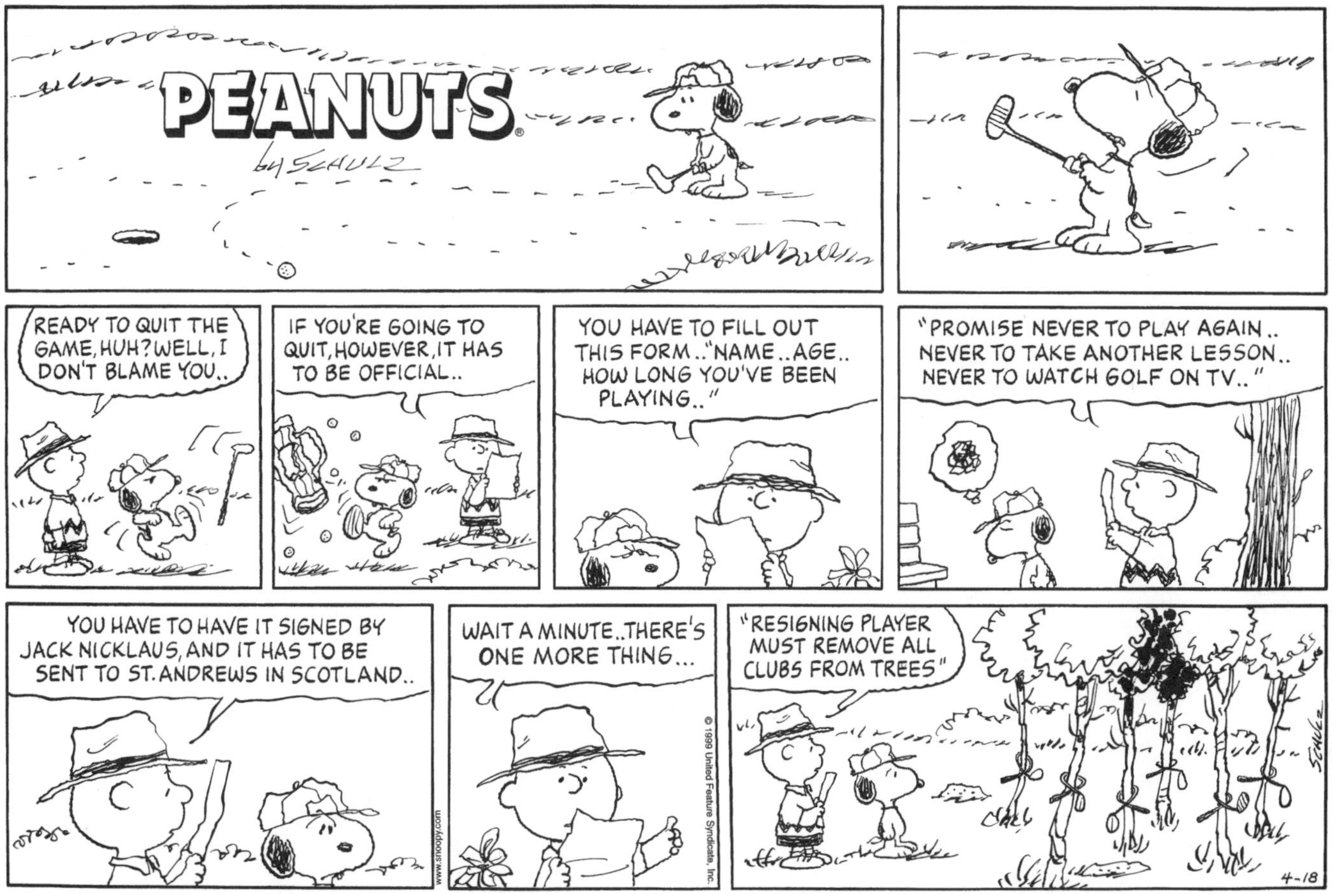
PEANUTS
by SCHULZ
READY TO QUIT THE GAME, HUH? WELL, I DON'T BLAME YOU..
IF YOU'RE GOING TO QUIT, HOWEVER, IT HAS TO BE OFFICIAL..
YOU HAVE TO FILL OUT THIS FORM.."NAME..AGE.. HOW LONG YOU'VE BEEN PLAYING.."
"PROMISE NEVER TO PLAY AGAIN.. NEVER TO TAKE ANOTHER LESSON.. NEVER TO WATCH GOLF ON TV.."
YOU HAVE TO HAVE IT SIGNED BY JACK NICKLAUS, AND IT HAS TO BE SENT TO ST. ANDREWS IN SCOTLAND..
www.snoopy.com
WAIT A MINUTE..THERE'S ONE MORE THING...
© 1999 United Feature Syndicate, Inc.
"RESIGNING PLAYER MUST REMOVE ALL CLUBS FROM TREES"
SCHULZ
4-18

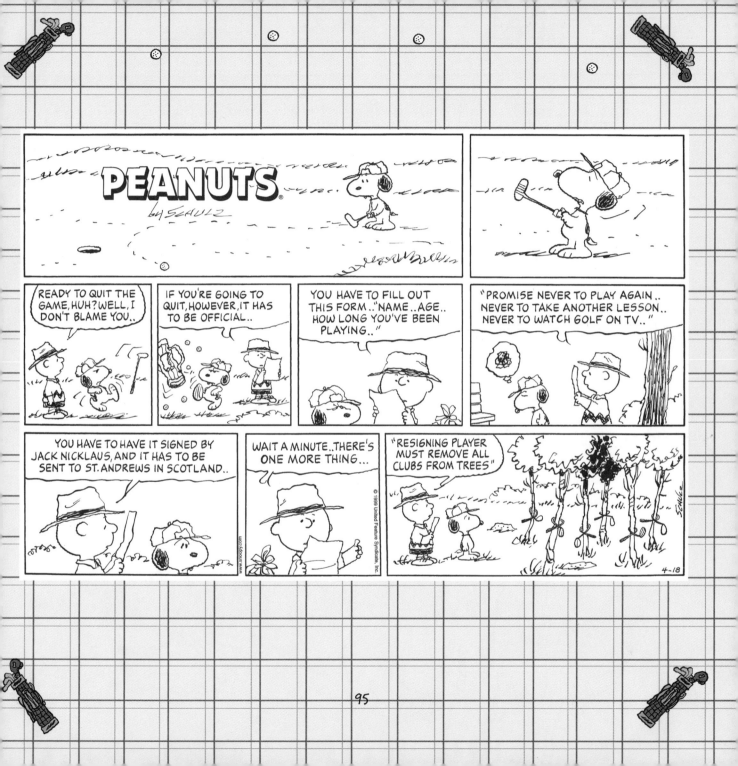

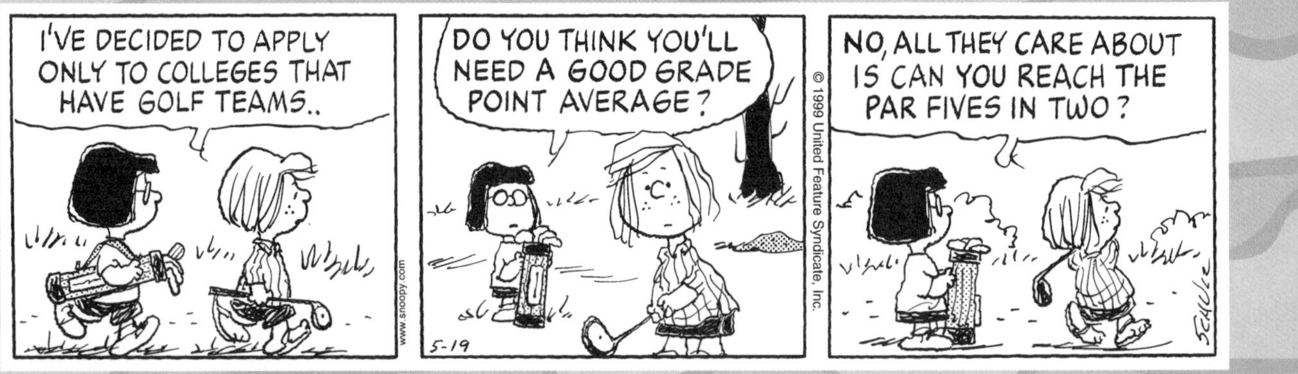
I'VE DECIDED TO APPLY ONLY TO COLLEGES THAT HAVE GOLF TEAMS..
www.snoopy.com
DO YOU THINK YOU'LL NEED A GOOD GRADE POINT AVERAGE?
5-19
© 1999 United Feature Syndicate, Inc.
NO, ALL THEY CARE ABOUT IS CAN YOU REACH THE PAR FIVES IN TWO?
SCHULZ

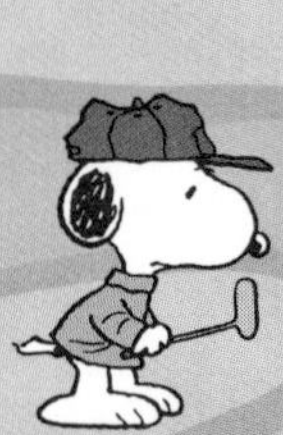